OSCAR BROWNING

OSCAR BROWNING IN OLD AGE

After a bronze head by Lerche

OSCAR BROWNING

by

H. E. WORTHAM

WITH ILLUSTRATIONS

CONSTABLE & CO LTD
LONDON
1927

First published 1927

Printed in Great Britain by Richard Clay & Sons, Limited,
BUNGAY, SUFFOLK.

NON SIT VOBIS VANUM MANE SURGERE
ANTE LUCEM QUIA PROMISIT DOMINUS
CORONAM VIGILANTIBUS

(Invitatory from the Roman Breviary
which ran as a scroll round the
frieze of O. B.'s bedroom at King's)

CONTENTS

LIST OF ILLUSTRATIONS

OSCAR BROWNING

CHAPTER I

INTRODUCTION

I

In June 1923 I received a letter from Oscar Browning in Rome. "I am writing to you," he began, "on a most important matter to which I ask for your earnest attention. You have probably seen in the papers that my dear friend, Lord Latymer, is dead. He was my sole executor and legatee. I had left him everything that I possessed in the world, for good reasons which I will not now explain. A large number of very valuable papers are now stored in the cellars of Coutts' Bank, I suppose in my name, but they may be in his. He had them because he wished to write my life, a duty which I hope you will now undertake. . . . It has always been a subject of controversy which is now as fervent as ever, and the truth ought to be told, which cannot be till after my death."

He went on to give some instructions how he wanted his property distributed, and said that at eighty-six he was in perfect health and, according to the doctor, "good for another fourteen years." A postscript in his own shaky hand—for some time he had been unable to hold a pen properly—added : "The weather here is lovely and very cool. The Royalties asked me to a private audience." Clearly

B   I

the old magnanimous spirit still inspired that portly frame, the weight of years had not destroyed his zest for the great world in which for so long he had loved to consider himself as playing a part.

I accepted the task without any foreboding that within a few months such a melancholy duty would devolve upon me. As to writing his life, I was more cautious; I pointed out that it was already a legend; by observing his wishes I might be destroying a picturesque corner of the Victorian era.

A genial letter by return of post would not have it so. " There are some things which can only be explained after my death and ought to be known. I heard the *Barbiere* last night very well done. To-night they have *William Tell*. I shall try to go for a part, but I cannot stay the whole time. . . . My doctor says I shall live another fourteen years." When a man of eighty-six goes to the opera two nights in succession and looks forward to seeing *William Tell*, in the same breath declaring that he expects to be a centenarian, one takes him at his word and allows him a provisional immortality. I should have reflected that O. B. had generally been disappointed in his ambitions and that he might fail to realise this, the last of many. In the light of the fuller knowledge of his character as revealed in his letters such an affirmation reads rather as intended to convince himself than the person to whom it was made. He guessed that the end was near, but he was going to play his hand out and, incidentally, see *William Tell* for the first time for over thirty years.

Towards the end of September the partial paralysis from which he was suffering had become complicated with other ailments. " I very much doubt," he wrote at this time, " whether I shall live through the winter, but when I tell people so they burst out laughing." Characteristically he pro-

2

ceeded to talk about Mozart. But his mind was busy on his papers at Coutts' Bank. He insisted that they were interesting and valuable, and asked me what I was doing about them. The story they contained about his Eton career must be told. "The work of my life is over," he added : "I don't suppose I shall write another book. My Memoirs have been a tremendous success, so I shall leave off with a good exhibition of fireworks. When I do write they pay me well. The other day I got eight guineas for a thousand words in the *Evening News*." A fortnight later he was dead.

II

Thus it happened that I found myself in possession of a formidable mass of papers and faced with at least a contingent liability to undertake the always ungrateful task of writing about a man who had already been his own biographer. But as I read through the correspondence relating to his years at Eton, it was borne in on me that O. B. was right. His work there had been remarkable, and if he had ultimately failed, the story of his failure was worth telling, both as a chapter in the history of Eton and as the attempt of a man of originality and vision to liberalise public school education. A. C. Benson has remarked in his chapter on Oscar Browning in *Memories and Friends*, that he had streaks of genius. Though the O. B. as a figure will doubtless always be identified with Cambridge, where he passed his middle age and the best of his later years, his own powers were shown in their fullest at Eton. It was there that the streaks of genius were brightest, there that his qualities were at their highest. But his Eton career, throughout marked by controversy and ending in a bitter quarrel with Dr. Hornby, was not one that he could have told himself.

3

" You've missed a chance," said the late John Lane to him, when he found that he had omitted practically the whole of that part of his life from the volume of his Memoirs published by the Bodley Head. O. B.'s comment, on repeating the remark afterwards, was " The vulgar fellow." The accusation is one which will doubtless be made against the story as I have told it. If so, I cannot help it. Oscar Browning wanted the story told, and I have done so with as much impartiality as I could command. I have told it all, suppressing nothing material of which I knew, and thus, I trust, have laid a ghost which always stalked through his subsequent career.

So recently as 1924 the present Vice-Provost of Eton, Mr. Hugh Macnaghten, in a note to his reminiscences of Dr. Hornby in his *Fifty Years at Eton*, refers once again to the ghost. Hornby, he says, in dismissing Browning showed high courage and deserved well of the school. " Granted that O. B. was a virtuous man, as I believe him to have been, he was none the less responsible for his own downfall. He talked very injudiciously and took a positive pleasure in risky situations "—the situation to which he refers in particular owing its " riskiness " apparently to the fact that it consisted of a tea-party of four boys in First Hundred and three lower boys, plus O. B. Still Mr. Macnaghten observes that it is something to be thankful for that there was " nothing, absolutely nothing, more serious in the background."

In order to make such apologies unnecessary, the fairest thing to do is to give the story of his Eton life as fully as possible. Those who read the following chapters about Eton will therefore know what happened so far as documents can reconstruct the story. If some things still remain obscure, one thing is clear, that Oscar Browning exercised a profound

4

influence at Eton over many of the best type of
boys, and that some of his colleagues and a great
many persons of intellectual distinction outside
Eton realised that he was doing work of a very valuable and original kind. If O. B. is to be remembered as one of the personalities of his time, it is
right that the nature of that work should be recorded
and that we should possess some data for forming an
independent judgment both upon it and on the controversy which arose out of it.

III

The present memoir may seem, therefore, to be
disproportionately concerned with that part of his
career which ended when he was thirty-eight and
belongs to the mid-Victorian era. But leaving aside
the intrinsic value of his contribution to public
school education, the story of his work at Eton
gives depth and tone to the picture of a rich and
curious personality which the world interpreted
rather by his foibles than by the qualities they
masked. The O. B. whom most persons now
remember was generally summed up by the judicious
as a genial, hospitable man with a *flair* for knowing
people, and possessing a boundless belief in his own
powers which was not justified on the facts, a man
whose egotism was so naïve as to be childlike and
so deep-seated as to make it impossible for him to
get on with his colleagues. To many generations
of undergraduates he was a joyous, epicurean don
who had nothing in common with the remote, if not
repellent, order to which he belonged. The queer
figure with the short legs which always seemed
uncertain whether they would continue to carry the
too ample body, and turned his gait into a nautical
roll, highly embarrassing for anyone walking with
him, the massive head and strongly marked features,

to which he gave a grotesque turn by his habit of inflating his cheeks like a piping cherub, his hearty manner and deep voice, all pointed to the fact that he was a fit subject for legend. So in the fertile Cambridge soil the O. B. myth, helped on its way by the vivid wit of J. K. Stephen, grew and was nourished by many stories turning on his vanity, his ready tongue, his partiality for the great, stories which he usually enjoyed as much as anyone. The myth did justice to his gaiety, his friendliness, his zest for life. But it grew till he became a figure of Falstaffian proportions beneath which the underlying gravity of his character and the seriousness of his purpose were hidden. Anecdote bred anecdote till one forgot that a man, with so deep an interest in human welfare and, despite the misadventures of his own career, so profound a belief in human character, must be something more than a gigantic joke.

There is, however, another side to the picture. If one lifts the protecting shield of egotism one finds the self-complacency turning to self-distrust, the inner happiness which he insists upon so emphatically to the courage which is grounded on despair. " I think that worry may be dispelled and averted," he writes in 1914, just before the war, to Lord Latymer, " if sufficient pains be taken. You know how I used to worry myself, but I never do now. I try to regard all worry about the *past* as quite useless and nearly all worry about the future, confining myself to the present day, hour and minute, trying to enjoy each of them as much as I can." In much the same strain wrote Voltaire to Mme. du Deffand from Fernay. But the philosophy is none the less dubious for a convinced optimist. This is hardly the Oscar Browning whom the world sometimes condescended to know, nor the O. B. who thought he knew himself, who declared with tedious iteration that he was happy and confident in the worth of the things which he had done, of the causes for which he had fought.

Nevertheless as the result of long practice he did create an ideal character for his own edification which as a rule kept him company. As he sped through his happy eighties on the wings of Christian Science and Universal History, with an income sufficient for himself and his Italian servant's family, and amidst the best society that Rome could afford, it seemed that at last he had tasted a degree of felicity beyond the ordinary hopes of man. The ambitions of his youth for fame had been satisfied, if not quite in the manner he had wished. He was a personality, he was someone in the world, which was more than could be said of most of the other dons. Indeed he saw himself at last winning the recognition which Cambridge had denied him. " My *History of the Modern World*," he writes in 1916, " will establish my reputation as a serious historian, which I have long wished for but have never been able to attain." Still there were doubts. Had he gone to Oxford instead of to Cambridge he felt he would have been " a greater man." There was always a provinciality about Cambridge from which Oxford was free. Had he been called to the Bar instead of returning to Eton as a master, had he set himself as a young man to make a reputation as a man of letters, he might then have been something more than O. B. And then he had been shamefully treated at Eton. And Rome, though the climate and society were alike delightful, was exile. Not even the music of Mozart and the satisfaction of being paid by editors for being a Nestor to Fleet Street could compensate for the loneliness and the regrets which refused to keep their distance.

But this is to anticipate. One cannot enter on one's task better than by once more recalling him

as he appeared when he trod the stage, impelled by
the force of an enormous vitality, in the full blaze of
life. O. B. combined in himself—or to the undergraduate imagination seemed to do so—the past and
the present, history and politics, music and gastronomy, Cambridge, London, Europe. It was a
portly, somewhat bewildering, but undeniably
entertaining synthesis. Like the Bourbons he never
forgot. His memory rotated securely in all circles,
and he was always ready to talk, as one man of the
world to another, of life in Rome under Pio Nono,
or of Florence under the Brownings, of the amours
of Metternich, of the proper method of cooking a
Spanish ham, of psychical research (in which he
believed), or of the beauties of the Bavarian High-
lands. Both literally and figuratively he was
omnivorous. What more can be said of a person
who records dining with pleasure off snails, frogs,
porcupine, hedgehog and wild boar, who took
lessons in Polish when eighty-five and preferred his
sermons long ? A man with such an insatiable
appetite is not easily to be circumscribed within the
limits of this dietetic age. One looks naturally to
the past and tries to measure him by other less
hygienic times, when we like to think that there was
more leisure and intimacy to savour the finer
subtleties of personality. " O. B. was by temperament, by sympathy, we might almost be allowed to
say by the date of his birth, an eighteenth-century
figure. In him its ideal of the scholar, the statesman in little and the man of the world was combined. That he should be remembered, as perhaps
he will be remembered, as the greatest Cambridge
don of the latter half of the nineteenth century seems
an anti-climax, such was the spell of his personality
on all capable of penetrating beyond its surface of
egoism and its whimsical adulation of the great."
Thus Mr. Osbert Burdett. Another King's-man,

Mr. N. Wedd, goes still further back : " Spiritually
O. B. derives from an age more spacious even than
Victoria's. You do not begin to understand him
until you realise that he is the hero of a lost play of
Shakespeare's, bearing in all his lineaments unmistakable traces of his Elizabethan origin. To love life
as well as learning, to regard rules as best kept when
broken, to give the world, the flesh and the devil
their due, to follow the gleam when it leads to Court
as well as to Cloister—these things were O. B.'s
by right of birth. They are the qualities most
needed and least liked in Schools and Colleges, and
their possession explains the paradox of a career at
King's and at Eton whose apparent failure was the
measure of true success. This union of high
spirits, high living and high thinking is such a rare
phenomenon in England since the Puritans that it is
liable to be grievously misunderstood."

IV

It is the business, however, of the biographer to
put his subject in proper perspective, to allow the
reader to form his own judgment, and if Oscar
Browning belonged in spirit to the eighteenth
century, or to the age of Elizabeth, his work was
done in the reigns of Victoria, of Edward VII and
George V. He was also sufficiently a child of his
time to like its inventions, which is perhaps the
truest test of being a modern. Though he had no
mechanical bent, he loved machinery. Clocks and
watches exercised a strange fascination over him,
especially the cheaper varieties. He was one of the
first persons, and one of the last, to ride a tricycle.
He was a pioneer at Cambridge in the use of the
telephone and the typewriter. The pianola found
in him an easy prey. In his old age he loved the
" pictures." If he disliked motor-cars it was

because they provided air without exercise, which he considered an impious combination. In any case, whatever the age to which he was spiritually most akin, he must remain a mass of contradictions, through which one may discern his achievement of what Montaigne asserts is man's most glorious masterpiece—to live *à propos*.

Thanks to our forbears and our environment we are what we are. A good many of Oscar Browning's characteristics may be explained by the known facts of his parentage, his birth and early upbringing. He was descended on both sides from families whose origins stretch back to the respectable mists of the Middle Ages. A Browning ancestor was high sheriff of Gloucestershire—if the assumptions of the genealogists are to be accepted—at the end of the fourteenth century, and supported, with a zeal for unpopular causes which marks Oscar as a true scion of the race, the failing fortunes of Richard II. Another held the same office in Surrey in 1740. Oscar's father received the education of a good bourgeois at the school in Ealing where at the same time John Henry Newman was dreaming his very unbourgeois-like dreams. But neither Brownings nor Bridges—his mother came of a branch of the Bridge family which had been long settled in Essex—had ever before the nineteenth century produced any members who rose above a respectable mediocrity, and it was with some complacency that Oscar Browning used to reflect that only in his own time had the name of his family become famous, even though the lion's share of that renown belonged to a certain Robert, with whom he was related by no ties of blood. In the purely English stock from which he was sprung there was no foreign admixture, unless we admit a tradition of his mother's family—a tradition which remains unverified—of a Jewish strain introduced through the marriage of a Bridge ancestor in the early eighteenth century with a daughter of the Chosen People. The jests that occasionally cropped up in the undergraduate papers about O. B.'s brains being derived from his Jewish extraction may therefore not have been altogether wide of the mark. To this strain it may not be fanciful to attribute his complete freedom from any prejudices of colour or creed, and the sympathy too which embraced all sects and religions, incidentally making him a Zionist long before Zionism was a thing of practical politics. There was an underlying quality of spiritual earnestness in Oscar Browning, a sense of the immanence of God unclothed in dogma, coupled with an appreciation of the value of ritual in the smallest details of life, which is by no means characteristic of the English temperament. And perhaps the crypto-Jew peeped out when the conversation happened to turn on some member of the race whom he considered had done him an injury. "Do you like Montagu?" asked the ingenuous undergraduate of Liberal convictions (unaware of the fact that O. B. considered that E. S. Montagu had been responsible for bringing his long tenure of the Treasurership at the Union to an end), only to be shattered by the question: "What, that circumcised Jew?" Maybe, too, his social exuberance had an Oriental as well as an Elizabethan tinge, and his egoism an exotic flavour. One doubts also whether any Englishman, in whose veins ran not some of the sacred Semitic fire, could have expressed such hatred for a political opponent as O. B. did for Disraeli. "What a brute Dizzy is," he writes, when he is an Eton master, to Arthur Sidgwick. "I should almost rejoice at his assassination. They tell me at the Castle that the Queen is devoted to him and does not in the least perceive that he is a snob."

11

Oscar Browning was wiser, or more fortunate, in his parentage than in his birth or the events of his infancy and childhood. His twin brother was still-born, and Oscar owed his life only to the rough-and-ready methods of the midwife, who, when the doctor thought the child was dead, gave him a vigorous slap—prototype of the many he was to receive in the course of his career—which caused him to make his first noise in the world. The puling and incredibly tiny infant passed precariously to a childhood of constant debility. Yet even as a baby he managed to obtain some glimpses of the great world. When he was six months old his parents had moved from Cumberland Terrace, Regent's Park, to one of the Canon's houses in Windsor Castle, and some of his earliest recollections were thus tinged with the gleam of Court splendour —the marriage of the Queen and seeing her and the Prince Consort, at the head of a noble cavalcade, go out riding in the Park—things which doubtless helped to foster his Johnsonian respect for royalty.

Those were Spartan days, and the feebleness of his health did not prevent him from beginning Latin when he was four and Greek when he was eight. Like his two elder brothers, William and Arthur, he was destined for Eton, and was actually entered as a lower boy in 1845, when he was eight years old. But his health was obviously not strong enough to stand what was then the rough life of Eton. His father's death too had left his mother in rather embarrassed circumstances, and since Oscar was clearly an intelligent boy, it was decided to wait and to send him into College. Ill-health and desultory teaching, however, interfered with his studies. He made more than one unsuccessful attempt, and it was not till he went to Thorpe and became one of the first pupils of his brother William, fifteen years his senior, that his scholarship was given the precision and suppleness which enabled him, at the Election of 1850, to attain the third place on the list. It was thanks to William Browning, a bluff, capable, unimaginative parson of the old school, who rode to hounds and celebrated saints' days by drinking champagne, that at the age of thirteen he had mastered the art of writing Latin verses so thoroughly that he was able to do his first copy of Latin Alcaics at Eton in his head whilst walking along the Slough Road. Greek iambics offered no more difficulty. Yet if William recognised the intellectual ability of his youngest brother, he was a stern mentor, and the delicate boy, whose languor was largely the result of a frail physique, would undoubtedly have been happier and less the prey of morbid doubts, against which his egoism in the end became a shield, had some more sympathetic influence counteracted the fondness of his mother. She, intelligent woman as she was, found it difficult to maintain the temperate mean between the harshness of her hard-headed eldest son, who believed that his youngest brother would never conquer his native indolence except by the most scrupulous discipline, and the remorseful and affectionate promises of Oscar to battle with the natural defects of his character. The result was that she quite shamelessly spoilt him.

PART I
ETON

CHAPTER II

SCHOOL-DAYS AT ETON

I

THE first full-length portrait we get of Oscar Browning is at Eton, which he entered in January 1851, a few days before his fourteenth birthday. He has drawn it for us himself in a diary which he began in 1853 and continued with occasional gaps until he left Eton. It was not till he was past forty that his journalising became an ingrained habit. With this diary, supplemented by his own letters, his tutor's reports, his mother's adoring exhortations, his brother William's rather priggish rebukes, he stands out as plainly as at any time in his life. More plainly perhaps; for at Eton Oscar Browning was unhappy and under no constraint about admitting it, at any rate to himself. Once a man embraces a vocation, chooses a profession, he resigns an essential part of his independence. As a boy, Browning disliked Eton; detested is not too strong a word to use. Then he was badly off, unpopular, in poor health. To Oscar Browning the successful house-master, Eton was the unrivalled school which had for the better part of two centuries provided England with those who made its laws and moulded its manners. Partly owing to the influence of the place, but much more, one suspects, because he had identified his own career with the greatest of English public schools, he became the most loyal of Etonians, the defender of the public school system. It wanted reforming, of course. But radicalism was young and ardent in the 'sixties, and it was thought that Parliament and zealous pedagogues together would be able to turn the older foundations, still asleep in their trivium of construing verses and " saying lessons," into more polished and more secular Rugbys. When Hornby cast him out from Eton he began to think differently, ultimately, as head of the Day Training College at Cambridge, coming to condemn the public schools and to exalt the elementary schools with which that institution was connected. Nevertheless, though in all loyalty there runs a strain of egoism, Oscar Browning, unjustly as he believed himself to have been treated, still possessed for Eton something of the passionate attachment of the *émigré*. He might declare that all boarding schools were a mistake, allow good of none except Marlborough, yet in 1908 he writes : " Still Eton remains Eton, and will be itself whether Warre or Lyttelton control its destinies. Bismarck once said that the Germans could not imitate England in certain branches of self-government because England was full of ' royal existences ' which were lacking in his own country. It is the function of Eton to foster these royal existences; they make her what she is and she suffers them to grow up as her destiny demands. What country but our own can produce a Viceroy of India, a man clothed for a short space of time with more power than any sovereign in the world, and yet ready to lay it aside when the time has come and return to the ordinary ranks of life ? " A question, we may surmise, prompted by his own friendship with Lord Curzon, begun when the future Viceroy was a boy at Eton and cemented by foreign travel together during the holidays. But it breathes the magnificent pride which some of the Gentiles have been known to call snobbery.

The interesting point is that this pride was absent

from Oscar Browning the schoolboy. "Bah, I hate Eton," he writes in 1854, and though in his last year at school he grew more or less reconciled to his lot, he was never under any illusions, then or afterwards, how the life had galled and bored him. The result is that we see him as a boy at Eton through a clearer medium than any in which he afterwards presents himself to our view. The mainsprings of his character are revealed, its mechanism stands open to our inspection. And instead of the assertive, self-confident, busy and expansive personality which Cambridge and the world afterwards knew as O. B., we are presented with a melancholy, rather unsociable youth, whose ambition is ever at war with a profound and native indolence. He is conscious of his abilities, believes in his powers, but, like so many clever boys, he is filled with a mistrust of his emotions. Oscar Browning was nothing of a Wordsworthian; if the child is father of the man, he took special pains to disavow his parentage.

II

His earliest years at Eton were the most unhappy. He was delicate, small, ill-fitted physically for the life in College. Though a Colleger's bills were very little less than an Oppidan's, the Collegers were badly fed and their accommodation was exceedingly rough. The only apparatus for washing consisted of a number of enamelled basins in a trough, at each end of which was a cold-water tap. The windows in the room were broken. The towels were deliberately drenched by the first-comers. Oscar Browning, who had a Roman passion for the bath, used to recall how he had often been kicked at his tutor's for being a " dirty tug," when the reason was merely due to the absence of the ordinary appliances of civilised life. At 7.30 they went into school, cold and unwashed. Breakfast was not till nine, and the famished boys were obliged to keep hunger at bay by buttered buns and coffee at Joe Brown's. Even when nine o'clock came the smaller boys, as fags, had first to look after their masters. Since they had to be in school again at half-past nine, little enough time was given them to consume the bread-and-butter which constituted their meal. Dinner was at two. Again this was prefaced by a visit to Joe Brown's, where the future gourmand used to indulge in brandy-snaps and lemonade. A whole sheep was provided daily for the Collegers' dinner, a relic of the time when the College rents were paid in kind. When the turn of the younger boys came, the breast was the only portion of the animal left, and on this unattractive and innutritious fare they had to make their one square meal of the day. It was washed down with small beer, " often flavoured with salt by waggish bullies." To add to the amenities of this dinner in Hall, there were not enough plates to go round and they had to struggle for knives, forks and glasses. It is not surprising that O. B. (then known as Bosque) used to get up from the table as hungry as when he sat down and, as he tells us, in a much worse temper. To the bad feeding at Eton he attributed his Napoleonic lack of inches. It was characteristic of him that when he himself became a house-master, he returned good for evil by keeping a table which would have been thought sumptuous even in these days, and created not a little annoyance amongst his colleagues, who saw their own household bills going up in sympathy.

At Eton his career was sufficiently distinguished without being brilliant. We find him at the age of sixteen in the Middle Division of the Fifth Form. In his last year he stood next to F. A. Bosanquet, the Captain of the School and his lifelong friend.

He was twice in the select for the Newcastle, and was a member of Pop, which then still maintained its literary character. In 1854 he was chosen to speak an address before the Prince Consort, who visited Eton for the Fourth of June celebrations, reciting a poem he had composed for the occasion. But on the whole his tutor, William Johnson seems to have been little satisfied with his pupil. And Oscar Browning was as little satisfied with himself.

He opens his heart without reserve to his " only friend," his *caro libello* as he calls his diary. " I commence this journal," he writes on October 20, 1853, " with the full conviction that it will be a short one. I never yet continued in the same state of mind for long together, and even with reference to this I have often the firmest resolutions to begin a journal, but before night they have passed away. Somehow or other the thought seized me late in the day. . . . This is the fruit. I want to follow the example of Lucilius." Neither the conviction nor the wish was destined to be realised. He became in the end a most methodical and perfectly dull diarist. During half a century he regularly chronicled his doings, how he had slept, whom he had seen, but rarely mentioned the state of his soul or recorded his opinion of others. Even in his last year at Eton his pen has grown disciplined. Always the freest of talkers, he ceases to show in his journal any Pepysian qualities.

But again let us not anticipate. Before reticence becomes a habit he is ready enough to scourge the vices and follies of mankind, not excluding his own. " This day " (October 20, 1853) " has been unpleasant, that is to say, I was called according to directions at 5.15 a.m. and did not get up till 6.30, which disgusted me with myself, and I am so conceited that when I am disgusted with myself I am immediately disgusted with my fellow-creatures, whom I think fools with few exceptions," an opinion, by the way, that weighed with him through life. On the eve of his seventeenth birthday he writes : " Half-past 11 of the clock. In half an hour's time I shall have completed my 17th year, assumed the toga virilis, etc. I know not if it be a matter of congratulation or no. I should be ungrateful were I not to thank God for giving me strength to live thus long and to have run I hope not last in my race, but I cannot help feeling it weighs on me like a nightmare how little I have done for fame. How much I might have. Alexander—J. Cæsar—Byron, all rise and reprove me. I always had an idea of perfect immunity from early death because I was reserved for greater things, but now I sometimes feel I have been weighed in the balance and found wanting and rejected for some worthier. To-night I prayed God that it might not be so, and I believe my prayer was answered, for of an instant a sudden calm as of angels' wings soothed me and I was happy. . . ."

III

Books filled the chief place in his life. He was perfunctory with his school work, but devoted himself with what can be truthfully called a passionate intensity to private reading. On a Sunday night in November, '54, he gives a picture of his room. " My Room at present is a faint shadow of my mind. It is strewed with books. Here is a list of the m On the table—Byron's works, Plymley's Letters, Ellis's Passage of the Alps, Horatii Opera, Livy, vol. 2, Spectator, vol. 5, Prior's Life of Burke, Addison's Works, vol. 3, Burton's Anatomy of Melancholy. On the small table, Byron's Life, vol. 6, Lighter Hours, Napier's Battles and Sieges.

On the water-pipes, Green's Life of Mahomet,
Gibbon's vol. 5, Mont Blanc and Back, Students'
Guide, Thucydides, various editions of Æschylus,
Gibbon's Miscellaneous Works, vol. 5, Elegant
Extracts of Poetry, Byron, Blessington's Idler in
Italy, Disraeli's Miscellanies of Literature. On the
sofa, Arnold's History of Rome, vol. 3, and the
first vol. of Cluverius' Italia Antiqua—such a
wilderness is my mind. I really must be steady and
noble (*morally*, I mean), and not loiter and fritter
away my time as I do at present, but perhaps it is
not my fault *only*."

Byron was his god. " In this journal," he says
at the beginning, "I dare say I shall fall into the
archaic style of writing horribly affected [and] so
much used by Byron, but although I detest and loathe
it I cannot help it." "I have just been reading
Byron's Life and the list of books he had read
before 19. I am ashamed of myself. I yearn for
fame and love him." A few days later the schoolboy of sixteen was consoling himself for not yet
having fledged his poetic wings. "I was talking
with M. M. B." (his mother) " about Byron to-day.
Said how odd it was that his first composition should
bear no proportion to his later ones, and that he
should have started up so suddenly ' one of the
giants of English Literature.' His letters, at least
his early ones, were full of bad grammar, and I
think that critique in the Edinburgh on his Hours
of Idleness, so much maligned because of his after
fame, perfectly just. I suppose every poet has a
certain quantity of scum which he must throw off
before the true flower of his poetry can come out.
Would mine were passed. Oh fame, I long for
thee, long for thee. And my mind storms, but
ah. . . ." There is no entry for a month after this
rhapsodical parenthesis.

His partiality for Byron did not cause him to

neglect the other poets of the romantic school. He
starts upon Moore. "Have begun to-day an arduous undertaking to read Moore right through.
However, it is worth while." A subsequent note
against this entry runs : "Found Moore was in
great measure not worth reading. However, got
through Lalla Rookh and Rhymes and the Road
and a good deal more." His reading was done at
all hours of the day and night. "This morning "
(November 3, 1853) " I awoke at 5 and read Coventry Patmore right through, and to-night I read
Arnold's Falcon, which I do not like so well as
Patmore's poem on the same subject." A few days
before he had been reading Keats, whom he
considered to resemble Spenser in his style and
imagination. He adds after this piece of criticism :
" Hate Southey and Wordsworth, more particularly
the Excursion and the Prelude, which I take to be
arrant humbug and egotistical." Tennyson and
Longfellow in his opinion did not equal Byron and
Campbell and " all the galaxy of beauty that dazzled
the eyes at the beginning of the century."

He longed to be another Byron. For some
months when he is seventeen he " lives and dreams
poetry." He seems to be really working off the
scum. Soon he will be drinking the clear and
shining waters. Then the poetic fit passes
off. He still writes poetry, but now he must
" labour every line." The waters grow muddier
than before. It is possible that he is not destined
to rival the fame of Byron. But there is always
prose. History as well as poetry can give the bays
to its favoured children. He has been reading
Gibbon's Autobiography, and suddenly it flashed
upon him that the author of the *Decline and Fall*
was born in May 1737, he in January 1837. " Not
much perhaps, but still enough to cling to. I
shall be able to compare his progress with mine, to

envy, rejoice over and emulate him by turns. O
God, turn it to my good." Thus was strengthened
his taste for history. He reads Gibbon constantly. "Have been reading Gibbon for the
Essay which we have to write on Mahomet next
Wednesday. . . . I shall support Mahomet intensely and shall think him a most awful trump. I
shall follow Gibbon mostly. His 5oth chapter is
wonderful—but wants attentive reading. He is
moderate and learned. I finished his Life last night.
It did me a great deal of good, but I don't understand what his reputed atheism is founded on.
He seems discreet enough to me, but I don't know.
Addio." The farewell is to his journal, which he
thus takes leave of in English, French, German or
Italian impartially. Later he tires of Gibbon's
magniloquence, for of chapters sixty to seventy he
writes : " His style worse and worse. His perpetual
love of antithesis which he somewhere complains
of himself in others makes his writing dull and
obscure and difficult to understand." But he took
Gibbon in his stride. Thirlwall's *History of Greece*,
Macaulay's *History of England*, Voltaire's *Charles XII*,
Stirling's *Charles V*, Thackeray's *English Humour-
ists*, Ruskin, " a 1000 novels," which included the
Brontës ("I do not like Villette nor any of the Bells
novels, the style is too strained and affected, and
that in the last degree. It becomes a labour to read
them," was his verdict then, which was reversed by
his later judgment), Mrs. Gaskell, whom he admired,
The Shaving of Shagpat, make up a formidable list for
any schoolboy's reading in his spare time.

IV

His tutor, William Johnson, for whom he had a
lifelong respect, thought he was inclined to dissipate
his intellectual energies. An early entry runs :

" My tutor says I am deficient in ' Vis.' I believe him. Must get up steam somehow or shall come to consummate grief." He hopes for a better mood on the morrow and then his pen runs off again to literature. "I admire Faust very much. Think the last scene beautiful and some parts of the beggin-ning (*sic*). Margaret is charming." Bad reports were the rule during those middle years at Eton. At the end of the Christmas half of 1855 he refers to his tutor's letter complaining of his " languor and inactivity as found by others. Says that my schoolfellows think me conceited, unsociable and cross. Also a jaw from Stephen H[awtrey], who is a humbug. Three cheers for the schoolfellows and their opinion." A year later he writes : " Have been having a long and important conversation with my mother. I have had a bad report from my tutor and a bad conscience for the last three weeks. My brothers have been uproarious. I am almost deter-mined to tell Arthur the proximate cause of all this misery. My social position at Eton. The way I have been treated. The way I have suffered. The way the flood of grief or madness, I know not what, has gradually melted away the feeble barriers I could oppose to it. My extreme sensitiveness, a failing I allow, but one of nature. How it has been tortured and how it has been disbelieved even by my friends, who can find no such corresponding feeling in their own breasts. How my joy has been turned into sorrow, my best resolutions into fruit-less gall, till at last with broken spirit, heart seared by disappointment and everything else which has happened to me, I have become what I am. I owe all this misery to two boys, Hicks and Pinchard. On them be the penalty."

This is the first indication we have of the persecu-tion mania which plays a large part in Oscar Brown-ing's life. He would imbibe a notion that someone was trying to do him injury, on any evidence or none, and nothing afterwards would shake his opinion. What Hicks and Pinchard had done we know not, probably they had been " ragging " him. Anyhow Oscar, who talks darkly of being " betrayed," was very bitter. " I here, if it be not displeasing to God," he writes, " register a vow for vengeance. I *will* have vengeance on them. They by their wanton foolery have—I cannot write it." Then follows this curious entry : " O my God, look upon me. Thou knowest what I say is true. If this vow be not wicked let it be fulfilled. I leave the vengeance to thee. Vengeance is mine, I will repay, saith the Lord. The Lord for higher motives give me energy and understanding. Counsel me in this strait, through Jesus Christ I pray. Amen."

The next entry, nearly two months later, begins : " Tandem rex sum." Pinchard, one of the two on whom he had cried for vengeance, had left. He took a commission in the Ceylon Rifle Regiment and died in 1874 as a captain in the 70th Rifles. They appear to have remained on friendly terms, corresponded with each other, and Pinchard visited him at Eton when on leave. The other lived the uneventful life of a country parson. Oscar Browning's prayers were not as a rule answered.

His unhappiness was due in part to his feeling that he was not a social success, and his spirits are lowest when he has been rejected for Pop in the Michaelmas half of 1854. But the vein of youthful melancholy, which persists through the pages of this diary until he is nineteen, in such contrast to the genial optimism of his adult life, can in part be ascribed to physical reactions. His " languor and inactivity " are really not surprising. An underfed boy of seventeen who led the life he did could hardly have been expected to show any other qualities. He rises at six or earlier, and we find him entering in his journal: "Am now writing this at 11.45 p.m. I must take a pill and go to bed, for I am not in health." "I wake up every morning with feverish hands and white tongue." "I went to bed this morning at 12.5, slept till five, dozed till seven, got up and went into the library for trials in the first three chapters of Hallam's Constitutional History." One does not wonder at anyone becoming morbid under such circumstances.

"I remember well," he writes in November 1854, "when I was nine years younger than I am now, that I could not help thinking how odd it was I was a man. I used to speculate on the position and the future state of men, and constantly the thought used to strike me and obstruct me that I was myself one of them. To-night but in a sadder way I have thought the same. I am here at Eton. I have been unluckily thrown among a set who do nothing but ridicule my peculiarities (whatever they may be) among them. Bosque (the name by which they are pleased to designate me) is only a subject for laughter. I am, according to them, incapable of performing in any way the duties of public or private life. Such things disgust me beyond measure, and I believe justly so."

This is the constantly recurring theme of his diary. "At present" (November 1854) "I am totally and thoroughly disgusted with Eton. I ought not to be, but am. Heaven send me prudence and friends." William Johnson's complaints of his unsociability were clearly well-founded. "Was reproved by my tutor for unsociability and consequent unpopularity. Felt rebuked, humble, but can't help it. By the bye, heard that Cookesley considers me out of my depth in my division work. A weakling forsooth. . . . May he some day find his mistake. A weakling—bah!"

Cookesley left Eton too soon to make this dis-

covery. But at the time Oscar Browning's low
spirits and inertia made his family apprehensive.
His brother William thinks him melancholy, "let's
hope not mad," adds Oscar. Not even the success
of winning the prize for the Address and reciting it
before the Prince Consort and the future King
Edward cures him of his habitual depression. "Both
in school and in private I have been unsuccessful
and unhappy, and now I would tell my griefs. . . .
4 (*sic*) or 3 years ago I was spirited, clever, successful
and everything else. Now I am effete, dilatory, unsuccessful and a fool. And this is attributable to
myself. . . . I am 17 and am reckoned clever.
Have done one or two things. But these, alas!
are but the fitful lightnings which expose the dark
gray and the barren moor else invisible. They
only show what I might have been. And possibly
may be. . . ." Michaelmas Day is a good occasion
for further heart-searchings. "I have fallen into a
very bad way of thinking, acting and a great many
other -ings during the last few months. I know the
cause but dare not tell, not even to my diary." It
was, one may hazard the guess, one of those
emotional crises not uncommon to clever schoolboys struggling with the problems of adolescence.
And then he records how he has got a nought for
his verses. He continues : "I intend to turn over
a new leaf this quarter. I had intended to begin
on the first of October, on which day a quarter and
my income (an allowance of £40 a year) begin. . . .
I have talents. Let me use them."

The mood, however, soon passed. In a few days
his good resolutions have all evaporated. "Can't
write and am in a wretched state as usual. I must
not dawdle. I must apportion well my time and
stick to it. At present I am going to hell fast, and
what is worse obscurity. Am not and have not been
over well. . . ." He is very much out of conceit

with himself when a few weeks later he says : " O that I could learn a lesson from the butterfly, who first appears as a worm crawling and despicable enough but still with its uses. Then encloses itself in a dark ugly skin and troubles no one, and asks not attention till it bursts out into the full glories of painted wings and downy colours, admired and caressed. So far let the comparison go and no further. . . . I have just been recurring to the entry in my diary of the 21st October last year." (His remarks about the romantic poets already quoted.) " I find it dull and conceited. It was a reflection of myself, but I am no better now. This notebook is full of that misery and wretchedness which has been my bane. They say cholera is produced by a most acrid vinegar-like poison which settles in the system and produces all the well-known effects. I have a pungent bitter in me. This is the effect of my sensitiveness, and I feel, or wish I could feel, I deserve it." Later he declares that nobody knows his faults better than he does himself, but he is " totally unable to cure them." So it goes on. As he grows older the tendency to self-analysis that is a common enough trait of adolescence becomes less. Yet when he is eighteen and a half it still persists. We find him writing on June 1, 1855, in an almost illegible hand : " I am in the lowest of spirits and believe myself not to be well. The only thing which would do me good is training, and that is too laborious and uncomfortable. However, it is next to necessary both for mind and body, the one a weedy wilderness, the other a wreck. I really must try to do something. . . . Oh, what I might have been."

But the Oscar Browning we know is beginning to emerge. He is already making friends and acquaintances in the great world. Part of the previous Easter holidays he had spent with Reginald Abbot, a fellow Etonian, who afterwards became the last

Lord Colchester. There he had been introduced to
Lord Ellenborough, " one of the master spirits of
this age." " He made my acquaintance warmly,"
the diary informs us, " and talked of the sameness
of the Eton lists of 50 years' difference in date."
And Oscar Browning " agreed with him." Another
day Lord Ellenborough dines with his host and
hostess, Lord and Lady Colchester, and is " gracious." The Crimean War had then begun to drag
its length along, and Lord Ellenborough "suggested
the enlistment of the King of Dahomey's army, all
black and all women, 7000 strong, in our foreign
legion, for they fight like devils." The butterfly
is certainly emerging. Lord Colchester takes him
to the House of Lords, and they have great difficulty
in crossing the Mall because the Emperor Napoleon
is returning to Buckingham Palace from his visit to
the Guildhall. The Empress was not so pretty as
Oscar expected, which he put down to the fact that
she probably " was not becomingly dressed." He
meets too Sir Robert Dallas, whom he has desired to
see all his life. " I remember," he says, " reading his
book, or rather the Percy extracts from it, and
thinking how much longer I should have the chance
of writing as he did. He told me of the Italian
order of the spur, a pretty one by the way which I
should like to have." And he is annoyed at a
certain Mr. Glennan, " Reggie's former tutor, who
much to my disgust rather treated me as in the same
boat with himself." Nor does he allow London to
interfere with his homage to literature. He re-
writes a poem he had composed on the subject of
Francesca, and presents the new edition to Lady
Colchester, " who received it graciously." He
spends an evening in the Strand watching the
illuminations, visits the St. George's Baths, eats ices
and enjoys himself in a perfectly schoolboy fashion.
In London he was obviously happy.

V

Yet if at Eton he had not many friends, he had a nature capable of romantic affection. "At school," says Disraeli in *Coningsby*, "friendship is a passion. It entrances the being; it tears the soul." So it was with Oscar Browning. On his seventeenth birthday he makes this entry : " To-day I received the greatest pleasure that for many days I have received, indeed a noble birthday gift, an hour of Prothero's " (F. T. E. Prothero) " society. For the last three weeks have I prayed to God that his heart might have changes and he might love, and my prayer hath been answered. For to-day I met him and walked with him. I told him that it was my birthday, and his lips wished me many happy returns of the day. Surely God will receive that prayer, surely I am blessed in that wish. Why I should love Prothero as I do I cannot tell, but I do love him and I believe that that love ennobles me and purifies me. It gives me an object for my work and my affections, truly a noble one." A year later there occurs in another page of self-analysis : " I know that what I want in life is someone to love. . . . My object is not love, but love without his wings, friendship. A half or two ago I saw a boy named Dunmore. I was struck by his eyes. I have been more so by his manner and everything about him. My wishes, my hopes and fears begin and terminate in him. I have found that he is a lord, but I loved him before. I never shall have a chance of knowing him, perhaps not one of speaking to him." An ideal passion could hardly go further than this.

Let us not think him, however, always a bookworm, a prig or a dreamer. Oscar Browning's days were much like those of other Etonians, more distinguished or obscure than himself. Though he never had the slightest skill at games he played them

all. His favourite was fives, which he considered
" beat football out of sight." Evidently he was
nothing of a cricketer. " Yesterday," he writes to
his mother, " on hearing that I played cricket my
tutor laughed immoderately and said he'd bowl me
out. I went and played with him in the Home
Park. He didn't, however, succeed in his object."
The sight of an Eton tutor, and that tutor William
Johnson, bowling to one of his pupils beneath the
Castle walls suggests more leisured and spacious
days than ours. But in the 'fifties organised games
were still in the womb of time. Naturally too the
river drew him. When he boats it is usually with
a book under his arm. He tells us how he and
another boy read Shakespeare aloud together on
summer afternoons. On a whole holiday he is one
of an eight which rows down to Richmond, and
they come home by train. Naturally he drinks
beer. " Nothing puts me in such spirits as pale ale,
though I don't like it. I have sipped liqueurs in
French cafés to no end of an extent. I have drunk
cognac'd coffee to the same, but I never felt in better
spirits." He meditates a breakfast party at Web-
ber's, " but must enquire as to £ s. d. etc." He
gets a passport for " up-town " because of the
" pig-headedness of the Eton tradesmen." The
evenings he sometimes passes at cards, though he
considers them rather a waste of time. " Spent the
evening somewhat unsatisfactorily. Played vingt-
et-un and lost 1/-." On the top of this dissipation
he " did 30 verses in ¼ of an hour." He adds :
" To-morrow I do nothing. I have been going it
tremendously with Evans and that set lately and
think them devilish pleasant fellows." In Brussels
during his holidays he develops a taste for billiards.
" Played Billiards all the afternoon. Cost me 40
centimes." Dances occupy his evenings. He complains not uncharacteristically of having received no

D   33

invitation to the King's ball, though he had been presented at Court the previous summer. And he submits like any other boy to the Crimean War fever. "Great news, glorious news," he writes on October 7, 1854. "All this kind of thing is going on and men are in the greatest state of excitement, and I with them, concerning the war."

Oscar Browning's thoughts, however, even as a boy never for long strayed far from the first person. His ambition, his desire to cut a figure in the world, never left him to enjoy his lethargy, his cards or his billiards for long. "I have been proposed for Pop and rejected by nine black balls. Not so many as I expected among 26 members none of whom scarcely I know. However, am not disheartened. . . . As there is only one more vacancy in Pop I am afraid I shall not get in." (He was, in fact, elected.) "It is and has always been my ambition. I wish I could write and speak English." The Bar had always attracted him, and indeed continued to do so long after he had become an Eton Master. But it had drawbacks. At sixteen he writes : "I have had my ideas about most things, more particularly my future life, much modified and changed. In the first place I am told on all sides that a barrister's life is by no means the most comfortable in existence, and that I shall after working like a horse (or an ass) for 6 years arrive at the attainment of £300 a year. . . . No, I am convinced that the only way of advancement, particularly to such as me, is *work*. I have no rank. I have no fortune. But I have a head and brains as good or bad as most." So he decides that what he must aim at is " high Academical distinction." " I am convinced," he adds, "that even literary distinction is gained by work and brains. It is all very well to say that geniuses are idle, but nevertheless 'tis a lie. If geniuses are idle they never come to good. Byron worked not perhaps at Latin and Greek, but read his life. Moore worked. Mat Arnold worked. Tennyson worked. May I."

One aspect of his life at Eton has yet to be mentioned, his love for music. "Good music," he writes when he is sixteen, "quite carries me away, it completely fills me. I forget that I am a man or walk the earth. The really most affecting music I have ever heard was at Antwerp at the Church of the Augustins. It was a fête day. The moment the procession entered the church the organ began, and with the organ the whole orchestra. I never was so entranced." He had a low opinion of the singing in Eton Chapel. "Yesterday we had Mozart's anthem, ' Plead thou my cause,' grand and noble in the extreme as all his are. But badly sung and worse played." Even at that early age he was under no doubt that Mozart was the supreme master. "There certainly never lived a greater or more perfect genius," is one judgment in his diary. And he runs on : "His masses are the best now existing. His comic songs surpass everything, and his tragedy and sentiment are as good. O that he had written an oratorio." A cantata of Sir Frederick Ouseley's he finds " good for nowadays but deficient in richness of instrumentation and harmony." *Israel in Egypt* is " very fine as music but not an epic by any means." He was not content with being a mere listener. He organised a choir which progressed favourably, or would have done so if only the members would have sung in tune. "I practise and practise, and din into their ears the difference between semitones and tones." The trebles, however, were unapt pupils. And he did not neglect the theory of music. "Read a treatise on music. I understand something of harmony and counterpoint. I cannot quite get all the intervals and chords. They must be the subjects of long study."

The world was too full of interesting things. There was Italian, in which he had private lessons, much to the disgust of his mathematical master, who saw in this an additional excuse for his neglect of mathematics. There was art and Ruskin: "I am learning the principles of taste; if Ruskin's system be false, it is at least a system and one of some stamina, to judge of the work and the man which produced it." And there was philosophy and Locke; his *Essay on the Conduct of the Understanding* had to be "read and re-read and meditated on thoroughly." Theology too attracts him. He is "really in danger of believing it an attractive study." He wishes he could investigate that "hard but interesting subject, the brethren of our Lord." And there were novels, *The Shaving of Shagpat*, which had just come out—"Wallahy, but it is good!"—and *The Heir of Redclyffe*. "I am not sure of the purity of the style, but Miss Young (*sic*) must be very superior in attainments, especially metaphysics." And there was the *Saturday Review* every week. No wonder that his last year at Eton was not marked by any great academic distinction and that he was hardly as high in the Select for the Newcastle as in the preceding year, and that his tutor considered he was wasting his abilities and in danger of becoming a dilettante.

But Oscar Browning was now nineteen and the time was fast approaching when he would have to leave Eton. At first there was talk of his going to Oxford. His mother's means were slender, however, and his brother William had many calls on his purse. Expense had to be considered. A scholarship was essential. It was suggested that he should try for a post-mastership at Merton. To this he was agreeable, but he demurred to the proposal of going to Oxford as a Bible clerk. "My energies," he wrote to his mother, "would be crushed by the constant irritation of a position which I knew I was not fit for. I should lose all the advantages of an education which I feel when finished will be my fortune." Nor was he favourable to the idea that he should supplement his resources by coaching in the vacations. "I do not think," he says, "you have a right to expect fruits of an education till that education is finished. If I have been working hard, as I sincerely hope I shall, for honours at Oxford, I shall probably be so tired in the holidays that I shall want recreation. Or, on the other hand, in most holidays I shall want to read myself. In neither of these cases could I take a pupil. As to my position. What is my position? One who has to work for his living, I know, but in company with many of his own class. I go to William's. I find him keeping horses and drinking champagne on fête days. I go to Arthur and find him most comfortable with his hunter and his champagne. I go to Brussels. I find you comfortable as far as your means go, associating with people of your own position. Am I not a gentleman, by birth, by education, by feeling?"

Not Oxford, however, but Cambridge was to claim him. His future was determined by the bounty of Henry VI. In the examination for entrance to King's, which at that time ensured a competence for life to one who remained a bachelor, he was placed fourth. John Witt, destined to become a well-known Q.C., was first; Churton, who, if the Anglican Church were not so incurably modest, would already be a candidate for beatification, was second; F. A. Bosanquet, who like Witt attained eminence at the Bar, was third. For a time it was doubtful if Oscar would obtain a vacancy. But his family by means of a douceur persuaded a Fellow of the College to resign some months before he had intended. So on July 27, 1856, Oscar Browning's gown was " ripped " by the Provost of Eton and he became a member of the major foundation of the royal saint, a connection that lasted for sixty-seven years and was only terminated by his death at Rome in 1923.

VI

The account of his four years as an undergraduate need form little more than a footnote to this sketch of Oscar Browning the schoolboy. They appear to the biographer as the dimmest and least documented of his life. Three slender and partially kept diaries show by their meagre entries and impersonal tone that he had emerged from the trials of adolescence and that he was happy, rather extravagant and moderately industrious. O. B.'s later description of himself as an undergraduate—a conceited prig, in his own words—give one no help. What able young man in the early twenties, who has enjoyed the advantages of being educated at Eton and Cambridge, is not conceited ? And though Oscar Browning had his foibles and idiosyncrasies, priggishness was not one of them.

If we judge him by his friends he comes through the test well, for the coterie of which he was not the least prominent member included Montagu Butler, Henry Sidgwick, R. C. Jebb, G. O. Trevelyan, F. A. Bosanquet, Calverley and Frank Cornish, the dearest of all his friends, who came up from Eton a year later than he did. Amidst this welter of youthful intellect O. B. discovered that he was no Whig, but a Liberal, even a Radical, that his political creed could rest securely on the writings of John Stuart Mill, and that his life must be devoted to the cause of humanity. He foresaw the advent of demos and meant to do what he could to make it a reasonable and a cultured demos. The social revolution seemed a very imminent thing to thoughtful and enthusiastic young men of the mid-Victorian era. They wished only to throw over its nakedness the decent cloak of Reform, to satisfy its hunger with the wholesome bread of Retrenchment. And over the whole picture there floated the dove of Peace.

There was, of course, much stupidity and conservatism to be overcome. At Eton the current of public opinion had been too strong to swim against with comfort. But King's was small, and if the little group of Eton scholars disapproved of his zeal and sent him to Coventry because he insisted on speaking at the Union, he could find congenial society in Trinity, where not Eton but Rugby gave its moral zeal and bracing tone to that august foundation. He wanted to fit himself to be a statesman and a trainer of statesmen, and as a stepping-stone towards that end he became President of the Union, the first King's-man to be so for nineteen years.

Though he aspired to "high academical honours," exact, professional scholarship had little attractions for him. Without undue exertion—" average reading three and a half hours," " average reading four and a half hours," are common enough entries in his diary at the end of the week—he succeeded in being one of the four candidates for University Scholarships who were called upon to do an extra paper, the other three being Peile, Abbot and Jebb. His success stopped there. He was fourth in the Classical Tripos, the three above him being bracketed together first. When the news was shouted to him from someone in the Court below, O. B., who was leaning over his window-sill, said "Damn." That seems to have been the sum of his regret to have missed by little the highest distinction which the study of the Classics could then afford to its pampered children at Cambridge.

For the rest he led the pleasant life of the undergraduate, passing no little of his mornings in breakfast parties at which College ale was still drunk, though only as a *chasse-café*, playing fives, or rowing, or swimming, or going for walks in the afternoon and devoting many of the long evenings which followed dinner in Hall at five to " wines." His polymathy was still as marked as ever, but he does not seem to have read with the insatiable zest of his Eton days. Talk, one may suspect, had taken the place of books, talk for which the Union, the " Apostles " meetings, and more intimate parties gave endless opportunity. So the years slipped by with young ambition preparing itself in that Epicurean *milieu* for the battle that was to come. The qualms of wasted opportunities, so strong at Eton, were still with him. After noting in his diary the names of the guests whom he had entertained to dinner on his twenty-third birthday he adds the first two lines of Milton's sonnet inspired by a similar occasion and similar regrets. Like Milton too, Oscar Browning felt himself to be ever in his great Taskmaster's eye. Religious observances played a regular part in his life, and on those Sundays when there was no celebration of the Holy Communion in King's Chapel, he used to repair to St. Giles', even marking Saints' days in this solemn manner. And in the vacations he would attend church regularly twice on Sundays and note in his diary his opinion of the sermons. Ultimately in the spring of 1860, after he had been teaching for a fortnight at Liverpool and was still quite uncertain whether he would devote his abilities to education or to the law, he received a telegram from Dr. Goodford offering him the post of an assistant mastership at Eton, and Saturn being the adverse element in his horoscope, he entered upon his new duties rather ominously on Saturday, May 12, of that year.

CHAPTER III

ETON AND REFORM

I

WHEN Oscar Browning returned to Eton as an Assistant Master he found an excellent field for his self-imposed rôle of reformer. Eton, governed by its Provost and Fellows, had so far resisted the changes that the times demanded. Montem and other abuses had been abolished. The material conditions of the Collegers had been ameliorated. But the old classical curriculum still held undisputed sway. And parents were becoming restive. They wanted their sons to know something about the modern world. Modern languages, modern history, not least science, were already surrounded with a prestige that adumbrated their future intellectual and commercial importance, and fathers were becoming anxious that their sons should not pass through their school careers in ignorance of these phases of human activity. The old classical education, which had reached its high-water mark under Butler at Shrewsbury, was suspect. It was growing doubtful whether a knowledge of Homer and the Latin poets was of itself a sufficient intellectual equipment for an English gentleman. Public opinion, concerned about the public schools in general, was specially concerned about Eton, and the currents of reform were beginning to swirl round its immemorial stones. It was full of abuses which no Government could afford to ignore much longer. The elderly clerics who as Fellows composed its

41

governing body were untouched by the intellectual ferment of the mid-Victorian era. The desire for reform was growing articulate, and something would have to be done very soon.

It was a golden opportunity for a young Radical, himself nurtured in this home of tradition, to march like David against the Philistines. And for fifteen years he did so. "I never worked so hard for anything in my life as I did to liberalise Eton," he says in his old age. The story of his career at Eton, though the thread is often difficult to follow in the controversies with which it was entangled, coincides with a definite stage in the transition of our public schools. On the one side was the "Old Eton party," represented by Dr. Goodford, Head Master till 1862 and then Provost during the remaining years Oscar Browning was at Eton, Dr. Balston, a splendid example of the scholar and gentleman parson of the old school, and by nearly all the senior masters. Chief among the younger Conservatives was Edmond Warre, who returned to Eton at the same time as Oscar Browning. Hornby, who became Head Master in the commencement of 1868, though for a year or two he was claimed by the Liberals, and indeed professed himself to be one, was really in sympathy with the party of tradition. The impression he gives is that of an able but narrow-minded man with the exaggerated sense of importance which Head Masters so easily acquire. He certainly was no Farrar or Temple.

On the other side were ranged Browning and a group of younger masters, Ainger, Wayte, Cornish, James and others. William Johnson, that attractive but elusive personality, stands alone and criticises both parties. There was little doubt which was the stronger. The reformers might be supported by what is generally called enlightened opinion, but the "Old Eton party" controlled the machine and in an emergency could draw on the loyalty that the public school spirit gives to constituted authority. It was an inherent weakness in Oscar Browning's position, that he seemed to be acting in opposition to his own chief. How true it was, the record of his Eton life will show. In any case his opponents did not fail to emphasise the point when the crisis came. He never in retrospect regarded Hornby as anything but a man of straw. His principal opponent he always believed was Edmond Warre. No two men could have been more unlike, either in temperament or appearance. "Usus optimus magister" might have been Warre's motto. "A life without discussion is not worth living" was Browning's. If Warre influenced Hornby against him, as he always firmly believed, there is no evidence in Oscar Browning's voluminous correspondence to show it. On the other hand, though their natural antipathy is undisguised, Warre's letters to Browning, unlike those of Hornby, leave an impression of sincerity. Both in conversation fulminated against the other. But at Eton in the 'sixties and 'seventies, it is clear that everyone talked about everyone else. The masters, and their wives and daughters, all discussed each other with candour rather than with charity.

II

Eton, however, is Eton. Oscar Browning, though he returned there as an ardent Radical burning to flesh his sword in the numerous abuses that he saw around him, was none the less a loyal son when it came to defending Eton against the outside world. "Sir," writes one who has been bold enough to raise his voice, "I have been favoured with your note in which you are good enough to give me your opinion that the education at Eton, moral, intellectual and physical, is the best in the world, and that my opinion to the contrary is the result of ignorance more or less wilful. I regret that I am unable to profit by this scholastic treatment of the subject, whilst there is obviously no room for improvement in your mind, and that our correspondence becomes, therefore, useless." "Snob" is the pencilled comment, snobbery being a failing he was quick to detect in others. Eton had to be reformed, but it had to be done by Etonians. Theirs was the responsibility, theirs too would be the credit. By becoming a schoolmaster Oscar Browning had sacrificed his personal ambitions. He had put by politics, the law, letters. It was some consolation to think that under his hand lay a task not unworthy of his powers. He pictured—and he had always that quality of vision which is one of the marks of greatness—a new Eton, educating a governing class in the delight of all intellectual pursuits, a governing class that would owe its position not only to wealth and privilege, but also to its Platonic virtues of wisdom and goodness. It was a fascinating prospect, a prospect which fascinated him to the end of his long life. "I always believe," he writes in 1913, "that if my party had won at Eton instead of Warre's, the Parliament Act would never have been passed. Warre and Hornby did their best to ruin Eton and the country, and a terrible responsibility rests upon them."

The task too, important as it was for the future of England and the Empire, offered immediate compensations. Eton, in the words of Professor Blackie, "was an elegant and refined seat of taste, learning, conservatism and wealth, where the masters make £2000 or £4000 or £5000 clear profit, and where the whole world appears to be walking with silk slippers on silk carpets." Oscar Browning liked walking on silken carpets. If he was a Platonist, he was also an Epicurean. On his library he spent £300 a year; no gentleman at that time could spend less, he used to observe in later days. But he had a care too for his wine-cellar and was already a curious though not, as in later years, an insatiable gourmandiser. He rode to hounds. When he travelled, as he did every holidays, he was attended by his personal servant. A courier added both comfort and dignity to his journeys. Thanks to Eton he was able to command these things. He took them as the return due to him for his renunciation of the greater world. "Why should a man," he asks in one of his letters to Arthur Sidgwick, "directly he becomes a schoolmaster, be thought as unfit for civilised society as if he had taken orders?" The lay schoolmaster, indeed, whatever his social advantages, was still seriously handicapped compared with his clerical colleagues. Oscar's elder brother thought it a misfortune that his haziness on questions of dogma prevented him from taking orders. An Eton mastership indeed was a kind of order, and many of his correspondents, including John Ruskin, persisted in addressing him as the Rev. Oscar Browning long after they had opportunity of observing the laicity of his mind and character. From the worldly point of view it was a pity that he remained a layman. He must look forward at some time to retiring. If he could not take a living, what was he to do? At twenty-three it was already obvious that he was not one of those who save money.

Yet though Eton offered both material compensations and spiritual rewards, the idea of being a schoolmaster all his life was often irksome. He still looked longingly towards the Bar and began to eat dinners. He will save £20,000. With that he will embark on the career of his choice. His brother William again turns his own common-sense on to this projected ladder of young ambition. " What good will it do you," he asks, " to be called barrister-at-law ? Any employment that would be given you twenty years hence would be given to you, not as a barrister, but as a distinguished Eton master. Then for the £20,000—it will take, under favourable circumstances, with unbroken health, without a wife, with strict self-denial, twenty years to make that sum. Do you think that at forty-five you will have the freshness of mind to turn to a new pursuit, to make your home and take your position in the world ? I think that you see only the outside of things and are taken with the tinsel and glitter of what is not gold." The elder brother, if he understood one side of his character, underrated the powers of the younger. Oscar continued to eat dinners. But the interest of his life at Eton by degrees softened his regrets. And he could always console himself with the reflection, which he makes to his friend Sidgwick, that if he were only a schoolmaster, he was nevertheless " in however humble a way, still forwarding the interests of humanity."

III

Young intellectuals took their Liberalism seriously in the 'sixties. They had the same earnestness as the Fabians of the early 1900's. They were Fascists in everything except violence. The youthful Radical schoolmaster never forgot that the world, as well as Eton, had to be set right. And to his hand lay the most splendid material. What finer opportunity was there of doing good than moulding the characters of those who as men would rule England ? Besides, he soon discovered that he had a peculiar genius for influencing and drawing out the young. This caused him, as nothing else could, to become reconciled to his lot.

So he threw himself with ardour into the task before him. He draws up an elaborate statement of his views for the reform of Eton. More than this he surveys the whole field of public school education and corresponds actively with his friends who are inspired by the same ideals in the other great schools, with Montagu Butler, Bowen and Young at Harrow, with Sidgwick at Rugby. There had never been a time when the ungrateful vocation of the schoolmaster attracted so many of the best brains and finest characters from both the Universities. Two or three times a term these young enthusiasts, who rejoiced in the science of pedagogics, met together in a society known as the " U. U." They dined together, often at the Star and Garter, and then one of them read a paper on some educational subject. These were sometimes printed for private circulation. One that lies before me advocates " inequality and so to speak caprice in punishment." It ends : " The perfect schoolmaster, if he is ever formed by the wisdom of a series of U. U. essays, will behave to his ordinary punishees as patients whose treatment is a matter for resource, experiment, curiosity, comparison and scientific interest. He will remember that boys are, on the whole, about as good as masters. He will never feel himself bound to any rules at all, and in speaking of faults he will, even with his culprits, be quite natural and honest." This paper was not, it may be said, by Oscar Browning. But caprice and favouritism were two of the offences his adversaries at Eton brought up against him, and it was for putting into practice such precepts as the writer of this essay inculcates that his difficulties at Eton multiplied upon him.

These, however, came later. During his earlier years he grew ever more optimistic. Success seemed within his grasp. In 1866 he writes : " I am so prosperous as almost to be astonished myself. No wish that I could have here is unfulfilled. Warre is crushed and Balston is becoming a reformer." Yet the old doubts emerge. Even here he adds : " But the more happy I ought to be, the less happy I am. I look back on my undergraduate days as the only bright ones of my life, and long for your society " (he is writing to Arthur Sidgwick) " and Jebb and the rest of the wise and good." It was not on this occasion any of the fancied ills, over which his mother used to accuse him of brooding, that inspired his thoughts. It was rather the restlessness, the demon of ambition that was ever at his elbow. His mother knew and grieved. " You mar your usefulness," she writes to him on one occasion, " by constantly looking beyond what you are for what you may be."

IV

What exactly did Oscar Browning want to do at Eton ? To foster intellect, to discourage the rising worship of athleticism ? That is how he answered the question himself. As regards athleticism he failed hopelessly. Its cult has long since spread from the public to the preparatory schools. The boys of the elementary schools are hardly less affected. If there is any dominant interest in England to-day it is games. Its only rival in the minds of the young is applied science, and science he utterly detested as a means of education. In his opinion the classics were the only basis of culture. In the battle for compulsory Greek at Cambridge, O. B. was a stalwart. It did not matter, he said, whether those who learnt Greek at school forgot it afterwards. A boy who had once construed a Greek sentence had thereafter his whole outlook on life changed. The classics were the bedrock of morality, citizenship, culture. He urged his views with paradox and jest. " All science consisted of looking through a very small hole for a very long time." Mathematics he disliked even more than science. It is evident that this conservative young Radical, who believed in Greek and the House of Lords and the principle of inheritance, who wanted to put games in their proper place and to keep the classics, suitably humanised, predominant in public school education, was ranged against stronger forces than he dreamt of. But he never changed his views. He considered that the attempt of the present-day curriculum to cover so many fields of knowledge was useless as education and very nearly so as instruction. Ultimately he reached the point of condemning the whole system of public school education. " The Great War," he said sententiously, " was won by the boys of the elementary schools."

Oscar Browning was full of the contradictions that to the hostile critic make the unpractical idealist. As a reformer, he used from the vantage point of old age to extol the Eton education of the 'fifties. At its best he claimed that the rigid discipline of instruction by the division master in school and the free intercourse between tutor and pupil in pupil-room were unsurpassed. It was a noble education which gave to many eminent Victorians that grandeur of style which our age lacks. But it was, like nature, wasteful. Forms in school were unwieldy. Tutors profiteered in the number of their pupils. Dr. Balston thought fifty a reasonable number. At one time he had seventy-two. As the sequel will show, the number was eventually fixed at forty. Even this was a large number for one man's supervision. The clever boys, as a result, got most of their tutor's attention. The rest were left to do the best they could. When a genius like William Johnson set himself to study the aptitude of every pupil, his colleagues considered him to indulge in favouritism. Oscar Browning, as I have said, was similarly criticised. He was thought too to be lazy; he regarded rules without punctiliousness, he did not sit up till the early hours at the thankless task of correcting work, which with some schoolmasters becomes a sacrificial obsession; his favourite method of education was talk, Socratic and unending talk. It was natural, if undeserved, that an Eton poet should describe " a strenuous sloth " as his " great gift."

The changes that he desired would have left the essential character of the old-fashioned classical education untouched. It would have been based on the culture and knowledge that are gained by the study of great literature. Only with this foundation could the philosopher-statesman be trained to comprehend the true dignity of human affairs. But modern languages and modern history were not less essential for anyone who wished to perform justly, skilfully and magnanimously all the offices, both public and private, of peace and war. Oscar Browning was a disciple of Milton. Amongst his educational works is an edition of the *Tractate*. And if a boy had a scientific bent and no taste for the letters on which civilisation rests, then it should be indulged by the study of chemistry and physics. We find this champion of a literary education providing, as a house master, at his own expense, the means whereby his pupils with aptitude for science could study those subjects; the first regular instruction in science, as he has claimed, ever given in Eton.

V

As the result of these views, Oscar Browning found himself in agreement neither with those who believed in the supreme virtue of Latin grammar and Greek verse, nor with the masters who wanted to see mathematics and science set side by side with Homer and the gods of Greece and Rome. Brandreth, a mathematical master, writes to him in 1863 complaining that he " has flung stones into their shop " (a lapse, one feels, from the dignity of Eton controversy), and pointing out that, allowing for there being " five decent boys " turned out annually by Eton and King's, which between them absorb £40,000 net revenue, each boy costs £8000 a year. He thinks this a dear bargain. " Now there are more matters in which the masters may reform, and instead of calling out to have more power put in their hands, show themselves faithful in that which is their own. Look on your pupils as a College, see where your treatment differs from that pursued in a successful College. There is probably no College in Cambridge where there is not a tutor assistant for every twenty undergraduates, usually, I should say, every fourteen." He ends on a more personal note. " Could you do nothing to prevent the use of cribs, particularly in Pop, or kickabout after ten ? Or the boys keeping their hands in those disgusting pockets ? And could you not set the boys an example of the religion you preach by occasionally coming to Chapel ? " Brandreth left soon afterwards in disgust and wrote a pamphlet on reform at Eton which he sent to Browning. " I see that it has not penetrated the serenity of your self-satisfaction," he says in a subsequent letter. O. B. was hardly likely to agree with a mathematical master, even when that master deplored with him " the honour and respect which successful idleness often ensured at Eton."

So much for the mathematical master who could not be expected to understand the virtues of a classical training, who showed its lack even in his style. But, on the other hand, the schoolmen with their trivium, their dry-as-dust grammar and their rhetoric, now sunk to mere learning by rote, were equally trying. Browning makes his Division learn English poetry, and thereby treads heavily on the Head Master's pet foible. A note is the result, curt yet polite, and ending categorically : " The learning of English poetry I do not wish to encourage." Even on the high ground of the classics they disagree. He gives an annual prize of £5 for Greek iambics very soon after returning to Eton. But it raises a correspondence between him and the Head Master which lasts on and off for five years, and finally ends in Dr. Balston returning the £5, as he cannot agree to the conditions which Browning asserts are to guide its adjudicators. Naturally, too, Browning wished to write to the papers. Nowadays, when Head Masters and Deans and Bishops are regular and highly paid contributors of the daily Press, it seems an innocent enough desire. But in the 'sixties the papers were " the public prints," and Dr. Balston, after stating a general disapproval, gives him leave " so long as only his initials are appended."

VI

All this talk of reform was given a *point d'appui* when in 1861 the Government appointed a Royal Commission to investigate the condition of the seven great public schools. The Commission turned its attention first on Eton, which was generally supposed to stand most in need of change,

and in 1862 inquired minutely into its administration
and organisation. Oscar Browning was not slow
to take advantage of the opportunity. He drew
up a memorandum of some 200 pages, which the
members obviously read with care, for they examined
him upon the views therein set out with the patience
that Royal Commissions always possess. His main
theme was the growing influence of athleticism.
He suggested that it might be countered by offering
more school prizes and surrounding them with
greater *éclat*. Every boy, he observed, knew the
names of the Eight. Few knew, or cared, who
won the Newcastle. "We want," he said, "a
thorough rearrangement, not only of our calendar,
but of our day." There were too many subjects
at one time. Modern languages and modern history
ought to become regular school subjects. Construing in pupil-room should be abolished. "On
the whole," said William Johnson to him, "I think
your reforming zeal *too* destructive and too much
like zeal for personal relief. Warre is set against
the cultivation of the intellect chiefly by your uneasy
cultivation of it." But he ranged wider than asking
for mere changes in the curriculum. He deplored
the habit of drinking at the Christopher and the
Tap, the slovenly nature of the Chapel services
(where music should form a part of the week-day
morning service with a voluntary choir recruited
from the boys), the poor sermons. Assistant
Masters, presumably lay as well as clerical, should
sometimes preach on Sundays. This would be "a
valued privilege." In one point he agreed with
Warre, who, as the Commissioners reported, had
"taken an active and lively interest in what may
be called the physical side of education at Eton."
This was in favour of the abolition of the Collegers'
gown. "I have never known," said Oscar Browning in his evidence, "a Colleger to have any great

or wide influence in the school at large.   A Colleger enjoys the privilege of being in the society of clever boys among whom work is general and fashionable and where he has every inducement to exertion. On the other hand, he breathes a somewhat confined atmosphere.   He does not drink to the full the spirit of Eton."   This proposal, however, was defeated mainly by the opposition of the Collegers.

In other respects the Commissioners' Report was a victory for Oscar Browning and the Liberals, a defeat for the Head Master and the " Old Eton " party.   A less conscientious man than Dr. Balston, whose obstinacy was as inflexible as his courtesy, would have resigned.   He was beaten on nearly every point.   " Not a day," he had said, " should be spent on the acquisition of French."   Now modern languages were to be a part of the work in school.   He had clung to the learning of the Greek and Latin poets by rote, " a thing which boys at any rate cannot get done for them."   The time spent upon this, the Commissioners recommended, should be curtailed.   Construing in pupil-room in pre-paration for Division lessons was to be abolished. All these reforms Oscar Browning had advocated The number of school holidays was commented on. The Chapel services were scathingly criticised.   The Commissioners thought that there ought to be music at the morning services.   On still another point the Commissioners reported on the lines that he had favoured.   The status of the Head Master had been in question.   Should he be given com-plete authority ?   Should he be practically free of the control of the Provost and the Governing Body in matters of school management ?   Oscar Brown-ing was of opinion that if the Head Master were to all intents absolute, as at Harrow or Rugby, he would be more open to receive suggestions. William Johnson, a shrewder judge of the forces that count in institutions, was against such despotism. The recommendation that the Head Master should have uncontrolled power of selecting and dismissing Assistant Masters was one that Browning would have supported when it was made. Around this point thirteen years later centred the battle with Hornby, when Browning fought against the Head Master's use of that very power which had been turned against himself.

CHAPTER IV

I

OSCAR BROWNING may have been restive at the checks placed upon him by the Head Master. He may have been impatient with colleagues who disagreed with him. As tutor and ruler of a house he showed a very different side to his character. His ability to shed every trace of intellectual condescension in his intercourse with his pupils partook, indeed, of genius. This and the undisguised pleasure which their society gave him were the secret of his influence. That reverence for youth, which Mr. Hugh Macnaughten has ascribed to Warre, can be accorded with equal justice to Oscar Browning. " A born master of novices " was how one of his pupils once summed him up. He watched, directed and tended with an apparent absence of effort that increased the effectiveness of his method.

The vice of systems, pedagogic and otherwise, is that they arrange and classify. His philosophy was based on the belief in the uniqueness of the human soul. That was an age when systems flourished. Following the fashion, he wished to formulate a body of theory for the complete schoolmaster. In 1868 he writes : " It would be well if schoolmasters could adopt the plan of describing their cases of education as methodically and accurately as a doctor describes his cures. In this way a mass of information might be collected which would be of the greatest use in forming a true

56

theory of education." It was Oscar Browning's supreme quality that he was, as he himself admitted, "hopelessly unscientific." He was an artist who followed no guide but his own intuition. His one working rule was that the stupid boy did not exist. If any seemed stupid, the fault lay in himself for not having found the exact spot in which their minds were assailable. He used to say that at Eton he only knew one boy who was hopelessly stupid, and that he subsequently took a high place in the competitive examination for the Civil Service. As he grew older it seemed a foible of his to detect genius. "My beloved Bob," he writes to Lord Latymer in 1919, "my secretary who was really a genius, has been killed by an accident in South Russia. I found him at Hastings when he was a poor boy minding a shop and knew that he was a genius. He had no money and was of humble birth." People smiled at his discoveries and regarded them as an amiable, or unamiable, weakness, according to their personal feelings towards him. O. B. courted smiles as he courted misunderstanding, and if at Eton a few masters sympathised and wished him well, the rest interpreted his neglect of the finer shades of routine as laziness, his readiness to talk on all subjects at large and at length as superficiality, and his wit, which sometimes appeared to them to coruscate dangerously, as unsoundness on those moral questions which lie at the foundations of society. They missed the underlying seriousness for which his humour was often a cloak.

How stimulating he was to the gifted few, Mr. A. C. Benson, who did not always say kind things about O. B., shows us in a few lines he contributed to *Eton in the 'Seventies*. He is writing on the high ideal of culture which characterised a particular generation of boys, very prominent about

1876: " J. K. Stephen, Sir Cecil Spring-Rice, Mr. C. Lowry (Head of Tonbridge), Archdeacon Burrows, Lord Curzon were among the boys who were all strongly under the influence of Mr. Oscar Browning. Indeed I remember as a small boy listening in the library to an animated discussion on some political point between Lord Curzon and Mr. J. Wallop; I was amazed and even stupefied, I recollect, at their eloquence and the maturity of their diction. . . . They talked about books and politics and ideas simply because they were interested and without any sense of superiority or any sacrifice of livelier practical issues. They were, I think, the palmy days of the literary society; but the resignation of Mr. Oscar Browning had dealt a severe blow to the intellectual life of the place for the simple reason that it was natural to him to seek the society of intelligent boys and to talk to them on terms of equality about the things which interested them. No one ever attempted the same thing on the same scale or with the same Socratic enthusiasm. He encouraged the shy boys to discuss bigger ideas, he put books in their way, and best of all he loved and practised leisurely talk." Leisurely talk—it is not in the atmosphere of a public school that one imagines this as flourishing. Schoolmasters always seem afraid of leisure for themselves, let alone their boys. And how many of them only talk freely on the subject of games, a topic which Browning, departing from his usual attitude of equality towards his pupils, would not allow to be discussed in his presence.

II

But a Socrates runs the risk of being suspected of impiety, nay, of worse. Tongues evidently wagged at Eton about his views and his methods with his boys. Fitz James Stephen, the codifier of the Indian penal laws, whose son, J. K. Stephen, was in Oscar Browning's house, writes him a hurried note one evening. He had just heard it stated in some London drawing-room that according to talk " in general society at Eton," Browning had lent to a boy a novel of Theophile Gautier's, *Mlle. de Maupin*. It was, Fitz James Stephen observed, a book which he had met with accidentally years before and was " nothing more than a mass of obscenity." Would Browning authorise him to contradict the rumour at once? The matter was too serious to pass uncontradicted even as gossip.

Oscar Browning was able to give the assurance Stephen demanded. In another note Stephen says that, though he does not wish to mention names, a man called Pater, whom he does not know, was reported as " approving the supposed proceeding." To clear up the mystery, O. B., evidently with a smile, sends Walter Pater the letters which have passed between him and Stephen. " My dear Browning," answers Pater, " I was not at all amused but much pained at the letters you enclose. You heard all I said to Graham. I think it is not possible that I mentioned the book in question. I should greatly disapprove its being lent to any boy or young man, or even allowed in his way, and it would be quite impossible for me to recommend it to any-body. I read it years ago but do not possess it. Please give an unqualified denial to the statement that I approved anything of the kind. Such statements misrepresent and pain me profoundly. . . . I remember that, the subject arising in the natural course of conversation, I mentioned an innocent sort of ghost story by Gautier as a very good specimen of its kind. I am sorry now that I did so, as I can only suppose that the report in question arose in this way."

The mystery is still unsolved when it is suddenly elucidated by a lady. "I have just heard," she writes to O. B., "that I have quite unconsciously been the cause of a mistaken report, and must let you know on how very slight a foundation the supposition grew that you lent books by Theophile Gautier to your boys. Mr. Pater was commenting upon the conversation in the boat the day after our delightful water-party, and saying how remarkable W. Graham's acquaintance with French novelists was, adding that when a boy of his years showed any kind of literary taste it was generally for poetry of a common-place nature, such as Alfred Tennyson's ! This profane remark I repeated to Annie Thackeray, mentioning also the names of Mérimée and Gautier, of whom you had talked with young Graham. She was as much surprised and impressed at the precocity of an Eton boy as Mr. Pater, and it seems to have made so deep an impression on her that she mentioned it to Leslie Stephen ! And so this piece of Russian scandal grew. . . ." The precocity of the youthful student of French romantic literature was unhappily never destined to flower, for Graham died whilst still a boy at Eton during the summer holidays of 1875. But the story, besides going to show the intellectual influence Oscar Browning exercised over the boys with whom he came into contact, proves how tongues wagged and how heads were shaken.

III

There was also the question of religion. Oscar Browning was one of those profoundly religious natures which can see virtues in all the sects, good in all religions. After running the risk as a boy of believing theology to be an attractive study, he subsequently approached the mysteries of faith with a reverent reserve, coupled with a prudent toleration that enabled him in after life to become a Christian Scientist whilst remaining within the fold of the Church of England. But there were not wanting those who looked askance at him for having an unsettling effect on his pupils in the matter of their religious beliefs. "I am told," writes an old pupil, Sir Stephen Spring-Rice, who had left Eton a year or two before, "that like Socrates you are accused of 'impiety' (in intention accused, if not in word). As to this I can only say that, though we had many talks together in the last two years, I am completely in the dark as to what your own form of religion really is, so much so, that on being told you were misleading the youthful mind in theology I could only ask : In what direction ? " Nevertheless another pupil, Charles Devas, afterwards to become a distinguished Catholic writer, stood out as an example of his disturbing influence. Devas was a poor classic, and at his tutor's prompting had read widely in history, including the whole of the *Decline and Fall*. Gibbon, oddly enough, had converted him to Catholicism. When he had decided to seek admittance to the Church of Rome, and before asking his parents' consent, he informed Oscar Browning, who said that he had so deep a respect for his character that he was convinced he could only do what was right. Devas was duly received. Lord Lyttelton, who had been examining for a history prize, writing to Oscar Browning about him, says : "I take it his general culture is mainly due to you and Wayte and a few more who lead the boys outside the school routine. I understand Devas is *now* a Roman Catholic, which I am sorry to hear."

In fact Oscar Browning, far from leaving this important part of a schoolmaster's duty alone or approaching it sceptically, took much pains in the

religious instruction it was his business to impart.
When he went to Eton he corresponded at length
with his friend, the learned and saintly Lightfoot,
who was to die as Bishop of Durham. Lightfoot
advises first of all the Greek Testament. "I do
not think that divinity can be presented in any
form which stimulates and interests both masters
and boys so much." (What would the Bishop say
if he knew that Greek was no longer a necessary
study in Theological Colleges?) "You can turn
from doctrinal teaching to verbal criticism and from
verbal criticism to history as you like and without
any unnatural interruption." Of Paley, that now
discarded champion, Lightfoot speaks highly and
urges that the question of evidences " should not be
shirked, since it often leads to an unnatural appetite
for such matters in later life." For dogmatic
theology he recommends catechetical lessons on
the Creeds. This advice Oscar Browning followed
in the spirit, if not in the letter. In his diaries
there are references to the " interesting talks " he
had had with confirmation candidates on Sunday
evenings, when he often used to read a sermon to
his boys, or as an alternative sing with them psalms
and hymns.

IV

Life in Browning's house was a pleasant combination of high thinking and good living. Artists
and men of letters, actors and musicians, Ruskin
and Solomon, George Eliot and Walter Pater,
Dannreuther, the brilliant pianist who was the
friend of Wagner and leader of English Wagnerites,
Sullivan, Sir George Grove, were more or less
frequent visitors and brought with them the atmosphere of the intelligent and civilised society to
which Oscar Browning liked to think that he
belonged in spite of his being a schoolmaster.

Theatricals used to be given by the boys in the dining-room, which was so arranged that it could be turned into a theatre for the occasion. Concerts were held periodically on Saturdays at which professionals from London performed chamber music. Both of these essays in the arts Hornby regarded with the suspicion which attached to everything in Browning's, ultimately putting his veto on the theatricals because they interfered, he said, with the school plays. Once a week there was house singing in Oscar Browning's drawing-room. He initiated inter-house competitions and presented a cup to popularise house-singing. And there was a house debating society to which boys of other houses were admitted. Arundel prints hung on his walls. Morris curtains framed the windows. Bronzes and marbles and plaster casts, especially the fragile plaster casts, helped to inculcate sobriety of demeanour. To play football in such corridors was as unthinkable as rough-housing in the corridors of the Vatican. Amidst these surroundings, in the genial warmth of the Pre-Raphaelite movement, the boys lived and grew from boyhood to adolescence, from adolescence to early manhood.

His house marked a definite step in the humanisation of the public schools. The little society over which he presided was "ruled by love rather than by fear." "Good Lord, how that man frightens me," a Lower boy is said to have remarked once of Warre. Browning never frightened anybody. His kindness of heart would get the better even of his dislike of Tap. "In July 1865," writes Mr. A. C. Trench, "I had sculled up to Monkey Island, and in running back to absence I had just time to rush into Tap for a glass of beer. In going out I ran into his arms. 'Come and see me to-morrow morning.' I went. 'I suppose you know the penalty?' he asked. 'Yes,' I replied, 'but I think it is very hard. I had been rowing for more than two hours, and I had one small glass of beer for which I shall be swished.' 'You are quite right. Go away and don't run into a master again when you come out.'"

Oscar Browning's aim was to make his house resemble the homes from which his pupils came. Thus, he argued, he would obtain the standard of conduct and the moral tone which every right-minded boy adopts unthinkingly when with his parents and sisters. He may sometimes have been deceived. He was more often justified. Here again he roused jealousies. The way he fed his boys was too luxurious, some of his colleagues thought, whose object it was to save £20,000 by their thrift and self-denial, virtues in which their pupils had the privilege of sharing. Even fagging, thanks to an unusually large staff of servants, was reduced to its lowest dimensions.

In such an unscholastic setting did Oscar Browning, helped by his mother, a beautiful and vivacious woman, and by his sisters, attempt to mould the characters of forty boys between the ages of thirteen and nineteen. "My host," I quote again the loquacious Professor Blackie, " is a man of large culture, liberal views and fine taste. His mother is a woman of breadth, decision and management, and his sister Malvina a genial, frank, laughing and talking English girl." Mrs. Browning had other qualities besides these. She too loved conversation not less than her son, and had a shattering power of reducing to silence anyone whom she considered to have taken a liberty. Every evening this *grande dame*, who in her youth had been educated in the fine arts by Old Crome, Cotman and Noverre, presided alone at the boys' supper-table and shed the light of her wit and charm on the responsive and generous mind of youth. No wonder that admission to his house was keenly sought and that some parents adopted the till then unheard-of course of entering their sons' names at birth.

One can imagine how in such company and amidst such surroundings clever boys took on the maturity of which A. C. Benson has spoken, and that few came under Oscar Browning's influence without being benefited. Nor did he confine himself to his own pupils. Warre and Mitchell, he argued, took up promising oars and cricketers; he was bound to do the same thing for those interested in intellectual pursuits. He thus drew into his circle many of the leading boys in the school and often its finest athletes. Neither Alfred Lyttelton nor his brother Canon Edward Lyttelton was in his house. But their letters to him show how they valued his intimacy, how high they put his moral influence in the school. If to come into contact with him was to be taught to submit all things to the light of rational inquiry, it was also to be convinced that the principles of morality were based upon the deepest strata of human character, on the control that springs from a well-balanced mind. This was also realised by the more far-sighted amongst his colleagues. Others had less prescience, amongst them Hornby, who grew more and more estranged from his remarkable assistant and ever less aware of his contribution to the life of the school. Dr. Hornby took the conventional view of schoolboy morals. Cases of immorality, when brought to his notice, he punished summarily. Otherwise he shut his eyes. Oscar Browning, on the other hand, thought it his duty to try and prevent such things happening, and when he saw that boys were in trouble and wanted advice and help, he gave them willingly. " Dangerous confidences " they seemed to Dr. Hornby. It was undoubtedly the Head Master's disapproval of the methods that Oscar Browning followed in his attempt to purify Eton which led to the break between them.

The view that Oscar Browning took of his duties and responsibilities, the way in which he treated his pupils as friends and companions, was a new thing in public school education. And he did not confine himself to his own pupils. Father O. R. Vassall-Phillips writes: " I was not one of O. B.'s pupils, but from the time that I was a small boy he was very kind to me, and evidently took an interest in the growth of my mind. When I was sixteen he took me with him to Florence and Rome one winter holidays. In many ways it was an epoch-making event in my life. O. B. at the time had a very considerable income, but at all times he found it difficult to live within his means, whatever they might be. We travelled *en prince*. We had a courier to do everything for us, and of course O. B. would only stay in the most expensive hotels. He knew everyone and took me to dinner-parties with the most distinguished people. . . . O. B. used to talk to me about everything and I became the depository of certain most intimate secrets. No doubt in many ways it must have been very bad for me, but in others it was excellent. For one thing at least I can never be sufficiently grateful —it gave me my first love for the Catholic religion as I saw it in Italy. On our return home O. B. gave me two things, a free invitation (which I knew that he meant me to accept) to breakfast with himself, his mother and his sister whenever I pleased, and the run of his library. The first was a great boon on one side of one's life. It was a joy to slip out of the cold of an Eton morning after early school into the warmth of the hospitable house, where Mrs. Browning, the most dignified old lady I have ever known, would ask me kindly what I would have to eat, sometimes remarking (I remember) that there seemed an *embarras de richesse*, as indeed there was. And all the time one listened to O. B.'s amusing and sometimes exciting conversation."

V

Oscar Browning, despite his anti-athleticism, was a stalwart for all kinds of physical exercise. He played football with his boys, undertook Homeric excursions with them on the river—though he always considered rowing as intellectually the most degrading form of exercise—he ran with the Eton beagles, and when he found time followed the drag-hounds or the buck-hounds. He was one of the earliest members of the Alpine Club. He toured the roads of England and Europe on his tricycle. His passion for swimming took him to the coldest waters. The uninviting stream of the Granta, though March hardly gave promise of spring, used to draw him to its chilly self when he was already in the October of his age. But whilst he shared games and exercise with the boys, he would not direct them. That was to admit them to be a part of the serious business of life, to mistake the frame for the picture. "Boys will always admire the body. It is the duty of the schoolmaster to make them admire the mind." Schoolmasters often take the easy course. Oscar Browning was obstinate and refused to do so. It perhaps made him unpopular amongst the boys at large. His own pupils appreciated his courage. One of them, who was in the Eight and President of Pop for two years, writes to him from Oxford about two fellow-Etonians who had matriculated at Brasenose " with flying colours." " The Dons couldn't withstand their reputation for athletics. You have an enormous enemy in these sporting Colleges, and I don't think you will get Etonians to think properly about 'sapping' until you get some worthy gentlemen up here to show them that cricket and rowing and idleness are not as safe a pass to a good College as scholarship and industry."

VI

They were indefatigable letter-writers at Eton in the 'sixties and 'seventies. Supposed slights are explained. Different points of view, which have cropped up in conversation, are put on record. The European Chancelleries could not have been more punctilious in their *aide-mémoires*. The Provost corresponds with the Head Master, the Head Master with the Assistant Masters, the Assistant Masters with each other. Even the boys fall into the same habit, catch the same rotund style and quote without self-consciousness the Latin or Greek poets. Everybody's pen flows with elegant ease, and as one reads through the mass of correspondence which Oscar Browning received from others at Eton during his fifteen years there as a master, one appreciates the advantage of a classical education in giving a command of our native tongue.

" Dear Browning, I am sorry to think my behaviour yesterday was inconsistent with my previous statements to you. I do not think it was. I was not annoyed at the expression *as coming from you*. I think it a pity anything was said about it. At the same time . . ." and the writer runs on the fourth page explaining his attitude. Yet Eton masters complained they were overworked. Or Oscar Browning thinks that Warre has been rude and writes to remonstrate. " My dear Browning," runs the answer, " I have in vain tried to find anyone who thought my manner discourteous to you this morning. I believe I was fully justified in calling your attention to Gooding's second exercise. . . . You of all men ought not to be offended in such a case, as you are so full of fault-finding with Eton and so ready to think we are retrograde and do not require work enough from the boys. Surely it would be well for one who is fond of expressing opinions with reference to how those much older than himself are conducting their work not to be in dudgeon. This is not the first case where your pupils have been pulled up by me. . . . All I want is a friendly correspondence about the matter. . . ." And he gets it.

On another occasion, Browning, smarting under what he thinks is the desire of the " authorities " to injure him for his reforming zeal, writes an Apologia and sends it to Warre, who replies on seven closely written sheets. " The great difficulty in treating with you on these points is that you will not allow anyone's account of himself to hold as true if it contradicts your preconceived notions and prejudices. This makes you impute wrong motives to those who differ from you and often to speak ill of others. At the same time you are so satisfied with your own opinions as to make it appear in voice and manner that you hold in contempt all who differ from you." He goes on to explain his " definite and very distinct opinion " about athletics, which, he says, " I have tried to give an account of to you, but have found that you would rarely give me a hearing." He develops his views and denies that they run counter to Browning's work for the improvement of Eton education, or that he is animated by any feelings of hostility towards him. " I do not know whether you include me as having tried to injure you. I am not aware of having done so. If you can point out anything in which I have I shall be happy to make all the amends in my power. . . . I have wanted you to see that the work I have done was not in reality so antagonistic to you as you suppose, but if you cannot do so, it can't be helped. If your object is, that as intellectual progress goes on, and education improves and certain changes take place in the direction to which you have pointed, you should say to all beholders, 'I am the protagonist and confessor of these opinions at Eton, I have fought and suffered for them; to my agency and to no other are they due,' which is the interpretation which your letter, so proudly excluding any working in concert, seems to postulate; why, I say then, it is a pardonable vanity and one that will be bettered by time, but still unworthy of an intellectual man."

Some years later Warre writes, after they had had a " pleasant walk together " : " Reflecting on our conversation of yesterday I see the difference between us is a fundamental one. I prefer liberty and think that fraternity is best preserved when that liberty is respected and recognised by all, and that equality though not seen at present will come in the long run and cannot be established by enactment. You, on the other hand . . . There is one other point. You said that Mitchell, and implied that I, were not 'high-minded' men. . . . I think that a little hard on us. However, I hope that all our conversations on this topic will be amicable. . . . I certainly see your drift now, which I did not know before." Thus the two champions correspond and argue about fraternity and liberty whilst talking impatiently with third parties about each other's failings.

They all pride themselves on their candour. " I will be quite open with you," writes William Johnson in 1869; " I should not have recommended any boy to you if he was meant to be a scholar. I perceived very soon after you came here that, as I have told you before, you did not throw yourself into what I call the school work. I am in the habit of doing you justice. In College affairs I have been your ally. I regret having spoken harshly in your presence of James and Walford."

Sometimes a correspondence attains the dignity of being circulated amongst the other masters. In 1862 a boy who was Browning's pupil was transferred from Marriott's, a dame's house, to his own. W. B. Marriott, believing that the boy has been filched by Oscar Browning, writes him a letter of protest. It ends : " I cannot help saying this much, that considering the relations on which we have hitherto stood, I am a little surprised at your carrying on negotiations as to the removal of boys from my house without a word to me on the subject—and that with regard to boys whose connection with you arose from my recommendation." Oscar Browning explains. Marriott replies that he is glad to find he has been mistaken. The usual four pages ends with the opinion that a longer experience of Eton would have led Browning to act somewhat differently. Another letter that same evening insists that three weeks' notice is not enough for the removal of a boy from his house. On the following day Marriott writes two more letters, making four in two days. In the second he regrets that the facts as Mr. Devas (the parent) has explained them, " place the whole transaction in so painful a light that I cannot but hope that they were really not as I understood them from Mr. Devas to-day." The Head Master, W. Evans, and others intervene. The correspondence lasts six months. Both sides draw up a statement. " In this matter," says Oscar

Browning with obvious enjoyment of the controversy, " there are two questions at issue : the first a public one, as to law or usage . . . the second a private one, as to the influence I have exerted." He ends by declaring that he has followed the plain course of duty. Under similar circumstances he would act in the same way again. Marriott's Memorandum runs to fourteen tabulated paragraphs. There are no quarrels so bitter as those between eminently reasonable people.

At other times no principle is at issue. A master writes to correct an impression " which you have had, and still seem to have, that I allow certain boys in my house to leave the dinner-table for the purpose of going to the ' Tap ' or the ' Cellar.' Going to the ' Tap ' is a thing of which I do not approve." . . . (Then in the true Eton style he slips from the particular to the general.) " I think you will find that when you have been fifteen years here, as I have, the management of boys is the last thing to be referred to any theoretical standard or code of rules, the disturbing causes and complications are so endless." . . . Or it is a note from a colleague, thanking him for his hint and saying that he has summarily dismissed the two female servants. He agrees with Browning that House Masters cannot be too careful in shielding the boys from this sort of temptation, though he always tries to take care that the " tempters shall be as old and ugly as possible." A similar case in another house, where O. B. was also able to pass on certain information about the character of one of the sewing-maids, causes a correspondence of a dozen letters, but happily ending in the removal of the exciting cause of evil.

Occasionally the letters have the actuality of a news bulletin. The boys in Browning's, true to the renaissance spirit, seem to have had a taste for the faction fights that were so congenial to the men of the *quattrocento*. Indulging this, they put Wolley-Dod's under fire. He protests in a letter which informs their house master that shooting has been going on from his windows. Oscar Browning's intervention appears to have been unsuccessful. A "second note" states that "at 12.5 a shot was fired (with a catapult or some such implement) from one of your windows (no others command the place) which struck the woodwork of my drawing-room window. My wife and a child were at the window and heard it, both the twang and the bullet or shot stroke." Still the hostilities continued. During the afternoon O. B.'s boys succeed in breaking the greenhouse with their "missiles," and Wolley-Dod writes that his children are in such constant danger that he can bear it no longer, and he has reported the matter to the Head Master.

Nor are the pleasanter fields of social intercourse neglected. "Come and drown your differences with Hornby in a stoup of wine at the Ascham," says one master. Edmond Warre thanks him for his very kind and beautiful present, which both he and his wife hope will remain for a long time safe and sound as a monument to the good taste of the donor. Or Mrs. Hornby, the Head Master's wife, writes to Mrs. Browning declining with regret the invitation to a Saturday evening concert, and mis-spells a word in so doing, a serious solecism in that academic and correct world. Mrs. Browning, herself "a fair woman without discretion," keeps it on her mantelpiece as a Museum specimen. A narrow world indeed.

Yet Oscar Browning, however its narrowness reminded him of his own baulked ambitions, looked in imagination beyond the pupil-rooms and playing-fields of Eton to that England whose governing class it educated. When disgusted or disheartened, he could pay homage to that future which his sanguine radicalism regarded with reverence and optimism.

CHAPTER V

OSCAR BROWNING AND HORNBY

I

AT the end of 1867 the majestic Dr. Balston resigned. He had preserved his dignity in the face of reformers both within and without, and so long as he remained he had been the best guarantee of the "Old Eton" party that change would be as gradual as the processes of nature. But public opinion was uneasy, and ever since the publication of the Royal Commission's Report it had been clear that his days were numbered. Lord Lyttelton in a letter that year to Oscar Browning says that he does not suppose Dr. Balston will remain Head Master much longer. If he had to resign, however, the "Old Eton" party amongst the Fellows was determined that his successor should be a safe man and that the "Young Eton" party amongst the Masters, many of whom had given awkward evidence before the Commissioners, should be kept in its place. None of them at any rate need hope to be promoted to the Head Mastership. If the idea had ever occurred to Oscar Browning he put it aside, as he had done five years before when Dr. Balston had succeeded Dr. Goodford. Yet in such a matter, which, as *The Times* observed, was of national concern, it was his duty to pull strings. He himself favoured Bradley, then Master of Marlborough. When rumours that the regime of Dr. Balston was nearing its end gained strength and probability he approached Bradley indirectly. The reply was non-committal. Dr. Bradley had doubts of his ability to overcome the innate conservatism in which " the Provost and Fellows were at one with the boys." Besides, with the modesty of the scholar over whose text-book on the composition of Latin prose many generations of English schoolboys have groaned, he said that he could not write Latin verse. Admittedly Eton was a nobler position than Marlborough. But he preferred to remain in a humbler sphere, where he had every reason to suppose that he was succeeding, rather than move to another where success would be " dubious or improbable." Finally, he recommended them to sound Benson. Dr. Bradley's answer shows at any rate that he appreciated the strength of the Conservative tradition at Eton.

Browning and others might sound whom they pleased, Dr. Goodford and the Fellows had no intention of allowing their hands to be forced. Dr. Balston would resign. That was understood. But his resignation would be placed in the hands of the Provost, and this would not be published to the world with any indecent haste. Oscar Browning was in touch with the *Pall Mall Gazette*, and that newspaper, which was nonplussed at Hornby's election, criticised the suddenness with which the vacancy had been filled. The *Guardian* replied that Dr. Balston had given the statutable notice to the Provost, who had a perfect right to keep the matter to himself if he pleased. As a matter of fact the appointment was exceedingly astute. James John Hornby, to give him his full name, came from Winchester, where he had been Second Master, with good credentials. He was a scholar and a man of the world, he had been a distinguished athlete, and through his father's mother, who had been a Stanley, he was related to Lord Derby.

He was said to be a Liberal. The break with the past was indicated by his having been an Oppidan and that he was an Oxford and not a Cambridge, or rather a King's, man, for previous Head Masters had been Collegers and King's-men. Everyone was pleased. "No other choice," said *The Times*, "would have commanded alike the confidence of Etonians and public school reformers." "Our new Head Master," Oscar Browning wrote to his friend Sidgwick a few days after the beginning of Hornby's first half, "promises to be a great success. We shall now be governed on the principles that universally obtain in human society." The only alarm that Dr. Hornby's advent caused was in the breasts of Eton boys. What could change mean but more work? And what Etonian worth his salt was not ready to resist this with all the doggedness of the Anglo-Saxon character? The new Head Master was from the first warned that Eton was a law unto itself. He was greeted with writing on the wall that Eton meant to remain Eton. "No Reform" was the cry that ran through the school and was chalked on the very doors.

II

The next two or three years determined, if not the future of England, at least that of Oscar Browning. At first he and Dr. Hornby get on well together. Modern languages, history, science, the despised geography, were given a place in the regular school work. O. B.'s own tastes were exactly suited in his being put in charge of the history teaching. Dr. Hornby even agrees with him that athletics at Eton "are no doubt practised to excess," though claiming that rowing is a fine training for the character as well as for the body. With Fourth of June processions and champagne

77

drinking he has no sympathy. But when Oscar Browning, disapproving of the training for Henley, wishes to put a stop to the Eight rowing at that regatta, Dr. Hornby confesses that to him it seems " almost an unmixed good," and he dreads the time when it is over, unless other races can be started. Still the Head Master " is very much obliged " for his letters and is very glad " to have an expression of his opinion on every matter affecting the interests of the school." He even welcomes his advice on appointments to the staff.

And whilst Warre is opposed to Hornby's reforms in the teaching of classics, Oscar Browning supports the Head Master. " My dear Browning," he writes to him in February, 1870, " many thanks for your very kind letter. Warre's pamphlet does not trouble me at all, for I think it is quite easy to show that it rests on unfounded assumptions of all sorts from beginning to end. . . . There are endless points which I feel inclined to challenge or contradict. Indeed I think it *very* unfair, though unintentionally so, and very shallow."

If, however, Oscar Browning thought that he was to be Hornby's chief lieutenant he was not long in being undeceived. They were too unlike in character and differed too widely in their ideas ever to have worked together harmoniously. Hornby believed in the value of exact scholarship. For him the classics were an intellectual training-ground rather than a door through which a boy entered on the inheritance of European culture. Madvig's Latin Grammar he held in particular to be a sovereign discipline for young minds. And Oscar Browning disliked Madvig. After a while too there cropped up the difference in their attitude towards the moral problems which inevitably occur where nature's balance of the sexes is disturbed. Their differences were not to be bridged by the zeal

78

OSCAR BROWNING, AETAT 31

After a drawing by Simeon Solomon

with which Browning urged his views or by the
lucidity of Hornby's replies. Those views embraced all subjects, not least the shortcomings of
colleagues. "You seem to me," observed Dr.
Hornby after one correspondence, "to show a
disposition to go beyond your own sphere of duties
rather gratuitously and to criticise others more
severely than you criticise yourself." What if all
the forty-four assistants wrote him long letters on
every conceivable subject? He would have to
leave them "*unread*," with the characteristic two
lines underneath it. On one point they agreed—
that the Chapel choir ought to be composed of
boys in the school. Even here there was a rift.
For Hornby was pleased that the Captain of the
Boats interested himself in collecting volunteers,
whilst Browning thought that this was bending
the knee to athletics. Hornby thereupon twits
him on his admiration for Harrow. "I think,"
he writes, "some of our friends elsewhere (at
Rugby pre-eminently) live in a regular fool's
paradise with regard to boys' notions on these
points. I believe at the moment the *one* point in
which we could not certainly beat Rugby, and perhaps Harrow, is '*cricket*.'" (In the inverted
commas one can detect something of the spiritual
pride of the rowing man.) He adds: "I hold
athletics to be in excess everywhere in our great
schools, but not more so at Eton than elsewhere."

Then Hornby began to be critical. Like Warre
he had been a famous oar. Both disliked the idea
of using the river for mere pleasure. "It is not
everyone who is so fond of water-parties," is a
remark in one of Hornby's letters. The Watteau-
esque atmosphere of water-parties, at which the
boys joined with elegant women and the conversation was adorned by the elegant mind of
Walter Pater, was not the sort of thing Hornby

looked upon as coming within the four corners of a public-school education. Sometimes the doubts are more openly expressed. " Certain verses might be looked over more carefully," Hornby writes on one occasion. When Browning replies that if the Head Master has any complaints to make he hopes he will do so unreservedly, Hornby says " that he will listen to no more idle tales." The " idle tales," however, seem to have persisted. Oscar Browning criticised others. He could hardly expect to be treated differently himself. And his wide interests gave such stories probability. He was admittedly not pre-eminent at his work in school, though he managed his Division with at least a modicum of success. But how could he attend to it properly, his critics argued, when he was so much occupied with other things ? Did he not go frequently to concerts and private views in London, and to the opera during the season ? Did he not examine for the Cambridge Local Examinations ? Did he not help the School of Art and Design which had lately been started in Windsor, and lecture to ladies on Italian literature ? Then there were the meetings of the " U. U." and George Eliot's salon on Sunday afternoons in Regent's Park, and political interests and the magnet of London's social life. . . .

III

Oscar Browning was not the sort of man to submit tamely or discreetly to those who did not appreciate him. Yet when it came to the point he was ready to take the lead in supporting his disapproving chief. At the end of the summer half of 1873 there was a question of increasing the boarding fees. The price of living had risen but the charges to parents had remained the same. The masters had urged the Governing Body to raise these fees and had met with a refusal. In spite of this a circular was sent out to the parents, on the authority of the Head Master, pointing out the facts of the case and suggesting that an additional charge of £4 a term should be made to meet the increased cost of living. To the astonishment of everybody, this apparently reasonable proposal raised a controversy in the papers—it was in the dull month of August—and *The Times* published letters showing parental indignation that such a step should have been taken without the sanction of the Governing Body. The Governing Body thereupon censured the Head Master for his share in the matter, though they allowed an increased charge of £6 a year to commence in the following half.

Hornby's position was naturally shaken by the action of the Governing Body, and the *World* declared that " it seemed scarcely possible for him as a gentleman to retain his post." The masters met and intimated to him that he should reply to this censure. Hornby answered that he would do so if they would back him against the constant interference of the Provost. Oscar Browning, who, it may be said, had disapproved of the wording of the original circular and had only joined with his colleagues in order to secure united action, was prominent in the party which supported the Head Master. He drew up a Draft Memorial which Hornby acknowledged: " Many thanks for your paper, which, I think, is *very* valuable, and would do great good to us, and perhaps through us to many other schools, especially if it came soon." The draft was afterwards amended. It offered sympathy and promised support in maintaining a position without which it could not be expected that the Head Master of a great public school could be " either efficient or successful." " My dear

Browning," he writes in reply, " I like the alteration in your draft of a memorial and think it an
improvement. I wish the masters would sign the
document as it stands, but of course in so large a
body it is very difficult to find complete agreement.
I trust that your draft will not be materially altered,
still less suppressed, even though some should
refuse to sign it." As usual the masters found it
difficult to agree. But if the Head Master did
not get full support from the staff, it was not on
this occasion Oscar Browning's fault. The incident
is in any case interesting as showing a certain
magnanimity on the side of Hornby's Assistant-
Master.

IV

But the Head Master could never get it out of his
head that Oscar Browning, who was paid to teach
classics, was slack in his Division work, and so far as
classics went slack even in pupil-room. And O. B.
did not disguise his opinion that it was a waste of
time for boys with no pronounced classical bent to
write Latin verses, an occupation that took much of
the time of his Division. He was suspect too
about " saying lessons," and he would not use
Madvig. So Hornby one day sends round for the
exercises of the various Divisions to be collected,
and returns Browning's with the comment that
" apparently none of them had been corrected."
" True, but they would have been if you had not
taken them away," was the answer, on which Dr.
Hornby observed that he had adopted the plan
in order " to catch him out." In the summer half
of 1873 there was an outburst over the " saying
lessons." Oscar Browning had made the boys
write out what they had learnt, and Hornby regarded this not as an " educational experiment,"
but as a method of saving trouble for the master.

The usual correspondence ensued. O. B. pointed out that the plan was a perfectly well-known one, being indeed a favourite method of Dr. Martin, the Warden of Radley, to ensure boys getting Horace and Virgil by heart in the " most accurate and permanent form." The storm subsides rather from the exhaustion of the parties concerned than from their having reached agreement.

Another time Hornby cites a complaint, which rumour afterwards states comes from none other than the Provost (" it is," says Hornby, " the first complaint I have ever had from a parent "), that the discipline in Mr. Browning's Division was so bad that the boys could learn nothing—Dr. Hornby, by the way, was himself a wretched disciplinarian. Oscar Browning thereupon procured testimonials from six of the tutors of boys in his Division testifying to the efficiency of his teaching. But before he had received this the Head Master had modulated into another key and come as near making an apology as a Head Master may in corresponding with an assistant. The testimonials he burnt, and told one of the writers that they meant nothing, receiving the answer : " Mine meant a great deal."

Dr. Hornby too was by no means happy about the history teaching. Oscar Browning, he thought, chose periods much too near our own time, the French Revolution, or the reigns of Queen Anne or George III. Oscar Browning liked these because they contained the germs of the controversies that were agitating the mid-Victorian era. Was he not educating the future statesmen of England and training them to weigh principles and movements in the fine balance of the human reason ? This was not Dr. Hornby's idea of the educational function of history. He was one of those who liked their history taken from the cold storage of the remote past. He wished the boys to read about the Norman kings, the feudal system, or, better still, "the great revolutions of Asia." O. B., whose ambition it was to train men of affairs, chafed and protested. Luckily he had success to argue for him. The history teaching at Eton was admittedly amongst the best in England. The University examiners extolled it; other schools recognised its superiority. Farrar writes to him from Marlborough: "If you could spare the time I should be very grateful to know what *method* you adopt with your history class." Bowen asks him to lecture to the Sixth Form at Harrow. Hornby alone was sceptical. He thought that O. B. was using history as a stalking-horse for his radicalism, or that he was chosing modern periods because they were easier to teach. So although he has no doubt that Mill's *Representative Government* "is an able book," he withholds judgment on its suitability as a foundation on which to lecture till he has had time to read it. This Laodicean attitude occasionally warms into open hostility. He regrets to see "any of the best boys of Division A join the history class." He writes to point out that history teaching must be given without prejudice to the classical teaching. "The classical teaching is the first thing to be considered in the case of classical masters, who are engaged to teach *that* and paid for *that*. If anything besides can be done in the way of History, Geography, Modern Languages, English Literature, etc., so much the better; but they must not be pleaded as a ground for diminishing classical study in any way."

V

Either consumed by his own mistrust, or prompted by others, one knows not which, Dr. Hornby nursed the idea of appointing a special master to teach history, and thus of taking away from Oscar Browning the thing which interested him most, the thing too which he taught with most success. The report of the Head Master's intentions became current at Eton and produced rather a remarkable letter from A. C. Ainger. "A rumour has reached us," he writes to Hornby, "that you intend to make a change in the history teaching by appointing a special master for the purpose of what has hitherto been done by Browning. Such a master would be either up to the standard of an Oxford history professor, or he would be a young man who had taken a good degree in the school. In the former case we should get more than we want in a place like this without any great increase in the efficiency of the teaching : in the latter it would be most improbable that the teacher would approach the present teacher either in historical attainments, power of imparting knowledge, or influence over the boys forming the class. This seems so obvious to very many of us who have had pupils in Browning's history class, and have been acquainted with the results of it, that we cannot be surprised that he should feel seriously hurt at the prospect of such a supersession. Possibly as compared with a Bryce or a Freeman, Browning's knowledge may be pronounced superficial, but in that or in almost any other literary subject it would be difficult for his habitual critics to substantiate any such charge. For my own part I think he is one of the most cultivated men I ever met, and I cannot comprehend the charge of shallowness so often brought against him. His undertaking the history teaching was an act of voluntary patriotism at a time when it was very much needed. This should entitle it to a somewhat tender consideration even if it had been a failure. Whereas, on the contrary, nothing of late years has been more successful."

It is not often that one Assistant Master is prompted to write to his chief about a colleague in such terms. Then Ainger goes on to speak still more boldly. " But behind all this I for one (and I believe many others, but I have no right to speak except for myself) am conscious of a painful feeling at anything which seems to cast a slight on Browning or to lessen his influence. It is, of course, a matter on which opinions may differ, but I do not think you can be aware how many of us feel that more than anything else we owe to Browning's exertions in his own house and pupil-room and in the school generally a very large proportion of any improvement which may have taken place at Eton in the last ten years. . . . Our standard in morals, in intellectual pursuits, in everything except athletics, is still miserably low—how low no one can know who is not in daily contact with the frivolity and carelessness about all serious matters which is the prevailing tone." (Hornby was notoriously aloof from the life and ignorant of the routine of the school.) " But whatever protest has been made against this muscle worship, whatever effort has been made to promote culture and industry and thereby improve morals, Browning has taken a leading part in ever since I have known Eton as a master. Again, you came here at a time when changes had to be introduced, and everyone in the place was ready to find fault with them whatever they were. During all this time Browning was your most loyal supporter, much more loyal than many who have always enjoyed a larger share of your confidence. This is so well known to us that we can hardly understand its not being known to you."

Ainger does not end without something more than an insinuation against Hornby's habit of listening to the " tittle-tattle " which was endemic at Eton. " We younger masters here . . . feel that we

86

cannot do better than follow the example Browning has set us, and which I hope he may long continue to set, for he is by far your most valuable assistant . . . I am well aware that the picture I have drawn may differ from that which some of us would draw, especially as I know from personal experience some of the older men. It is possible, though I have no right to say so, that you hold their views and have been in some degree influenced by them."

A letter like this, written, of course, without Oscar Browning's knowledge, throws a good deal of light on the cabals at Eton and Hornby's inability to stop them. How much effect it had is indicated by the fact that Hornby informed him a few weeks later that he had written to Oxford with the intention of getting someone to teach history in his place. O. B. replied that this was treating him in cavalier fashion, and that if the project were carried through he should probably leave Eton. The Head Master made " various uncomplimentary remarks," but gave up his plan on the representations of a large number of the masters. The following half we find Oscar Browning, as already related, taking the lead in supporting Hornby against the Provost and the Governing Body. Quixotry could hardly go further. But O. B. the man, as distinguished from the boy, was always an optimist. " I always look at the best side of things and avert my mind from the worst," he writes nearly fifty years after the events here recorded. He seems actually to have hoped to convert Hornby to the merits of his history teaching. The Head Master had withdrawn sulkily. His dislike of Queen Anne and the French Revolution was no less than before; his mistrust of Oscar Browning rather greater.

Oscar Browning would have done well to let sleeping dogs lie. To himself, however, his own merits were so obvious that he could never understand others failing to appreciate them, and being a philosophic Radical with a profound belief in the goodness of human nature, he attributed Dr. Hornby's opposition to misunderstanding. So when Dr. Benson, later to become Archbishop of Canterbury, who had been examining for the Newcastle, said in the course of a speech that one of the candidates, also afterwards to be episcopated, owed his place to his history, Oscar Browning writes to Hornby to point out that here was a proof that history did not interfere with classics, since on Dr. Benson's own showing it had assisted a boy to translate Thucydides. The Head Master begins his reply ominously : " I would gladly pass your letter by in silence, but I feel that I ought to protest most strongly against it. . . . That a clever, well-trained Colleger should distinguish himself in your history class is not surprising. But to turn the matter round and say that the history class produced the clever Colleger is too monstrous. . . . I will not speak now about your history teaching, but I hope you will allow me to say really as a friend that you do not know the disadvantageous impression which you produce on examiners and other clever men who come here, by these efforts to advertise your claim." The recipient of this very candid letter sent it on to his friend and counsellor on the Governing Body, John Hibbert, asking whether it was the sort of communication a subordinate should receive from his chief. Hibbert sympathised but could do nothing.

In the face of Hornby's hardly veiled hostility it is remarkable that Oscar Browning had not already resigned before the relations between himself and the Head Master could have produced such a contemptuous letter as this. Henry Sidgwick was anxious that he should return to Cambridge to help develop the nascent history school there, and had proposed that he should be offered a fellowship at Trinity. There was a task to his hand amidst friends and congenial surroundings. Various reasons, however, weighed with him. To leave Eton would be to desert the cause for which he had been fighting for fifteen years, to hand over the citadel of English secondary education to the Philistines, to abandon the party he was leading, to sacrifice all the efforts he had made for a purer morality, a truer sense of the values of life. There was his mother too, an old lady, who, if he went to Cambridge, would be ill provided for—as he himself would also be. And there were the actual boys in the school who relied upon his influence. Could he in justice desert them? More than once he thought of resigning, but he always found reason to put the thought aside. Besides, if it came to an open battle with Hornby, there was always the chance that it might be the Head Master and not Oscar Browning who would have to leave.

CHAPTER VI

' THE LIE '

IF Oscar Browning had determined to leave the onus of dismissing him on the Head Master, Hornby, eighteen months before his explosion about the history teaching, had already held the threat of dismissal over O. B.'s head, a threat which had caused that former protagonist in favour of increasing the powers of Head Masters to try and persuade his friends in Parliament to draft a bill amending the Public Schools Act of 1868. He corresponds with G. O. Trevelyan and others on the subject. Ironically enough, the trouble in this case between Hornby and O. B. arose out of the proposal to increase the boarding fees, which had brought Oscar Browning forward as the Head Master's champion amongst what William Johnson called " the obscure mob of assistants." The controversy is interesting from its mere pettiness. Oscar Browning had disapproved of the wording of the masters' original circular. It was certainly a flabby, inconclusive document. It pointed out that " it was necessary to reduce the scale of comfort in which the boys lived or to increase the cost to the parents." Then it asked the parents to say what they wanted. The question was obviously absurd. Supposing, as was probable, that some agreed to pay more and others would not do so. What was to be done then? Oscar Browning, therefore, whilst falling into line with his colleagues, took the view that the circular intimated a definite

intention to raise the boarding fees by £4 a term.
And in September he sent out another circular to
the parents of his boys, emphasising the reasons
and the necessity for the charge. The answers he
received speak well by contrast with those which
other parents of Etonians had written to *The Times*.
Sir William Gull, the famous physician, thinks it
perfectly fair and " regrets the tone " in the papers
on this matter. Lord Portsmouth says that " his
decided opinion is, that the weak point of the
boarding at all public schools, is that the boys'
breakfasts are insufficient." He adds : " I know
that I am addressing one whose House is famous
for boarding the boys *most liberally*. . . . I do not
think this is a question for the Governing Body.
I think it would be placing them in a position over
your heads of boarding houses which would be
most unpleasant. They would be like the Poor
Law Board prescribing the dietary in a work-
house."

So too thought Oscar Browning. He was, as
it happened, quite wrong. Under the new statutes
the Governing Body alone had authority to alter
the scale of fees. The latitude of the old regime
was a thing of the past. After all he might have
remembered that one cannot have it both ways.
He had wanted changes. If the new Eton was not
what he had hoped for, and if the Governing Body
had acted in this matter with their customary
stupidity, still they had many more rules and
regulations than before. " Progress in public
school education," he had written to Sidgwick,
" can only come through attention to detail."
This meant organisation, and organisation meant
rules and regulations. However, he had said
that he intended to make the additional charge, and,
with what one of the papers afterwards characterised
as " undue zeal for the petty emoluments of his

position," he duly made it. When he sent out his bills in December he enclosed an explanation defending the increase. "The arrangement," he said, "proposed by the Governing Body is not considered by us as final or satisfactory. We have protested against it, and it is not certain that it will ever be carried out: under the circumstances I thought myself justified in complying with the wishes of parents by securing myself against a loss which I have borne too long. At the same time it must be understood that the extra charge made by me for board is entirely unauthorised, and can only be regarded as a private arrangement between the parent and myself."

After his bills had been sent out a bundle of circulars arrived from the Head Master explaining the new scale of charges sanctioned by the Governing Body. They were meant to accompany the school bills, but there were no definite instructions, apparently, about this, and in Oscar Browning's case the bills had already been posted. The circulars of the Head Master accordingly remained in his study whilst he went abroad and forgot about the trivialities of Eton routine in the delights of Florence and Rome.

When he returned the circulars were still there. Though this for the moment was not realised by the Provost, it was evident that Oscar Browning had put himself in a situation from which there was no escape except by retreat. The Governing Body asserted its rights most emphatically and Hornby passed on its admonitions to his assistant. Browning gave an assurance that for the future he would make no more unauthorised charges. In reply the Head Master thanked him and observed that it relieves him from all anxiety about the future. All seemed to be well. And Hornby in asserting the authority of the Governing Body had taken the opportunity to refer again to the discontinuance of the " saying lessons "—still rather a sore subject —whilst the Provost had concluded his letter to Hornby with the observation that " the Governing Body forbore to make any remark on the style and tone which Mr. Browning had thought fit to adopt." Most decidedly Oscar Browning had been badly snubbed. He was unconscious of the fact and wrote to the Governing Body expressing sorrow for any language that had been taken exception to. Certain letters, he supposed, " which could not have come into their hands without a breach of confidence," had been shown to them.

This barely veiled reference to the Head Master, which the Provost naturally did not keep to himself, made Hornby extremely angry. A letter of four foolscap pages was its fruits, a letter with so many words underlined and doubly underlined that it might have been the protest of a jilted swain rather than a solemn indictment by a grave pedagogue whose emoluments were equal to three average deaneries. Hornby was angry. Angry that he had been accused of a breach of confidence, but angrier still that in the four days' interval which had elapsed since the incident had been closed, a new piece of evidence had come to light which showed that Oscar Browning was a man whose word could not be trusted, a man capable of telling a lie. Since the lie *motif* recurs later it must be briefly annotated.

What had happened was this. The circulars were still in Oscar Browning's study when he heard one morning that the Provost was extremely annoyed that all the masters had not sent them out. Accordingly, he posted them at once. That same evening an open letter came round from the Head Master. This contained two questions : " Have the circulars been sent ? " " Were they sent with the bills ? " " Without a thought," O. B. related afterwards in a statement to the Governing Body, "I signed my initials below the answers already given to the question by other masters, and after them the words, 'Yes, but not with the bills!'"

Hornby used this to give the *coup de grâce*. "I could not conceive, no honest man could conceive, that you had suppressed my notice *till that very morning*, and that when you wrote *Yes* (twice underlined) you knew that the notice had only just been posted and that it could not have reached any parent whose complaints might have caused the Provost to institute this inquiry." And he ends with what amounts to a provisional dismissal, though he says that he will take no further step until Browning has had the opportunity of speaking in his own defence. On reflection Hornby must have decided not to push matters to extremes. For he gave Browning the choice between resignation or recalling his previous letter of apology to the Governing Body. Oscar Browning therefore wrote to the Provost asking him not to present his letter, only to be told that it had already been presented. Yet when he inquired of Spencer Walpole, the ex-Home Secretary, whose sensitiveness had been shown by his weeping before a deputation in connection with the Hyde Park riots of 1866, that gentleman assured him that so far as he knew no member of the Governing Body had ever accused him of dishonesty or proclaimed any feeling of diminished respect for him. Two other members, Lord Lyttelton and John Hibbert, answered in the same strain.

In a controversy of this kind casuistry is never far to seek. If Oscar Browning's reply, which moved Dr. Hornby to such righteous indignation, lacked the complete candour which should invest every answer that a man of honour may be called on to give in life, neither perhaps can Dr. Goodford or Dr. Hornby be said to have been perfectly frank. Much play, for instance, is made in the Head Master's letter of a " serious complaint made by a parent." This was with reference to a charge of £10 for furniture which Oscar Browning made to all boys entering his house. It was a practice he had begun under the old regime, when house masters made very much their own terms with parents and continued subsequently, though it had never been authorised by the Governing Body. Dr. Goodford, learning that Oscar Browning was making this charge, had written to the parents of one of the boys to inquire. The parent, who was perfectly satisfied with the arrangement, gave the information asked for. Upon this so-called serious complaint the Provost and Head Master had acted. Those who emerge most creditably indeed from this particular controversy are the parents, who, as their answers to his circulars show, fully appreciated the care he lavished on his pupils and were ready to support him in his contention that it was impossible to board the boys properly without an additional charge. Their cordiality and friendliness are in contrast to the suspicious attitude of the Provost, the ill-considered nonchalance of O. B. and the rather silly moralising of Dr. Hornby.

CHAPTER VII

I

IF Oscar Browning meant to stay on at Eton, his friends warned him that he had better keep quiet. But he could no more help putting himself forward than a sunflower can help pointing to the sun. His " swallow flights," as William Johnson called them, were a very part of his being. Though he might annoy the Provost and the Head Master and the Eton Conservatives generally, he could not refrain from tilting at abuses. Edward Hale, another master, writing to him some months after the events recorded in the last chapter, reminds him how on three separate occasions recently he has neglected his advice to keep in the background. " After your speech at the masters' meeting, when you condemned the want of support given to masters in maintaining discipline—also when the Head Master proposed to bring Creighton here to take your place as a history teacher, and when your proposed re-rating college property and inquiring into parochial churches. I told you, not for your own sake only, but for your mother's, to cease for a time acting as reformer, because such a step must bring you into collision with the authorities, who did not always like being rubbed up the wrong way."

96

II

Re-rating college property, inquiring into parochial churches, discipline in school, even the
teaching of history, important as these might be,
were as nothing, however, compared with the
great central idea of education, which was the
inculcation of a pure morality amongst the nine
hundred or so boys thrown together into the
vortex of Eton. And it was on this very point,
the most vital and the most delicate of all, that
Oscar Browning was next to come into conflict
with Hornby.

The state of morals at Eton was far from satisfactory. There was abundant evidence that the
vice which called down the judgment of Heaven
on the cities of the plain did not excite that repug-
nance of public opinion amongst the boys which
it should in any healthy society. Immorality was
discussed under the name of " spooning," and
though, of course, detected cases were summarily
punished, the culprits were not viewed, it was
thought by the reformers, with the reprobation
which was shown under analogous circumstances
at other public schools. A party amongst the
masters, searching for the reason of this laxity,
attributed it to the secrecy with which such matters
had been treated, and determined, as far as they
were concerned, to adopt different measures.
Oscar Browning had long laboured for this end,
and his own house was generally considered to
be, in this respect, one of the best at Eton. Now
under his influence the work was to be carried on
more intensively. Those masters who agreed with
him in the way the evil should be eradicated, or at
least kept within bounds, drew up a set of rules
for their own guidance; cases of detected immor-

ality were to be thoroughly investigated. All such cases were to be reported to the Head Master, though not necessarily with names, and they were also to be reported to the other masters. Thus it was hoped the standard of morals would be raised and Eton become worthy of its illustrious place at the head of English public schools.

These proposals excited fierce resentment. Many of the Assistant Masters looked upon them as the result of a conspiracy to carry on a general espionage. The boys, or a large proportion of them, shared these sentiments, and one of Oscar Browning's pupils, who had exposed a scandal and been hooted and mobbed for his pains, was held up as typical of the effects of such a system. Oscar Browning himself was believed to invite confidences from boys in a spirit which was quite alien to the sturdy independence of the public school atmosphere. Fitz James Stephen, afterwards the well-known judge, than whom no mid-Victorian worthy was a sterner censor of morals, followed his efforts with sympathy and encouragement. Another distinguished Etonian has left on record some account of how Oscar Browning proceeded in these matters. Far from being anxious to extract confidences from boys, we are told that he never held any conversation upon "esoteric anthropology," or any matter connected with vice, in the school unless he saw clearly that a boy, for some reason or other, was unhappy, or in ill-health, or consumed by a morbid curiosity, and then he acted always with extreme caution. He made an exception in the case of boys in authority, from whom he often appears to have had voluntary statements and disclosures, as being one of the few masters to whom boys could appeal without "unwholesome restraint." This attitude of his was intensely distasteful to Dr. Hornby amongst others. For some time the Head

Master was able to vent his griefs only in chance remarks, but in the summer half of 1874 an incident occurred which showed more plainly the suspicion with which the Head Master regarded Oscar Browning's moral influence.

III

Two years previously a bright and clever boy, George Nathaniel Curzon, had entered Wolley-Dod's house. That same autumn Oscar Browning, who was taking another master's Division, first made the acquaintance of the young Curzon, who impressed him at once, in his own words, as one of the most brilliantly gifted boys he had ever come across. Curzon was subsequently "up to him"— that is to say, he was his form, or, in Eton phraseology "Division," master—and this impression was confirmed. Oscar Browning, who had given himself a roving commission to take an interest in any boy of intellectual promise whom he considered was neglected by his own tutor, was anxious about the future Viceroy. He had no opinion of Wolley-Dod's insight, and he believed too that his house was in a bad state. This anxiety was increased in the following Michaelmas school-time, when the captain of Wolley-Dod's house told him that he was deeply concerned at the companions with whom Curzon was associating. Oscar Browning advised the boy to speak to his own tutor, saying that under the circumstances he did not see how he could interfere. On consideration, however, he wrote to his father, Lord Scarsdale, with the result that at the beginning of the ensuing half Curzon went to see him, and the beginnings were formed of a friendship which was destined to last uninterruptedly for half a century.

That the dangers which surrounded this gifted lad were real and did not cease at once is shown by a letter to Oscar Browning from a boy high in the school and a distinguished athlete, which was written in the summer half of 1874. The boy had borrowed a rug in Upper Club which chanced to be Curzon's, with the result that its owner was chaffed. "It made me feel," says the writer, who afterwards also became a well-known man, "what a state of public opinion there must be when a big fellow cannot even come across a little fellow in the most casual way without its being remarked, and (as might happen in some cases) the most hideous construction being placed upon it. I feel it more particularly in this instance, as Curzon is a boy among many whose acquaintance for various reasons I should much like to make, knowing of what a superior quality he really is and how often he has been in a dangerous position here. But bearing in mind the state of feeling about these matters, I have, of course, relinquished the idea, fearing the harm it might do other boys. As I know the interest you take in him, I should be much obliged if you would let him know how sorry I am if I have got him into the least trouble accidentally in this matter, and I write to you about it as I see no other means of safely letting him know what I feel." It is a commentary on the position of unofficial *custos morum* which Oscar Browning had come to occupy that two boys, both high in the school but neither of them his pupils, should appeal to him about a third who was likewise not in his house.

On the same day that he received this letter his right to the position was to be sharply called in question. As with not a few other boys in whom

he was interested, Oscar Browning had developed
a close intimacy with the young Curzon. He had
given him the run of his library, invited him often
to breakfast or tea, supervised his work. To the
stimulus thus received Curzon doubtless owed his
winning of the Prince Consort's French prize in
1874, much to the surprise, it was stated, of his
own tutor. In the summer half of that year Curzon
had been struck by a cricket ball in the eye, an
accident which had prevented him from taking any
part in the normal school life. It was the interest
which O. B. showed in Curzon at this time which
impelled his tutor to complain to Hornby. "I
strongly object," Wolley-Dod wrote to Browning,
"to your taking Curzon out for drives without
leave from me or the Head Master, to your writing
to him by post, which you have done several
times, when he is only two doors off; and most of
all to your doing his verses for him, as I have
suspected several times, and as he admits in the
case of his iambics this week. I think the whole
case is one which justifies an appeal to the Head
Master, and I have accordingly made one, specifying
the points on which your dealings with Curzon
seem to me objectionable." The three things
were all susceptible of explanation, and they soon
dropped out of the ensuing controversy. An
invitation to breakfast had found its way by accident into the post; leave had been obtained for
the drive, taken when Curzon had been incapaci-
tated and left to his own resources; the only
occasion when Oscar Browning had "helped"
Curzon with his iambics was one afternoon in his
study when Knatchbull-Hugessen, afterwards the
first Lord Brabourne and a friend of Lord Scarsdale's, had been present for the greater part of the
time. The assistance had been "very slight" in any
case. The fact was, as O. B. pointed out to Wolley-

Dod, that Curzon was a very clever boy, and as his tutor he should have recognised it.

The unpleasant tone of Wolley-Dod's letter was emphasised when Hornby, who had sent for Oscar Browning on the strength of Wolley-Dod's complaint, received him with the remark: " So I hear Mr. Wolley-Dod has a good-looking pupil."

" Do you mean to say," Browning answered with some heat, " that you have allowed any master to tell you I took notice of a boy because he was good-looking ? "

" I don't know, I am sure," was the ambiguous reply.

It is not the sort of remark one expects a Head Master to make casually to one of his subordinates, and one wonders how Oscar Browning, as he did on his own showing, allowed the interview to continue without a full explanation or a withdrawal. Was he so astonished as to be reduced to a silence usually foreign to his nature? Was he overpowered by the prestige which surrounds a Head Master? Surmise gropes for an explanation, and one can only say that the pedagogic mind works in a strange way. However, if conversations were unsatisfactory it was always possible to continue the discussion by letter. Oscar Browning, searching for an explanation of the Head Master's innuendo, was informed by Wolley-Dod that the summary of his "complaint" was that he considered Curzon a boy likely to be made vain and to be spoilt by the notice and attention he got from Browning. He ends drily: " The Head Master has misunderstood me if he thinks that I attributed your attentions to Curzon's personal appearance. I have written to the Head Master to correct that impression." And two days later he adds: " The suggestion which you say was made to you by the Head Master is one for which I should have been very sorry to give any authority whatever, nor was it, as you say you heard from Wayte, made by one of my colleagues." Wayte, it may be explained, had told O. B. that a colleague whom Wolley-Dod had consulted on the matter had remarked that he supposed it was a " case of spooning." It was also to Wayte that Wolley-Dod had spoken of Oscar Browning's " irrepressible attentions " to Curzon. It is pretty evident, even if one accepts Wolley-Dod's assurances about his communications with Hornby, that gossip was busy and that the Head Master was again listening to " idle tales." Wolley-Dod on his side was clearly blind to his pupil's qualities. He does not think that he has " improved." " Every master," he writes to O. B., " who has had him under him except you has complained of want of straightforwardness in him, and I am sorry to say that I have seen too many instances of it. He has lately become querulous and spoilt in manner." He goes on : " I regret nothing I have said or done, for I feel that it is impossible for us to do justice to our pupils if counter-influences are at work amongst ourselves to undo the good we try to do."

Dr. Hornby, " who does not wish to dwell on the subject," begins, when he takes up the pen, by explaining his exceedingly equivocal remark. " I want," he writes, " only to say first that in speaking of Curzon as an attractive boy I did not wish to impute any motives to you, only to point out that in a public school appearances must be taken into account, and that, independent of a tutor's expressed wish, there is good reason why such an intimacy as seems to have arisen between you and Curzon should not continue." Hornby imagines that even Oscar Browning's most intimate friends, while justifying his motives, would admit

that there had been " some indiscretion " on his
part. Then he shifts from the particular to the
general and the real point at issue emerges. " I
think that I ought to say that the habit, which if
I am not mistaken you have formed of entering
into very confidential talks with many boys (not
your pupils) about the character and conduct of
their schoolfellows, seems to me to be a very
dangerous one and to do great harm without really
effecting anything for what, I believe, you have as
your object in such intercourse, the eradication or
diminution of gross vice in the school." He concludes with an almost cordial apology for touching
on the wider subject, which often " causes him
anxiety."

Any chance of the matter being discussed in a
friendlier spirit was dashed by Oscar Browning's
reply. The charge of " indiscretion " had roused
his indignation, and the Head Master's condemnation of the methods which he had deliberately
chosen to improve the morality of the school
struck, he believed, at the very root of his work.
And he asks how Dr. Hornby could listen to such
reports, " which were quite untrue and unfounded."
A long reply is the result, a reply which begins by
recording the Head Master's " sorrow " that his
previous note had not drawn any expression of
regret, " nor any assurance that you will not continue to act as you have hitherto done in this
matter." Hornby proceeds to make two demands :
firstly, that Oscar Browning shall discontinue his
intimacy with Curzon at once, and secondly,
though he cannot lay down exact rules about his
intercourse with other boys, or his reports to other
masters regarding his belief in particular boys'
conduct and influence, that O. B. should be more
careful than he has hitherto been in reporting
confidential communications affecting the character

of others, and also " in encouraging boys to make such confidences." Oscar Browning, thus attacked in what he considered the most vital sphere of his influence, protested. But it was in vain. Another long letter from the Head Master declares that he had reasons for thinking Browning " indiscreet " and for regretting that he " should have taken a prominent and very mistaken line about some delicate matters relating to the temptations and vices of boys." A reference to that unfortunate affair of the bills, about which Hornby had accused him of prevarication, shows that this too was not forgotten.

Should Oscar Browning give the promise ? Would it be right to do so ? He had made a friend of Curzon with the father's permission and approval. He could hardly let that friendship drop unless he desired it. Let them, therefore, he suggested, appeal to Lord Scarsdale. But Dr. Hornby declined any mediation of this kind. " There is much," he observes, " in such cases of which a parent can hardly judge, and which I could not without neglect of duty waive my own right to decide." And again he demands the assurance.

Oscar Browning was strongly advised by his friends to give nothing of the sort. If the matter was one of principle, he was stultifying himself by submitting to this deliberate curtailment of his activities. He was admitting his own error. The proper and dignified course, they held, was to refuse the Head Master's unprecedented demand and to leave upon him the onus of taking further action. Thus he hesitated. In the meantime he wrote again to Dr. Hornby asking why he should require such an assurance and what exactly it was meant to imply. Supposing he met Curzon in the street, as was exceedingly probable, was he not to say

" Good-morning " or acknowledge a similar greeting on the part of Curzon ? " What I mean," answered Hornby, " is that *all* intercourse should now cease between you and Curzon. Nothing short of this will do. It is impossible to define degrees of intimacy in such a matter." His reasons, the Head Master says, are clear. The boy's tutor considers the intercourse bad for him, and the marks of an " unusual intimacy " are known. " Boys speak of such matters in somewhat plain-spoken and possibly coarse terms." FitzJames Stephen, commenting upon this letter, observed that the hints and suggestions it contained would scarcely, if at all, bear the ordeal of the Courts of Law when the peculiar atmosphere of Eton, as shown in preceding letters, was taken into account. " Dr. Hornby's language," he writes, " is so framed as to contain an implied excuse for the boys' ' coarse language,' and something very like belief in the justice and applicability of it. A severe condemnation of that ' coarse language ' might naturally have been expected. The absence of it alone would constitute a very near approach to the charge of immorality. Hints and insinuations of this kind are sometimes worse than simple accusations. On the Head Master's own showing it indicates that the school was in such a frightful condition that no intercourse beyond the most ordinary could take place between master and boy without a filthy and obscene meaning and intention, language which the Head Master calls ' somewhat plain-spoken and possibly coarse ' ! "

The perplexity in which Oscar Browning found himself, further increased by a letter from Lord Scarsdale, who said that he did not wish the kindly relations existing between him and his son to fall through, led O. B. to consult Knatchbull-Hugessen. After reading the correspondence that man of affairs drafted a letter for him to send to Hornby, which first registered "an indignant protest at any such complexion being given to the relations between himself and the boy as the terms of the Head Master's letter implied," and concluded as follows : "If I were conscious of the smallest impropriety in these relations I would readily give the assurance you desire. My doing so, however, especially after your last letter, would imply my admission of that which I indignantly repudiate, and I cannot feel justified in taking such a course."

In his answer to this, Hornby, avoiding the more dangerous ground of his previous letter, falls back on the " admitted facts " as regards Browning's intercourse with Curzon. In any case the tutor and the Head Master disapproved. That should be sufficient. And he asks again for the assurance that his wishes shall be carried out. An attempt at mediation by E. D. Stone was fruitless, and finally Oscar Browning, faced with a final and peremptory demand from the Head Master, consulted the Provost. Dr. Goodford advised compliance, and accordingly he sent the required assurance, pointing out at the same time that its exaction showed a want of confidence in him which ought not to exist, and that if the intercourse between him and the boy had been the subject of comment, as the Head Master seemed to have feared, its sudden cessation would " probably be so to a greater extent." It only remained for O. B. to inform Curzon that he could see no more of him during the school-times. Curzon, on discovering the way in which his name had been used, was not unnaturally annoyed and hurt. This his letter shows : " I can't say," he writes, " how distressed I am to think that I am prevented from seeing you, and all through the unkind, ungentlemanly and obstinate conduct of my tutor, whom I detest the more I see him. But I must thank you with my whole heart for all the inestimable good you have done me, for you have always been open to me as the best of counsellors, and have opened my eyes to the company by which I am surrounded and have warned me against evil companions." He adds that he has written to his father, who he is sure " takes a right view of the case," asking him to write at once to the Head Master and call upon the latter to revoke " his unjust decision," and that in any case there can be no obstacle to their communicating in the holidays.

The affair, one would have thought, was now closed. Such an assumption, however, would be far from the truth. Oscar Browning had written to Wolley-Dod to say that so long as the Curzon interdict lasted there could be no friendly intercourse between them. " Dear Browning," answers Wolley-Dod, " I have never expressed a wish, either to you or the Head Master, that all intercourse between you and Curzon should cease." Yet the Head Master had written : " You formerly pleaded that the boy's tutor had not made his disapproval plain to you. You now know his wish and mine as regards this intercourse." It was all very puzzling. Did this statement of Curzon's tutor justify Oscar Browning in supposing that the prohibition was already removed ? It was at any rate worth while inquiring. But Hornby's answer only repeated what he had already said. " I have consulted Wolley-Dod," he says, " who does not think a renewal of your intercourse with Curzon desirable." Nor did a letter from the boy's parents to Dr. Hornby, drawn up in consultation with Knatchbull-Hugessen, meet with any more success. An interview which Lord Scarsdale and Knatchbull-Hugessen, that active friend of Oscar Browning's, had with the Head Master shortly afterwards was equally unfavourable. Dr. Hornby had spoken, and he was not to be deflected from his course by argument or entreaty.

It is clear that Hornby had made up his mind that his assistant's influence in the school was a bad one. The correspondence apart, remarks he let drop prove this quite conclusively. Thus in conversation with E. D. Stone he observed that he could attend to nothing Lord Lyttelton's sons, then high up in the school, might say, as they were under " sinister influence." On being asked whose he replied : " Browning's." True, the Head Master on being written to by Lord Lyttelton denied that he had said it, but his informant adhered to his story and sent it in writing to Oscar Browning. To Cornish, who pointed out the obvious truth that if Oscar Browning was unfit to hold intercourse with Curzon he was unfit to be a master, Hornby replied : " So he is." And he informed another master, who had asked him why he had required a written assurance, that he had done so because he could not trust Browning's word.

During the holidays O. B., whilst in Norway with the Bryces and Bishop Welldon, who wisely preferred sleep to reading Curtius's *History of the Greek Verb* with him in the long summer afternoons, returned again to the question. He regarded himself in his own words as under a stigma, and until it was removed he felt that his work and usefulness at Eton would be seriously impaired. But Hornby was not to be mollified. In an answer that extends to eight closely written pages he says that Browning is " most perverse " to make a grievance of the question. " It is intolerable that an Eton Master should come between a tutor and his pupil and even bring the boy's parents into the unpleasantness. Even if I thought that the cessation of your intercourse with the boy would give rise to unpleasant reflections in the school I should not hesitate. A man cannot plead his own wrong-doing and be allowed to continue in it for fear of possible scandal." An extraordinary statement. O. B. had certainly never pleaded any "wrong-doing." On the contrary, he considered that he had been acting throughout in accordance with deliberately chosen principles which were endangered by the Head Master's attitude. And as for the "scandal," it was, of course, Hornby who had given this as one of the reasons why he should have nothing more to do with Curzon, O. B. having merely replied that the scandal (if any) would probably be greater if their intercourse ceased entirely.

His most dignified course would have been resignation. But this was now more difficult than before. Resignation unaccompanied by a full statement of the circumstances would have placed him in an impossible situation, whilst other considerations made it difficult, if not impossible, that the truth could be told. "I doubt if any of you," writes E. M. Young, afterwards to become Head of Sherborne, who had been in close touch with Oscar Browning throughout, "who have breathed the Eton atmosphere for so long appreciate what the effect upon public opinion will be of disclosing the fact that at the greatest of our public schools it is a possibility that one master should throw out casual innuendoes against another, as Wolley-Dod has made against you, and that the whole body should not feel itself outraged and rise as one man against the accuser or accused—that the fairest youth in England should have been entrusted to a body of men who could tolerate such a state of things with patience." Clearly it was difficult to resign and leave the question to the public verdict.

It was almost as difficult for Oscar Browning to believe that the Head Master and Wolley-Dod could be really of the opinion that his influence on the young Curzon could be bad. Reflection added to his incredulity, and one afternoon in the following November he wrote a note to Wolley-Dod asking him if he would permit Curzon coming to tea with him, as Knatchbull-Hugessen would be there and wished to see him. He marked the note " private," intending thereby to prevent its reaching Dr. Hornby. Armed with Wolley-Dod's consent, which he fully expected to obtain, he believed that he would secure from the Head Master a revocation of the Curzon interdict. But the thing turned out otherwise than he had expected, for Wolley-Dod sent the note on to the Head Master, and Dr. Hornby at once jumped to the conclusion that Oscar Browning was trying to evade his promise.

Though one may dismiss this assumption, it was, as his friends admitted, " very foolish and unbusinesslike," and laid him open to renewed attack. Another letter from the Head Master again threatened dismissal unless the assurance were renewed, the third threat he had received within a year. Again he was torn with doubts whether he should give it; again acting on advice, this time given by Knatchbull-Hugessen, he submitted. And the end of what has been described as an " affair without parallel in school history" was reached with the letter of another Eton master to Lord Lyttelton asking whether it should not be made incumbent on the Head Master to place his threats against his assistants before the Governing Body, as he was bound to do in the case of dismissals.

Undoubtedly this incident, to which afterwards he was always loath to refer, caused him, in his own words, "the acutest pain he had ever experienced." He had never regarded his duties as an Eton master as confined to his own pupils or his own Division. He was a master of the School. Ever since he had been at Eton he had thrown open his library and his house to any boys who cared for literature, music or art, and he did so the more willingly because he felt that some counterbalancing influence was required to that exercised by masters over boys who were not their pupils in games. For the future he had to work under the declared hostility of the Head Master, and it was obviously only a question of time before Dr. Hornby would seize an occasion to rid himself of an assistant whom he suspected and completely failed to appreciate. It is worth while mentioning that some time after Oscar Browning had left Eton, Lord Scarsdale arranged that his son should change his tutor, and that in the following year, as the result of the more congenial atmosphere of Stone's pupil-room, Curzon was in the select for the Newcastle; and it should be added that the Head Master's ban only applied to school-times. In the holidays O. B. was at liberty to write to Curzon and to see as much of him as was agreeable and convenient to Lord Scarsdale and himself.

CHAPTER VIII

OSCAR BROWNING LEAVES ETON

I

BY staying on at Eton Oscar Browning might be still, as he had conceived himself to be twelve years previously, forwarding in a humble way the interests of humanity. But it had become also an exceedingly disagreeable way. The battle was going against him. Whereas in 1869 he had written to Alfred Sidgwick : " You see that after ten years' fighting we have at last beaten the Provost and Fellows," it looked now as if the victory would be on the side of the big battalions. Should he fight to the finish, or leave the field to the Philistines ? All through the ensuing winter half he was beset by doubts. George Eliot helped to persuade him not to despair, and in the end he decided to remain. " I am glad," she wrote to him, " that you have made up your mind to endure and persevere— words easy to write as advice but hard to follow out in the patient action of days, months, years. Perhaps the most difficult heroism is that which consists in the daily conquest over private demons, not in the slaying of world-notorious dragons. Certainly it seems to me that the finest course of action you can pursue will be to impose the utmost restraint on impatience and look on your life simply as the problem of carrying out your ideas of useful- ness at Eton as far as may be without dangerous collisions. To further this happiness and benefi- cence of your life—even apart from the question of your dear mother's feeling—you should have the precise conception of an alternative to your present task, an equivalent social contribution, before you unlink yourself. But I gather that your resolution is thoroughly formed and I rejoice."

It was all very well for George Eliot to write thus. His own private demons, his own impatience to make Eton a microcosm of a better world, might be restrained. FitzJames Stephen promises to help him with any advice or assistance which he can offer. "I feel," he says, "that you deserve it on every account, and especially because you have been a kind and judicious friend to James (J. K. Stephen) in all sorts of ways." As a mere matter of discretion, however, he thinks that Oscar Browning should try to lead boys rather to grave and hard books than to poetry and criticism, and he is sorry that he should have lent *Omar Khayyam* to one of his pupils. It is a lady's book, and he has both lent and given it to ladies though he has been told " the original is as bad as anything can be."

But even if O. B. avoided introducing his boys to Fitzgerald, there was always Dr. Hornby regarding him with a cold and critical eye, ready to pounce upon him at the slightest opportunity. And there was gossip to misrepresent his activities. Stephen is true to his word, and in May 1875 he writes that he has taken steps effectually to stop all further repetitions of the " infamous slander " (with which Walter Pater had been connected—clearly an echo of the *Mlle. de Maupin* story) that had grown from out of a perfectly innocent and natural conversation. Perhaps it would be possible to make peace, to compose the troubles which filled not a few of the Eton Fellows with misgiving. " The wrath of man," wrote the good old Bishop Chapman to J. L. Joynes, who a few years later was to become Lower Master, " never did and never will work the righteousness of God." And Joynes, in replying to Oscar Browning's suggestion that he should act as peacemaker, says that if ever he could help as a colleague in that way it would be both right and a pleasure, although

" Who would in quarrels interpose
Will often get a bloody nose."

" But this," he adds, " one ought not to mind."

II

The wrath of the Head Master did not slumber for long. It was next aroused by an alleged piece of carelessness on Oscar Browning's part. There were three brothers called Leatham in his house, and the second had been removed gravely ill. Sir William Gull had despaired of his life, and in the absence of news O. B. had concluded that he had left for good. In consequence he omitted the boy's name from the school list in the Michaelmas Term of '74, and did not pay the usual fee of £8 to the Head Master. Leatham mi. subsequently returned, and in May '75, Oscar Browning received a note from the Head Master stating that the fees had not been paid in for three school-times. He replied that he would forward Hornby's letter to the father, and that as soon as he received the money he would pay it into the school fund. This evoked an angry answer, which accused him of "carelessness," expressed surprise that he had made no apology for the trouble he had caused, and requested that the money should be paid into the bank " without further delay or evasion." In the end it was discovered that only £8, and not £24, was owing for Leatham, so that if there was carelessness it was not only on one side. Oscar Browning sent Hornby's letter to John Hibbert, who agreed that his "correspondent" certainly did not write in a pleasant style. He added: "You must submit, as he carries the guns, and an appeal to the Governing Body (of which Hibbert was a member) would be most unpleasant, and I think fatal to you." And then, like the others, he recommended great caution and great forbearance. During the same half there was some trouble in which Leatham mi. was implicated, and the father, after interviewing both Oscar Browning and Dr. Hornby, said that he would prefer to have his boys in another house, as the relations between the Head Master and his assistant were evidently of such a nature as to make it impossible for boys in Browning's house to have a fair chance.

Dr. Hornby was always on the watch. O. B. tells him casually that he had been to a meeting in London. He ponders over it, and the result is a rebuke. "Till you mentioned to me in Chambers on Tuesday that you had attended a meeting in London about the Hawtrey Memorial, I had no notion that you had given up some of your schools on Monday. It is an old rule, not of my making, that one master should not take another's school without the Head Master's sanction." The reply was that on Monday Oscar Browning had given up no schools whatever, as whilst he was away his Division was up to a mathematical master. Hornby was rapidly, at least in his dealings with Oscar Browning, falling into those habits of inaccuracy and slovenliness of which he accused his assistant. As Wolley-Dod remarked to Browning after his dismissal, the Head Master's feelings toward him "amounted to monomania." "Hornby has no charge against you which is not absolutely frivolous, and you can state this whenever you like on my authority." So said Wolley-Dod, who had no prejudices in Browning's favour.

III

The last act of the comedy, however, had begun before this. There existed a regulation that no master should have more than forty boarders, though by special permission he might have forty-three. This had never been enforced before Christmas 1874. Then one day the Provost's daughter, to while away the leisure of an idle hour, reckoned up the number of boys in each house and discovered that some had more than their complement, Browning's naturally being one of them. Dr. Goodford told this piece of information to Hibbert, who said he had better send round and have a return made. The Provost found it sufficient to write to Dr. Hornby, who forwarded his letter to Oscar Browning. The Head Master naturally made the most of this unexpected piece of good fortune and required him " to state at once *in writing*" whether he was prepared to begin the next school-time in due compliance with the regulations. Oscar Browning, angry that he was being thus picked out for the infringement of a regulation whilst others equally culpable were left alone, failed to overcome his private demon of impatience and answered in a tone which the Provost described as defiant. Thanks, however, to the intervention of the peace-maker, John Hibbert, he placed himself " unreservedly " in the hands of the Governing Body, and expressed his regret at having contravened the regulations. Thus in the summer half of 1875 he had forty boarders and three Colleger pupils, the maximum allowed by the special sanction of the Governing Body, which had to be renewed every school-time. He looked upon the granting of this leave as a matter of form. It was hardly possible that it would be refused, as it would mean that he would have to keep three empty rooms in his house for the sake of the three Colleger pupils, whom the Head Master would not allow him to give up, and would inflict a severe financial sacrifice on himself as well as a hardship on the parents who were clamouring to obtain admittance for their sons into his house, admission to which, as one of them complained, " could only be obtained after a regular process of siege." He would, to be accurate, be losing £400 a year from his boarders and gaining £31 10s. from his Colleger pupils, a point which he emphasised at various stages of the ensuing controversy, and which led *The Times* to deprecate these " disputes among schoolmasters on matters of petty gain."

At the end of the half, however, two brothers were removed from his house to another on the ground that they were overworked, and the vacancy thus caused he promised to give, after some discussion, to Knatchbull-Hugessen's son, who was already high in the school. On the last day of the half a circular came from the Head Master asking the masters to say what new boys they expected. O. B. replied from London that he expected no new boy in his house who was not already in the school, and that if the permission of the Governing Body, given in the half then terminating, were extended, he would have the same number of boys as before —forty in his house and three Colleger pupils. (The two brothers had occupied a single room and counted as one.) He enclosed a formal application at the same time to the Governing Body which he asked the Head Master to forward. In reply Dr. Hornby said he was sure that the application would not be granted, for one thing because it was too late, and for another because a similar request made by C. C. James had already been refused.

Oscar Browning was indignant. He wrote to Knatchbull-Hugessen to tell him that he could not take his boy. Knatchbull-Hugessen at once appealed to the Provost, who replied that as chairman of the Governing Body it would hardly be right for him to act as counsel in a case which might come before him as judge. "One thing," he said, "I cannot advise, that Mr. Browning should take the boy and ask for an indemnity afterwards. The Governing Body gave notice in May last that they would not entertain applications for an increase of the number of pupils from masters who first increased their numbers and then asked leave to do so." A week or two later O. B. saw Dr. Hornby at Keswick, when he was "very civil" and promised to write to the Provost hmself. The letter in which Hornby acquaints him with the negative result of this attempt is also perfectly friendly. There was nothing more to be done, and Oscar Browning again told Knatchbull-Hugessen that he could not take his son. Shortly afterwards the circumstances were changed through other boys leaving, so that it became possible after all to accede to Knatchbull-Hugessen's wishes. In the beginning of September Mrs. Browning sent the Head Master a list of the thirty-seven boys who would be in their house, and on September 6, only ten days before he formally gave Oscar Browning his notice of dismissal, Dr. Hornby wrote to Knatchbull-Hugessen : "I have received the list sent by Mrs. Browning. If there is no misunderstanding (and Mrs. Browning is very careful and accurate), all will go smoothly, and I shall be very glad of it." There was no hint here of the storm that was about to burst. It is evident that Dr. Hornby on September 6 had no prevision of what he was going to do ten days later. Neither had Oscar Browning. When he returned to Eton he was concerned with the question of his three vacant rooms. It was clearly hopeless to expect the

Governing Body to agree to any extension. The only way to avoid the loss of the £400 a year was by giving up his Colleger pupils. This he could only do with the Head Master's sanction. True, Dr. Hornby had already said that he would not consent to such a step. Still Oscar Browning evidently thought it worth while asking, and so on September 15 he called with the object of making this proposal. Fresh from his summer holidays abroad, he was no doubt less subtle than ever in his diagnosis of what the Head Master's thoughts and mood might be. He felt it to be absurd that when parents were clamouring to obtain admission for their sons into his house he should have to keep three rooms vacant in order to satisfy a regulation which other masters, besides himself, had habitually broken. The conversation, nevertheless, from the account which Oscar Browning sent immediately afterwards to Lord Lyttelton before there had been any sequel, appears to have opened amicably. They talked of the holidays, of Switzerland and mountains, the Lakes and the Alps. Then Oscar Browning walked to the edge of the precipice. He said that he supposed there was no chance of the Governing Body giving leave, as they seemed determined to stick to the number of forty, and he added that he was sorry he had not made it clear about the transfer of the young Knatchbull-Hugessen.

Suddenly Dr. Hornby lost his temper. His "griefs accumulated" were too much for him, and he called O. B. a "shuffler" because he had not asked for leave. Browning pointed out that leave was never asked in the case of an amicable arrangement. "Worse shuffling then ever," Hornby declared, not without something of the self-righteousness which was natural to this Head Master, "to excuse yourself by others' delinquencies." Oscar Browning asked whether he had called C. C. James a shuffler for receiving the two brothers into his house without leave. The Head Master replied that Browning had told him they were going. "Whose business is it then," he inquired, "to ask leave? The tutor who surrenders, the tutor who receives, or the parent?" "Both," replied Hornby. "You are the greatest shuffler I have ever met. You shuffle in everything you do. Your character is known to the Governing Body. You neglect your work. Why don't you read Madvig's Latin Grammar? You lecture to ladies; you examine here and there; you give musical parties on Saturday evenings. Why don't you stick to your work? No one ever treated me in a straightforward manner who did not find me straightforward."

O. B. declared that his conduct had been candour itself. But Hornby, now "grown white with rage," was in no mood to listen. "Why, you are a liar!" he went on. "You told me a lie two years ago. I wish I had dismissed you for it then." "If you use that language," Oscar Browning replied, "I had better leave the room, and you had better make a complaint to the Governing Body," and he moved towards the door. But the interview did not terminate thus. For Dr. Hornby at once, plunging into the affair of the bills, now nearly two years old, went over that story once again, and concluded by saying that the relations between them had better cease. Oscar Browning answered that he would not resign and that Hornby must take the responsibility of dismissing him. On his side he poured out his grievances, how he had endured "constant persecution" at Hornby's hands for two years, how he had only stayed on for his mother's sake, how Hornby had written him indefensible letters, how he had never had a chance of clearing himself of the charges brought against him. There was no tribunal to which he could appeal. All he wished was a fair and impartial hearing before someone or other on the questions at issue between them. He had often thought of appealing to the Governing Body. "If you do that," said Hornby, "you must take the consequences." Browning replied that he would write to Lord Lyttelton and take the consequences whatever they might be.

After this undignified wrangling the two discussed the question of the Colleger pupils. Dr. Hornby wished to lay exact restrictions on their hours of going out in the evenings, because he believed that O. B. "made the boys idle." O. B. does not appear to have made the obvious riposte that in that case it would be better for them to have another tutor. But when he asked if he might give them up, Hornby replied: "If you do I will dismiss you. No, you shall not give them up." "Why then," asked O. B., "was C. C. James allowed to give up his outdoor pupils?" Hornby denied this—one of the inexactitudes which creep into controversy, for James two hours later received the written permission of the Head Master to this end. He made his denial more emphatic by saying: "Clear the dirt off your own doorstep and don't mind your neighbours. I shall do what is perfectly right. You shall not give up your three Collegers." And once more the conversation turned on the exact times at which the three Collegers were to go to and return from Browning's, that home of wasted time. Hornby ended, in fact, by relaxing the restrictions which he had wished to impose. Thus after two outbursts the discords of the interview were more or less satisfactorily resolved. Hornby had resumed his natural colour. Oscar Browning had neither been dismissed from the Head Master's presence nor had he himself left the room as a protest. But the relations between the two had grown one degree worse. Mutual recriminations by word of mouth were a new thing. And that same day Oscar Browning wrote an account of the interview to Lord Lyttelton, substantially in the terms given above, pointing out that his own attitude had been throughout that of one trying to remove misconceptions. He had remained perfectly cool and had done nothing either to excite or aggravate the anger of Hornby. Should he now resign, or should he appeal to the Governing Body?

Lord Lyttelton returned a very cordial answer in his usual illegible hand, discountenancing resignation, but saying that advice he could not give as he was himself a member of the Governing Body. But before he had received this letter Hornby had forestalled either course. For on the following day he wrote this letter to Oscar Browning:

"Eton College,
September 16th, 1875.

" Dear Browning,

"After our conversation yesterday you will, I think, have expected some communication from me.

"I have purposely put off writing for a whole day, that I might not, in a very serious matter, act hastily or under any feelings of irritation.

"I must remind you that, in the interview which you sought with me yesterday, you charged me with prejudice, unfairness and constant persecution in my dealings with you; and you tried to justify your recent breach of well-known rules, which I am bound to enforce, on the ground that you believed that some of your colleagues had broken them. Such a plea hardly needs an answer; but I must remind you that, in your case, particular

123

attention had been called to your violation of the rules last winter—that you had in consequence received a reprimand, and very definite instructions in writing as to your future course. I believe that your colleagues will be found to have kept within the regulations; but if there has been any violation of them (and I shall at once proceed to investigate this), it cannot in any way justify what you have done.

"For two or three years, hardly a school-time has passed in which I have not been compelled to undertake the very painful task of calling you to account for neglect of work or violation of rules. I feel that I have carried forbearance, in your case, beyond the limit which I ought to have observed in strict duty to the school. I have done so because of the extreme gravity of dismissing a master from Eton, especially one of your age and standing, and because I tried to indulge the hope that your conduct might yet be such as to make this extreme measure unnecessary. I feel, however, that after recent events, and after our conversation of yesterday, it is not possible for me to feel that confidence in you which is absolutely necessary to our working together, and to my entrusting you with the important duties which belong to an Eton master.

"I must therefore give you notice that your mastership will terminate at the end of this school-time.

"Yours sincerely,

"J. J. HORNBY."

This curious document, with its self-commendation—the writer has allowed a whole day to elapse in order that he may not act "hastily, or under any feelings of irritation," and he extols his own forbearance—does little to increase our opinion of the writer. It starts by a misstatement, that Oscar Browning had tried to justify his recent breach of well-known rules, when all he had done was to attempt to obtain a relaxation of a rule that he had not broken, and proceeds to show that the Head Master was unaware of what was happening elsewhere in the school on this very matter. How well founded was Hornby's belief that Oscar Browning's colleagues were keeping the regulations which he himself had infringed the previous winter is shown by a letter Wolley-Dod wrote to Browning shortly after the interview just recorded. In this he says that when he heard a year ago that the rule of forty pupils was to be strictly enforced he wrote to the Head Master explaining that he had forty-three, and asking leave to keep them. "As I got no answer I took it for granted that no objection was made. I have neither received nor made any further communication on the subject until the beginning of this school-time (September 1875), when in answer to a circular from the Head Master I wrote to say that I did not understand that leave had to be obtained every school-time. . . . I have heard no more of the matter."

"The simple fact," observed FitzJames Stephen, who was closely acquainted with the whole series of differences between Hornby and Browning, "was that Dr. Hornby's dismissal of Mr. Browning was a petulant act, resolved upon under the stress of extreme irritation and never really deliberated upon in the proper sense of the word. Even the interview might have been supposed to have been concluded and done with, since there was no sudden, angry parting or anything of that nature. Dr. Hornby never actually dismissed Mr. Browning during the conversation. On this view his own words condemn him, for if Mr. Browning by any words he said did not bring down on himself

actual and instant dismissal, even from a man in
an ungovernable rage, how can Dr. Hornby justly
bring forward Mr. Browning's language as con-
ducing to his dismissal? It was evidently only
the after-irritation produced by the memory of an
interview in which he was entirely in the wrong,
that caused him to do so." Knatchbull-Hugessen
also points out the suddenness of Hornby's decision
to dismiss Oscar Browning in his own Memorial
to the Governing Body. "If Dr. Hornby," he
remarks, " as he says, exercised forbearance towards
Mr. Browning in time past, his letter to me of
September 6, deliberately sanctioning and approving
that my boy should go to Mr. Browning's house,
implies that such forbearance extended up to that
date and that he had then no intention of getting
rid of Mr. Browning. If, therefore, the charge
against Mr. Browning of ' breach of rules ' falls
to the ground, it cannot be just or fair that old
offences, if they be offences, which have been
condoned, and for condoning which Dr. Hornby
claims the merit of ' forbearance,' should now be
raked up against Mr. Browning solely in consequence of an alleged ' offence ' which he has *not*
committed." For once in a way Oscar Browning
was technically in the right. No Head Master on
the stated facts ever had a weaker case in dismissing an assistant whose length of service was
double his own. That was one reason why rumour
kept on referring to the things that lay behind, and
persisted after O. B. had left Eton in throwing out
hints of the same nature.

IV

Dr. Hornby's letter, though not altogether unexpected, came nevertheless as a very unpleasant
surprise. For the moment it was kept a secret,

only one or two other masters who were his intimates being told in confidence about the Head Master's action. Besides being an unprecedented step, there were doubts whether the Head Master's powers, as laid down in the Public Schools Act of 1868, could be taken to apply in the case of Oscar Browning, who had been appointed before the passing of that Act. In his answer to Hornby's letter of dismissal, which he wrote after consultation with FitzJames Stephen, he refused to admit that his tenure was regulated by the statutes of 1871. "What the precise legal effect of this state of things might be " he did not, however, at the moment inquire. But he pointed out that he had reached an age when it was hardly possible for him to turn to any other profession, and he could not in justice to himself and those dependent upon him " acquiesce in disgrace and ruin " without using every lawful means at his disposal to avert them. If, therefore, he made an appeal to the Governing Body, his only object would be to bring about a recall of his notice of dismissal, not to attack the Head Master, with whom he was still ready to co-operate " faithfully and honourably." Hornby curtly brushed aside the olive branch, contenting himself with asserting his right of dismissal. On his side there was no hint of compromise. In the meantime Lord Lyttelton, who was the most influential layman on the Governing Body, had written to Oscar Browning deeply deploring the step Hornby had taken, and saying that he would tell the Head Master and the Provost his mind. But he warned him at the same time against following in Hayman's footsteps and thinking of legal proceedings.

Early in October Oscar Browning wrote to all his colleagues at Eton, informing them of his dismissal and offering to show them the correspondence which had passed between himself and Hornby. At first public opinion ran strongly against the Head Master, and on the morning after the affair was generally known he was very coldly received in Chambers by the other masters. The security of tenure of Assistant Masters in the great public schools had been placed by the Public Schools Act in the discretionary power of the Head Master. Though there had been cases where Head Masters had used their power tyrannically, Eton so far had remained free from this abuse. The evil was generally recognised by those interested in education. A writer in the *Spectator*, calling attention to it, says that it had hitherto been supposed that Assistant Masters had sufficient security in the good feeling of the Head Master and the force of public opinion. "Now," the correspondent continues, and he is writing before Oscar Browning's dismissal from Eton, "we know the value of this security. The Head Master may, if he is a selfish man, calmly and deliberately, or, if he is an impulsive man, in a freak of ill-temper, work the ruin of any of his subordinates. He may take from them their employment and their income and turn them adrift to begin the world again. And public opinion will take the matter very quietly." Incidents at Rugby, Felsted and various grammar schools had shown the danger of giving despotic power to Head Masters, and it was for this reason that Oscar Browning, with many others, had been endeavouring to secure the right of appeal for Assistant Masters in such cases to the Governing Bodies. He had had himself considerable correspondence with Grant-Duff and G. O. Trevelyan on the subject. Two years before this, Forster, then Secretary of the Board of Education, had pointed out that although under the Act an Assistant Master, if dismissed, had no right of appeal, the

Governing Body had the power of dismissing the Head Master. This proved to be a very accurate forecast of the position in which Oscar Browning was subsequently to find himself.

Nearly all his colleagues expressed their sympathy with warmth, F. E. Durnford, the Lower Master, one of O. B.'s most inveterate opponents, who had never allowed any of his boys to frequent Browning's house, being the only one to content himself with formal regrets. J. L. Joynes, the senior Assistant Master, was " distressed," not least at the thought of Mrs. Browning and her long and anxious care of the boys. " Indeed," he remarks, " the whole matter is extremely painful." Edmond Warre had received his note with surprise and regret. " I was not aware," he writes, " that matters between you and the Head Master had assumed so serious a phase, and had indeed hoped, from not having heard anything more of them lately, that they had been peaceably settled or were at least quiescent. . . . Personally you and I have been in many matters antagonistic in opinion, and no friendship, so to speak, has existed between us. On the other hand, the Head Master and myself have always been on friendly terms. But my wish had always been to stand aloof on all matters of disagreement between you and him." He is anxious to maintain the same attitude. Nevertheless he ends with the assurance that the " news is in no sense a source of satisfaction but rather of pain and regret " to him. T. P. Carter had also heard the news " with astonishment and extreme regret," and he cannot refrain from saying that in his opinion the Head Master has at various times shown less regard for the feelings and rights of his subordinates than he, for one, could have wished. He adds : " I could not repose implicit confidence in his verdicts." There was almost unanimous agreement that Hornby's action was likely to produce grave evils. Many indeed seem to have regarded it as a threat rather than an irrevocable decision. H. W. Mozley, who is of this opinion, offers to join in any remonstrance Browning's colleagues may make, and gives his personal opinion that Oscar Browning's departure would be as great a loss to the school as well could be imagined. St. John Thackeray advises him to make " a full apology "; Henry Daman cannot conceive that anything has happened to warrant such a proceeding as the Head Master has taken, and H. Gilbert Wintle, who had that term gone to Eton as a master, has not forgotten the many kindnesses which he had received at Oscar Browning's hands in former times, and feels confident that Assistant Masters and Old Etonians alike will join in unanimous approval of his conduct.

Clearly O. B.'s dismissal was a matter which touched them all. Everyone's interest was concerned, and a meeting of masters was called to discuss what steps should be taken. Had there been any general agreement to make Oscar Browning's cause their own, Dr. Hornby would have found himself in a position from which he could only have extricated himself by resignation or by withdrawing the dismissal. But there were two parties in the school, and Hornby did not rely in vain on the division between them. The Hornby party, headed by Warre, first of all managed to secure the postponement of the meeting for twenty-four hours, so that when it met the sharp edge of resentment had already begun to be blunted. And when it was proposed to submit a resolution calling on Dr. Hornby for his reasons, one master said that he would decline to agree to anything of the sort. Ultimately the meeting, by the votes of forty-four out of the forty-six present, agreed to a " memorial " which did no more than deprecate Oscar Browning's dismissal. To this Dr. Hornby, who had refused to meet the masters in a body, returned a non-committal answer and the matter, so far as the staff was concerned, was at an end.

An attempt had already been made by some of Oscar Browning's friends at Eton to secure the mediation of Dr. Balston, who had remarked that if he had ever found it necessary to dismiss an assistant he would have called a meeting of the masters and informed them. But Dr. Balston saw Hornby and declared that it was useless to ask him to reconsider his decision. Others also tried. Sir George Young, not the least distinguished of Etonians of the 'fifties, told Hornby that whatever grounds he had for getting rid of Browning he had absolutely no case for a penal dismissal, and was astonished to find that the matter had never occurred to Hornby in that light before. He also expressed his astonishment to O. B. at having "ever managed to quarrel with so easy-going a person." Chief Justice Coleridge was another who expressed himself as ready to mediate if the parties wished it. But Hornby, well aware that so long as he did nothing his action could not be seriously challenged, refused the overture.

In the meantime sympathy came from all sides, from pupils, parents and friends. "It seems worth while to suffer a catastrophe if only it enables us to know what our friends think of us on this side of the grave. The letters are a credit to human nature." Thus, a few months later, wrote William Johnson, as whose supporter, at a masters' meeting three or four years previously, Oscar Browning had perhaps first incurred the suspicions of the Head Master. Certainly they are a notable collection. Frederic Harrison writes: "I have just heard from Maxse some rumours of an outrage with which you have been threatened or assailed at Eton, and I share his indignation and that of all honest men at the attempt. I trust whatever shape it take that it will fail. I will do anything I can to back you up. . . . I cannot doubt that with all your many and powerful friends you will come out all the stronger for the attack." Lord Morley, then, of course, plain John, says that it is all very painful and hopes that he will find some way to avoid leaving Eton. " To do so will be a loss to the school and, as you seem to feel, a damage to yourself. . . . An individual fighting against an accepted system of school (or other) government is unluckily placed." Walter Pater had just met one of O. B.'s old pupils, enthusiastic in his favour. " All I can say is, that you know how much I admired your work at Eton when I was with you in the summer, and I was very glad to hear, not for your own sake only but on public grounds, that you had decided not to leave Eton without a struggle." John Ruskin's feelings were shown, when he went to lecture at Eton, by his walking arm-in-arm with Oscar Browning the whole length of the Library.

His Eton and Cambridge friends were even more emphatic. Kegan Paul, once master in College, then a country parson, afterwards founder of the well-known publishing firm, was wholly unable to understand, not only how such charges as Hornby had made could be substantiated, but under what strange misconception they could ever have been formulated. " I have never doubted," he says, " that your general influence on Eton was one of almost unmeasured good." S. H. Butcher, to become one day Member for the University, lamented Browning's dismissal not merely for his own sake but for that of Eton. " You have indeed fought the battle of culture against an engrossing athleticism or a would-be gentlemanly nonchalance, but you have done much more. Culture and moral indifference sometimes go together. But I cannot too strongly express how much I believe morality is indebted to you and to your courageous struggles against all that was vile, though not always condemned by public opinion. It is easy enough to utter protests and lamentations, but it is a different thing to act, as you have done over and over again in the face of odium." And he goes on to dilate on O. B.'s " fearless and unflinching moral earnestness."

The parents, to whom he had sent a circular acquainting them with his dismissal, were angry as well as sympathetic. They had taken unusual trouble to secure admission for their sons to what they thought was the best house at Eton, and now their trouble was not only vain, but they had to find vacancies for them elsewhere. Lord Portsmouth, three of whose sons were in Browning's, declared that he would call a meeting of parents at the White Hart and head a procession over Windsor Bridge to the Head Master. He did not carry out the threat, for ultimately the parents met in London and petitioned Dr. Hornby that he would reconsider his decision, which if it were carried out would mean that their sons would be cast adrift and be either compelled to pass under the care of other masters not originally selected by them, or be forced to leave prematurely, " to the injury or absolute destruction of their future prosperity," Needless to say the Head Master was unmoved by these parental outcries and the majority of the parents began to lose their zeal when it was hinted to them that if they made a fuss their sons might indeed be forced to leave prematurely through finding other houses closed to them.

But William Johnson in his comments was

thinking rather of the letters Oscar Browning had received from his pupils, letters which in themselves were sufficient justification of his work at Eton. "My dear old tutor," "my very dear tutor"—they begin with every mark of affection and contain every mark of respect. Some might think that in their insistence on the moral, as well as the humanistic, qualities which their tutor's influence conveyed, they err perhaps on the side of priggishness. But one remembers the charge, or at least the suspicion, of impiety which was attributed to Oscar Browning by his enemies and finds justification for their attitude. "You have not only had the intellectual, you have also had the moral good of the boys at heart, and I believe that no one has exerted himself more to lessen the prevalence of vice at Eton." Thus wrote a Balliol scholar, himself afterwards to become a distinguished Eton master. Many others destined to become famous were amongst those who supported him whole-heartedly. Alfred Lyttelton, the glory of Eton, his brother Edward, who was to succeed Dr. Warre as Head Master, Mr. Gerald Balfour, Selwyn the future Head of Uppingham, Bishop Welldon, who had left Eton two years previously and was now in the middle of a brilliant career at Cambridge—these were some of the young men who felt that a gross injustice had been committed and ardently wished to see it redressed. Perhaps the most impressive expression of sympathy, because it is not prompted by any feeling of personal affection, is one from F. W. Maitland, afterwards to breathe new life into the dry bones of early constitutional history and to revivify the study of the origins of English common law. Maitland, who was never O. B.'s pupil, writes: "The conduct of the Head Master is to me inexplicable. He surely must be able to see that a man may be a good schoolmaster though he be neither an athlete nor a pedant. However, happily it is not my place to make excuses for him. I will only say (what I never should have said to you except in circumstances as the present) that you were one of the very few masters who attempted to give me an interest in reading as opposed to cramming, and that is a debt which I cannot forget. . . ."

Oscar Browning had no lack of friends. Foremost amongst them then, and not less his intimate nearly half a century later, was Lord Latymer, then Francis Money, who afterwards took the name of Coutts and later exchanged that of Money for Burdett. He asks him to come and live in London and to allow him to help in any work he undertakes. "I should like to write a book and publish it," he says, "about the things of Eton in reference to you only," though the opinion he held in the generosity of his youth was so far changed by the caution of age as to lead him to advise his octogenarian friend not to revive "a sad story." But for O. B. neither friends nor the consciousness that he was entirely in the right, a feeling, by the way, which also sustained Dr. Hornby through the whole affair, was to prove of any avail against the machinery which had been set in motion against him. Dr. Hornby had only to sit tight and do nothing, and Oscar Browning and his " powerful friends," however they might storm, were unable to win a single point.

In the meantime the whole business was discussed in all its bearings in the little world that is Eton. The " reprobates " amongst the boys were glad that his sun was setting. A good many of the masters looked forward to the peaceful days when Oscar Browning would be removed to some other sphere, and some of the highly placed ladies in Eton society were said to be rejoicing that Mrs. Browning would no longer overshadow them with her charm and her malicious wit. The affair seems indeed to have become almost an obsession, and Dr. Farrar, when early in November he preached a sermon in Eton Chapel on Saul, was thought to have been inspired by the topic of the hour. This draws from him a " private and confidential " letter of protest to Oscar Browning. To have done such a thing, he points out, would have been in glaringly bad taste. As a matter of fact, it was an old Marlborough sermon. He had intended to preach on Belshazzar's warning, but a Marlborough friend had said, " ' *Do* preach that sermon on Saul and the Philistines,' his reason being *not* Eton affairs, of which he knows nothing, but the fact that the concluding pages on self-reverence as sons of God would be useful." The thing has pained him very much and he gives it his " surprised, unqualified and indignant denial."

Even the local shopkeepers took sides. " Dear sir," one signing himself a Slough Tradesman writes. " Having Seen The Dictation you are Subjected to the Thought Forced into My Mind That A Good House at Upton Slough Near The Old Church Belonging To The Nixey Family his Now Vacant and Would make a fine Seminary and Home."

V

There was nothing to be done except to appeal to the Governing Body. Oscar Browning therefore drew up a memorial in which he recounted the story of his more recent relations with the Head Master, printed the correspondence which had passed between them, and ended by submitting a twofold request, to prevent Dr. Hornby from " illegally " interfering with the discharge of

his duties " as a master of Eton College not liable
to dismissal by him at pleasure " (this was based
on his plea that he had been appointed under the
old statutes), and if they declined to comply with
this, to interfere, as the ultimate authority, to
prevent the Head Master from making an oppressive
use of his powers. FitzJames Stephen, it should
be said, had given it as his considered opinion that
Dr. Hornby had no right to dismiss Browning at
all except as agent for Eton College, and the College
had no right to dismiss him, except for misconduct,
without reasonable notice. The Governing Body
could, however, if it thought proper, adopt the
Head Master's act.

The Governing Body was placed in something
of a quandary. It could not in any case intervene
directly in the dispute. Supposing that the weight
of opinion had been on Oscar Browning's side, all
it could have done would have been to force Dr.
Hornby's resignation, which in itself would not
have reinstated his victim. In fact the majority on
the Governing Body were ready to support the
Head Master. He and Dr. Goodford were on
very different terms now compared with two years
previously, when Oscar Browning had led a party
amongst the masters to back Dr. Hornby against
the constant interference of the Provost. At the
same time O. B. had two or three influential friends
on the Governing Body who were anxious that he
should be treated with all possible consideration.
They were supported by a strong element of liberal
feeling outside Eton, which considered that Oscar
Browning had been made a scapegoat for his
reforming zeal. Even the more conservative members of the Governing Body saw that the dismissal
of a popular and successful master required some
sort of justification.

VI

In addition to Oscar Browning's memorial, the Governing Body was presented with a long and closely reasoned complaint by Knatchbull-Hugessen. In this he went over the ground which is already familiar to anyone who has read the account of this strange case, pointing out that Browning had broken no rule and that he had done nothing more than give legitimate expression to a desire to obtain the relaxation of a rule, which was a totally different thing. Earnestly and not without many italics he asked for a fair consideration of the case. He sent also a copy of the correspondence which had passed between him and Dr. Hornby, in which the Head Master seems unaware of the sorry figure he is cutting. Knatchbull-Hugessen was a person of some weight. He was chairman of the South-Eastern Railway, a Member of Parliament, and was subsequently raised to the peerage. Since it was over the affair of his son that the dispute had arisen, he considered himself in some measure responsible and made it his duty to try and find out the precise grounds on which Hornby had come to his decision to dismiss Oscar Browning.

In this correspondence he begins by pointing out that on September 6 Hornby had written that if there was no misunderstanding about Browning's list all would go smoothly, and he for one would be very glad of it. If, as Knatchbull-Hugessen observed, the Head Master had entertained the idea on September 6 of getting rid of Browning, the words would have been scarcely ingenuous in themselves and very unfair and misleading to him personally as a parent. Therefore the cause of the Head Master's decision must be found in something which happened between September 6 and 16, and he hoped, since in so short a time it could hardly have been anything but trifling, that the matter might be amicably arranged. The Head Master answers that on September 6 he did not foresee this rupture. "The point, of course, is simply this—is his dismissal right or wrong?" and Hornby, with that soundness on moral questions which he shares with Dr. Skinner of the Shrewsbury of fiction, has "no doubt whatever what answer would be given to this question by any impartial person who knew the facts."

The facts, Knatchbull-Hugessen answers, the facts—that is exactly what we all want to know. There are clear and definite charges of offences committed by Oscar Browning of the nature of which he himself is ignorant. If that is so, why not submit them to some person above suspicion of partiality, such as Spencer Walpole?

Hornby sees that he has made a mistake, has weakened his position in referring to "facts." So he avers that the reasons of dismissal are set out in his letter of September 16, and as for the "feeling" against Browning, which he has admitted to Knatchbull-Hugessen before now both in conversation and writing, it is not "malicious or unworthy," but merely a "moral disapprobation." And he goes on to say that he cannot burke his responsibility and admit the matter to outside mediation. He must take the burden of this "most painful act" alone.

Very true, answers Knatchbull-Hugessen in effect. Naturally there is nothing malicious about your feeling. Still you have admitted certain sentiments which may have insensibly led you to put a construction upon words and actions of Browning's which they would not bear in the eyes of others who have not that prejudice. Of course you may have facts in reserve which put a wholly different complexion on the whole affair. But if so they have never been made known. "If you refuse all mediation," he adds, "I must fairly and openly tell you that I shall feel bound to take every step in my power to secure for Browning the reversal of the sentence passed upon him, or at least the opportunity of vindicating his character before the world." In a further letter he remarks that if necessary he will introduce a Bill into Parliament to amend the Public Schools Act, and so take the opportunity of stating Oscar Browning's case in the House of Commons. "All this could do no good to Eton and would be *very* disagreeable." But he sees no escape for it if the Head Master is inflexible.

Hornby's moral sense was roused by this. Threats, he says, make it now quite impossible, even if it had been possible before, to hold out any hope of a reversal of Browning's dismissal. "I pity the man indeed," he writes, "who binds himself hand and foot in such a way as this and fears to face full inquiry into his conduct. Of course there is an evil in having Eton affairs discussed, but the public soon gets tired of mere mud-throwing, especially if done with a wrongful motive." He adds in a postscript to what he apologises for as a "hasty letter": "I cannot understand why, if Browning and his friends really think there is anything frightful which needs disclosure, they should not desire to have it made. I would far rather in such a case have the truth out. I have never lived under any fear of disclosures and trust I never shall." To which Knatchbull-Hugessen answers that his letter is absolutely unintelligible. "So far from fearing to have full inquiry into his conduct, that is precisely what I understand Browning to desire. There must be some strange misunderstanding somewhere."

140

There was, however, to be no such investigation, or categorical statement of charges, as Oscar
Browning had demanded. The Governing Body
when it met never even discussed whether it
had competence to enter on the question of the
Head Master's dealings with the Assistant Masters.
There seems to have been some discussion whether
or not Dr. Hornby's resignation should also be
demanded, some members of the Governing Body,
including Dr. Thompson, the Master of Trinity,
John Hibbert and possibly Spencer Walpole,
favouring this step, whilst Lord Lyttelton was
notoriously critical of Dr. Hornby's regime. But
whatever passed, the only decision taken was to
ask the Head Master for a statement of the circumstances under which he had resolved on dismissal.
The Governing Body then adjourned for four days
till it had been received. This was in no sense a
victory for Oscar Browning. The statement was
duly drawn up and presented, but its contents
were not divulged, and though he formally asked
both the Provost and the Head Master to see a copy,
as Dr. Hornby had seen copies of the documents
he had submitted to the Governing Body, his
request was refused. When the Governing Body
met after its adjournment, it decided that no case
existed for action on its part. It was this refusal of
Dr. Hornby to divulge the charges he had brought
against Oscar Browning that caused the most
influential of the weekly papers to observe that
Dr. Hornby " can hardly be surprised if he chances
to meet with some hard words which are ordinarily
used against those who stab in the dark."

VII

The decision of the Governing Body led to
Knatchbull-Hugessen's writing to *The Times*, much

to the scandal of old-fashioned Etonians, who deplored the affairs of their school being discussed in the " public prints." Once more he stated the facts of the dismissal, to be answered by an anonymous correspondent who attacked Oscar Browning with all the courage a pen-name inspires. J. L. Joynes, anxious to be on the side of the big battalions, wrote to point out that the master's Memorial to Dr. Hornby had " carefully disclaimed expressing any opinion on the merits of the case." A leading article, whilst regretting that the matter should have been made public, said that the account of the interview between Dr. Hornby and Mr. Browning " afforded the public a singular view of the social relations possible in a great public school, when such expressions as are alleged to have been used, fly about casually." It descended, however, from its pinnacle of superiority on the side of authority, said that Mr. Browning showed a very troublesome disposition to violate rules, and finally observed that " these exhibitions of temper between masters of schools on trumpery points of profit" were the worst possible example to the boys.

The thing became as near being a Press " stunt " as the demure manners of Fleet Street in 1875 would allow. That November there was little news. The sinking of the *Thunderer* was beginning to be forgotten, and India was too remote for much interest to be taken in the Prince's visit. For a day or two Oscar Browning and a small boy of six who had been taken up in Liverpool for being drunk and disorderly held the attention of the public between them. Papers took sides according to their political bias. *The Times* and the *Morning Post* backed authority, the *Daily News* supported Oscar Browning, the *Daily Telegraph* shook its head and deplored " the idleness, extravagance and luxury of Eton." Hard words were visited on all.

142

The public was told of the deplorable scenes of cabals and intrigues among the Eton masters. It was informed that the Public Schools Act had really made those places of education less efficient than before, that the Governing Bodies with which " Parliament afflicted the great public schools of England had done little but mischief since they came into being." The prosperity of Eton, one paper remarked, had never been greater, but that was " because the prestige of Eton is extraordinary and because the first thing which a *nouveau riche* does, to give his children caste, is to send his sons to Eton." Though a good deal of water has flowed beneath Windsor Bridge since then, and all the principals in this controversy have passed to other, and perhaps more charitable places, Eton still remains true to itself.

And all the time whilst the pros and the cons were being argued in the clubs and in the Press there was an undercurrent of gossip which sometimes emerged into print. It was impossible that Oscar Browning could have been dismissed on the published facts. There must be more behind. What was it ? A raising of the eyebrows, a shrug of the shoulders could convey columns of innuendo. Dr. Hornby himself had little control over his tongue. He said things without reflection. He even wrote things, things which appeared to give authority to the rumours which continued to circulate. He ended by writing a letter to Ainger which FitzJames Stephen declared was libellous, and prompted O. B. for many months to nurse the idea of bringing an action for damages against Hornby in the courts.

Oscar Browning's friends were anxious that these rumours and this gossip should be scotched. Hornby, when he was approached by those who had observed an attitude of neutrality, declared that he could not stop the idle talk of people, and that the remedy of publishing a full statement would not, in his opinion, tend to diminish it. It was then proposed that Oscar Browning should apply for a pension which the Governing Body had power to grant to any master who had been more than fifteen years at Eton. If this were given it would be in itself an answer to malicious reports. It was felt too that it would only be an act of bare justice that Oscar Browning should not be turned adrift from Eton with only the slender means of subsistence which his King's Fellowship gave him. Public opinion at Eton, which had been divided on the merits of the controversy between Hornby and Browning, was in this matter unanimously on Browning's side, and a petition was addressed by the masters to the Governing Body praying that a pension might be accorded him. In the attempt to secure the support of the Head Master in this not unreasonable request, and to clear Oscar Browning of the aspersions that were being made about him, Ainger, always one of O. B.'s most loyal colleagues, wrote to Hornby.

"My dear Ainger," ran the reply, "I am sorry for Browning, but I cannot possibly say that I do not think ill of his character. I have not charged him with *immorality* in the ordinary sense of the word. His own admissions have proved evidence enough against him as regards want of truthfulness, and this though his statement omits and distorts things in his favour as far as possible. Public opinion is clearly dead against him already; what would it be if the whole truth were known? A pension is utterly out of the question. I do not want to press hard upon a man in trouble, but I cannot help Browning in the way you suggest. The more I say, I am afraid, the worse his case would be. I have said as little as I possibly could help saying and nothing of any doubtful kind of which I have not full proof." Lord Lyttelton, who was shown the letter by Mrs. Browning, wrote at once to advise O. B. to make a formal demand of Hornby in writing for a full statement of the charges to which he alluded, and to lay it before the Governing Body for their next meeting. The Governing Body, however, did not deviate from the policy it had already adopted. The reply about the pension was that they were precluded from taking the claim into consideration. Oscar Browning received no more enlightenment than before on the question of the offences with which he was charged. After the meeting Lord Lyttelton writes again : " What moves me to write, is that I do still feel able and bound to repeat to you that I fully admit *no one* would sit down under such imputations as are conveyed and insinuated in Hornby's letter of November 19, charges which are only very partially explained and retracted subsequently. I conceive you are, and will be, fully justified in doing all you can to have everything in that letter fully and publicly investigated." But though O. B. toyed with the idea, the advice of another friend, who counselled him not to bring an action, " neu matris validos in viscera vertite vires," prevailed.

So concludes the story of Oscar Browning's career at Eton. The two great requisites in a Head Master, the Rev. R. H. Quick has observed, are energy and sympathy with the staff. By the standards of that eminent educationist, Dr. J. J. Hornby can lay no claim to the second quality, and every account of Eton under his rule shows his deficiency in energy. Oscar Browning too had his faults. He was impetuous in giving expression to his feelings, impatient of the routine which is the schoolmaster's way of letting off steam and preventing himself from thinking, careless, though not probably more careless than many other school-masters, about business matters. But any man of strong character has defects proportionate in scale to his virtues. It is these that matter. And to these qualities in Oscar Browning, Hornby was blind. He was fated to remain Head Master for another nine years. During that time the discipline of the school steadily deteriorated, to be restored under the capable hand of Edmond Warre, of Warre whom O. B. had looked upon at Eton as his rival, but who, as he always realised, was a far stronger and abler man than Hornby.

There can be no doubt that Oscar Browning never really got over the shock of his dismissal from Eton. In 1920 he writes to a former colleague who had published a book about Eton : " You are too favourable to Hornby. Writing at the age of eighty-four, forty-five years after being dismissed from Eton, I can honestly say that I never in my life met a man of more despicable and contemptible character. His treatment of me, as I look back on it, was unpardonable, although I was very glad to go. I was, as you say, one of the most popular masters of the school and certainly one of the most successful. My house was full for five years to come, and in some instances boys were entered for it as soon as they were born. I was dismissed at three months' notice on the charge of having broken a rule which I had never broken and had incurred considerable loss by keeping. My income was reduced from £3000 to £300 a year. My mother, to whom the school was under deep obligations, was turned on to the streets at the age of seventy-five, my named branded as an enemy of Eton, and you know what that means, and Warre, who was the real cause of my dismissal, continued his vindictive jealousy till the day of his death."

CHAPTER IX

THE AFTERMATH

I

When Oscar Browning left Eton at Christmas, 1875, there was anger in his heart and the desire for vengeance. He wanted to go to law, to sue Hornby, to obtain the rehabilitation of swingeing damages, to have his case brought up in Parliament, in short, to leave no stone unturned in letting the world know how disgracefully he had been treated. It was of the utmost importance that his character should be cleared and the true story of his dismissal made known. All that winter while he was abroad with four Eton boys he toyed with the idea of bringing an action against Hornby. But Fitz-James Stephen gave him little encouragement; for he pointed out that the Head Master undoubtedly had absolute power of dismissal with reasonable notice, and on a trial on the question of what was reasonable notice, no facts about O. B.'s character and life at Eton could have been elicited, whereas on a suit for libel no damages could have been obtained unless " special " damage, apart from the loss of his Eton mastership, could have been proved —which was doubtful. Besides, a lawsuit would have been costly, and O. B. had no money, whilst as he explained in a letter to a friend, he " shrank from the effect on the school which litigation might have produced." And finally he found that in the " public estimation " his character had been in no way impaired. On the whole, therefore, he decided not without reluctance on leaving the matter as it stood.

So the question was at length closed in the following April with a debate in the House of Commons when Knatchbull-Hugessen brought forward a motion that a select committee be appointed to consider whether any alteration was desirable in the existing relations between the Governing Bodies, the Head Masters and the Assistant Masters of the seven schools under the operation of the Public Schools Act of 1868. Throughout the affair Knatchbull-Hugessen, whose son had been the occasion of O. B.'s dismissal, had worked for him, and now he carried out the threat he had made to Dr. Hornby in the previous October of bringing the case before the notice of Parliament if all other remedies failed. Knatchbull-Hugessen did not spare his rhetoric. It was a strange anomaly, he said, that those who doubtless wished their sons to inherit that freedom of thought which Englishmen prized as their most cherished possession had been content that the men to whom they entrusted the education of these sons should be obliged to submit to a system under which their tongues were tied, their very thoughts suppressed and their independence crushed out beneath the pressure of a degrading thraldom. Such had been the experience of Oscar Browning, who to that hour was unaware, as his friends too were unaware, of the real reasons for his dismissal. There should be, therefore, he urged, some appeal from the Head Master, or at least some check on the Head Master's unlimited power to dismiss any member of his staff. In support of his arguments he brought forward a petition signed by masters at seven of the Public Schools, including sixteen signatures from Eton, and quoted a letter from Dr. Montagu Butler, then Head Master of Harrow, warmly upholding the

OSCAR BROWNING

*After a medallion by William Story in the
possession of Mrs. N. B. Bainbridge*

cause of the Assistant Masters. The debate was perhaps chiefly remarkable for the fact that amongst those who spoke on the side of Oscar Browning and the "helots of English education" was Lord Balfour, then a private member of some two years' standing. Spencer Walpole opposed the motion, and since, as one of the papers observed, the "Rugby question (when Dr. Hayman, the Head Master, had been compelled to retire after a quarrel with one of his staff) had left in Tory minds a feeling unfavourable to Assistant Masters," the debate was not pressed to a division.

II

The best way for Oscar Browning to prevent the past from rankling was to forget it, to forget that such a place as Eton existed. When he had gone into residence at Cambridge he wrote to his mother to say that he wanted to hear nothing of Eton. "If it prospers," he said, "I shall put it down to the good effects of my work there; if not, to the way it treated me." His mother did not take this too seriously, and since she continued to live at Windsor she was able to keep him well informed of what was going on. And O. B. soon forgot his own resolutions and told her of anything Etonian that bore on his case: "Donaldson said to Welldon," he wrote, for instance, two or three years later, "that he attributed the decline in numbers at Eton to the effect of my leaving, which was just beginning to make itself felt." And naturally his letters to her were full of references to his old Eton pupils, who of themselves would have effectually prevented him from attaining that Lethe of oblivion, so far as Eton was concerned, which he had professed to desire.

There was another thing too which made it more

difficult to forget the past. Rumours kept on coming to his ears, whisperings that there was more in his dismissal from Eton than appeared on the surface. Cambridge, so far as it was interested at all, took his part. Oxford inclined to the side of Hornby. In any case the tranquillity he desired was disturbed by gossip. He had not been long at King's when he hears that Edmond Warre had said " to at least one person, and probably to more," that he had not been dismissed from Eton for the reasons Dr. Hornby had ostensibly assigned to the Governing Body. O. B. accordingly wrote to the alleged author of this slander, who replied: " I do not think that I have said anything which is untrue concerning you, or anything intended to injure you. I need hardly say that I should have been very sorry to have done so." O. B. also persuaded John Addington Symonds to find out from Jowett —both Hornby and Warre being Balliol men— whether he had heard anything of a libellous nature about him, but Symonds reported that though Jowett sympathised with Hornby in the matter, the Master had not heard anything derogatory to his moral character.

When O. B. went shortly afterwards to stay with Walter Pater at Brasenose, he found indeed that nothing could exceed the kindness of his reception by everybody, dons and undergraduates alike. "I really think," he wrote, " that the tide is turning and that people are beginning to find out the real nature of my dismissal from Eton and are taking sides accordingly. I am constantly meeting with proofs of it." In the street he had run into Warre, who was up in Oxford preaching in Balliol and had taken " the opportunity of cutting him." It was not a very bold cut, however. " I did not look at him," he told his mother, " because I thought he might be impertinent enough to come across to me. When I think of all you are suffering it is impossible that I can forgive him." If O. B. when at Eton had steered his course, as his friends advised, with a moderation inspired by his responsibilities towards her, such sentiments would ring more true, but they would be less characteristic. The egoist and the idealist, however, jostled each other here as always with O. B., and in the next sentence we see him, after visiting the rooms of W. R. Paton, one of his old pupils, and finding them littered with the latest books in French, German and Spanish, lamenting that the machinery which had turned out this sort of a boy was for ever smashed.

Yet there was nothing really vindictive in O. B.'s nature, and it began to grow irksome to him that he was not on speaking terms with Hornby. They ran into each other occasionally at Harrow Speech Days or at meetings, and finally he decided to break the silence. The opportunity at length occurred, and he told his mother about it with some complacency. "A great event happened to me yesterday. I shook hands with Mrs. Hornby and Dr. Hornby. Since I met him at Marlborough House, one or two people have said to me that I should be putting myself in a superior position with regard to him if I spoke to him the next time we met. Yesterday at a Garden Party at Lambeth, finding them in the corridor, I shook hands, first with Mrs. and then with him. He was very cordial and friendly. She seemed rather 'out of it,' that is, she walked on whilst I spoke to him. I felt very much pleased afterwards, and I am sure that I have done the right thing." His mother did not share his satisfaction. "It is a Christian virtue to forgive those who have injured you," she said. "But I am sure that Mrs. Hornby afterwards called him a fool."

He might be on speaking terms again with

Hornby, but this did not, of course, alter his opinion of his character or abilities. The death of Dr. Goodford in 1884 left the Provostship vacant, and much to O. B.'s disgust Dr. Hornby was appointed. "I am very sorry," he wrote to his mother, "because I had hoped for something better. It shows that the Eton party is too strong and that there is no real or efficient desire to see the school reformed." He was not alone in his surprise. A few days later he told her that he had met his old pupil, Gerald Balfour, who said that he "had been quite ill since he had heard of Hornby's appointment." O. B. goes on to moralise. "Success," he said, "cannot alter the foundations of right and wrong. It is marvellous to me that a man whom I respect as much as I respect Gladstone should have made so serious a blunder." When he attacked one of Gladstone's private secretaries about the scandal of the appointment, he was told that Hornby had asked for the post and had intimated that he would not resign unless it was given to him. In such circumstances, the secretary argued, it was surely a good service to Eton to place Dr. Hornby in the position where he could do least harm to the school; but O. B. disapproved of this justification of the practice of kicking upstairs.

It seemed certain now that Warre would become the new Head Master, and Mrs. Browning, from her post of observation in Windsor was able to tell Oscar, not without a certain spice of malice, how all were paying court to the rising star and how they foresaw at Eton the advent of another golden age. There may have been malice too in her suggestion that O. B. should stand. But if that was impossible, there was no reason why he should not do what he could to prevent the disaster that Warre's appointment would be to Eton. The best candidate obviously was Dr. Welldon, then Master of Dulwich,

and O. B. did " everything in his power " to get him
made Head Master. He took him as his guest to
the Eighty Club dinner, where Gladstone shook
hands with them both, and it seemed as if there
really might be a chance that Liberal principles
would triumph for once at Eton. Needless to say
his hopes were unfulfilled, and Edmond Warre was
elected without the Governing Body so much as
discussing the claims of any other candidate. " A
great calamity," was O. B.'s comment; " how great
only the future can show."

With Dr. Warre too there was a partial reconcilia-
tion. On one of his rare visits to Cambridge he
called on O. B. and they appear to have chatted
amiably. But the old animosities were not to
be so easily stilled, as O. B.'s account of a
Founder's Day Feast at King's, at which Warre
was a guest, shows : " Warre was here and made
what everyone thought was a very bad speech.
In fact I don't think that he created much of an
impression. I was called on suddenly to speak
and received a most warm and affectionate greeting
from the undergraduates which lasted several
minutes. I looked at Warre whilst it was going
on and he seemed extremely disgusted." Relations
once more became strained between them over an
invitation which O. B. received from the President
of the Eton Literary Society—the Society which
he had founded—to lecture before it. This rehabilitation as an Etonian gave him great pleasure
and he accepted the invitation with alacrity. The
date for the lecture was fixed, and O. B. after some
hesitation had chosen George Eliot for his subject,
for one thing because he had recently delivered one
on that novelist and it was ready to hand, and for
another because her teaching contained great
ethical and moral qualities. But difficulties arose.
The lecture had to be postponed. It was getting

near the end of the Easter half. There was no other convenient date. Finally, O. B. became suspicious and made inquiries, from which he gathered that the Provost and the Head Master were opposed to his coming. He wrote to both. Dr. Hornby replied that he had no power of veto over the lectures of the Literary Society, but that being asked his opinion he had said that he thought he ought not to lecture at Eton. With Dr. Warre there was a longer correspondence in which O. B. considered he had " scored." And when his mother advised him to have no more to do with them, he agreed, adding that they were " a cowardly and ungrateful set of people."

III

But it was easier for his mother to give this advice than for Oscar Browning to follow it. He might say that he looked on his time at Eton as an " unpleasant duty " which he had performed on the whole better than he could have expected, and that if he were to return he would pursue the same course as he had pursued before. He had done nothing to regret, nothing he could wish undone. And as he went over in his mind the history of his career at Eton and its many controversies, one thing stood out as inexplicable—Hornby's attitude over George Curzon. Other things he might forget, but he could not forget how Hornby had misunderstood his motives in what was his most successful example of scientific pedagogics. So when Curzon made his maiden speech in the House of Commons, a speech which at once drew prophecies that a new Conservative statesman had entered the political world, Oscar Browning wrote to Dr. Hornby, going once more at length over the events which had caused him " some of the acutest pain" he had ever experienced. This recital of a twelve-year-old controversy threw no new light upon it, and indeed O. B. confessed at its close that "the only reason" he had for writing such a narration was that the matter had been much in his mind "in the last weeks," and he thought it possible that Dr. Hornby might never have known all the facts. Besides, so long a time had now elapsed since their occurrence that O. B. could now "think and write of them with a calmness which some time before would have been impossible." But Dr. Hornby was not to be drawn into the discussion of the past, even when it could be viewed with calmness. He answered briefly and with polite coolness. "I am sorry to say that your letter does not mend matters. I am very unwilling to revive old controversies, but I feel bound in justice to Wolley-Dod to say that your language with regard to him is unjustifiable. I wish you knew him better. George Curzon is, I think, a much stronger man than you imagine."

PART II

CAMBRIDGE

CHAPTER X

THE NEW KING'S

I

IN September 1876, Oscar Browning went into residence at King's, where he was to remain for a third of a century leading what he called the unnatural life of a don. He had no tutorial functions in the College, which then was small, consisting of less than fifty undergraduates, and he had nothing to live upon except his Fellowship, then worth about £300 a year, but to drop afterwards during the hard times of agriculture during the 'eighties to less than half that amount. This and what he could make by lecturing and writing were insufficient to gratify tastes that he himself complacently described as extravagant, let alone to pay his Eton debts. For these friends came to his assistance. But during the rest of his life he was fated to be more or less continually in want of money, and when he died the value of his estate did not exceed two hundred pounds.

There were compensations, however, for the " poverty and obscurity " into which he had fallen. He had already been assured of a warm welcome from his friends in King's and Trinity, yet the cordiality of his reception agreeably surprised him. King's was still very closely allied with Eton, and he had feared that the jealousy and spite which had pursued him there might continue to do so at Cambridge. Of these he found " no trace whatever." Everybody, on the contrary, made a point of being kind. They drank champagne in Hall on the evening of his arrival, and Henry Bradshaw, the most distinguished member of the College, who invited him to his rooms afterwards, told him that his coming up opened a new era for King's. The Provost, Dr. Okes, who had been a reformer in the 'forties but had now settled into a caustic conservatism, alone was cool and reserved. Yet even the old Provost after a few weeks " is gradually growing civil," a fact which Oscar Browning records to his mother with some pride. With Whitting he was very friendly. Nixon he regarded as a fellow-reformer. During his years at Eton O. B. had always supported the measures of W. R. Churton, who had for many years been Dean of the College, for the liberalising of King's, and with Augustus Austen Leigh he had enjoyed a friendship cemented by common struggles in the past for the future of King's about which they had common views. G. W. Prothero he found " very pleasant and agreeable." And at Trinity his two intimates, Henry Sidgwick and Richard Jebb, were as delightful as they had always been and made him recall the happiness of his undergraduate days. Altogether there was a geniality and an intellectual freedom most refreshing after the stuffy atmosphere of Eton under the tyrant Hornby. Even the Cambridge climate was bracing by contrast. " As far as I can see," he writes after he has been at Cambridge a week, " my work here will be everything I hoped and expected—only I shall make no money," and he comforts himself with the reflection that the want of money is the least of evils.

Indeed for the ascetic life he meant to lead the lack of it would be a positive advantage. He began at once to order it as he had planned. He awoke at five, six or seven, read till breakfast at 8.30, then worked till luncheon at 1.30, which consisted of a "plate of soup and a cigarette." A walk followed. At five he went to Chapel, where he generally read the lessons. After Hall, which was at six, he spent the evenings in the diversions of a don, in reading Goethe, or in some other intellectual pursuit. Such was the methodical existence he had planned, and his one regret at the first was that morning Chapel, which he had been looking forward to, had not yet begun, so that his day, in this respect, was still incomplete. But the change from the restless and exciting life of an Eton master to the studious calm of the historian, which for the future was to be his, was not to be so easily compassed. He could not accommodate himself at once to the Cambridge habits of dining late, of drinking wine and of going to bed after midnight. It was difficult also to settle down " in the ways of the place and read steadily every morning." He was nervous too about his lectures. Lecturing to undergraduates was a very different thing from lecturing to schoolboys. On this point he soon reassured himself, possibly without sufficient justification, for from the start he had twenty men attending them, and they " appeared to be interested."

His mother, knowing his character, was afraid that in the absence of routine work he might become idle. The reputation for idleness, she reminds him, still clings to the Fellows of King's. He tells her in reply that there is not the least chance of this, though as to reputation that must be left to take care of itself. His mother's " one wish " to see him famous may or may not be realised; in any case fame " cometh not by observation." Still he realises that he needs a basis if he is to establish his reputation as a historian, if only in Cambridge, and both Sidgwick and Jebb have impressed upon him the necessity of writing a book, so he is going to begin on a history of George I. For the moment he is writing an article on Bulgaria for the *Academy*.

II

Ten years before this he had remarked to Arthur Sidgwick that he too was rather losing his interest in history. Many things had happened since then, and in his revulsion from the classical curriculum at Eton and the mechanical turning out of Latin verses he had identified himself with the teaching of history and had eagerly supported the nascent Historical Tripos at Cambridge. But he was still a little dubious whether history was to be his master passion, or only the solace of an educationist's spare hours. Once a schoolmaster . . . He wanted to teach, and though he was sure of the future of King's, he was not so sure whether there was any scope in the College for himself. Prothero had just been put in charge of the history teaching in the College, and he was more than sufficient for the few historians in King's. O. B. had dismissed the idea of standing for the High Mastership of St. Paul's, the vacancy of which had seemed to his mother " as if it were the piece of good luck which was to turn up " after all his trials, because the governors were notoriously Tories. He had considered more seriously being a candidate for the Head Mastership of the newly-formed County School at Cambridge. There he would be in a position of responsibility and he might succeed in doing what he had failed to achieve at Eton, " where to gain anything like a reputation was impossible for a subordinate." But on reflection he decided against it. It would keep him from writing, and besides it was badly paid. His elder brother William, who was as meticulous in money matters as Oscar Browning was careless, recommended him to take pupils as an obvious way of getting some money. This plan O. B. quoted Jebb in calling short-sighted, since it would make him lose caste, besides occupying much of his time. No: he must make his mark as a serious historian—there was George I ready to his hand. In this way both money and reputation would be his. Thus he quieted his doubts and his family, and for this reason too he decided not to compete for the Head Mastership of Skipton Grammar School, or for a post in Owens College at Manchester, both of which had been brought to his notice by his mother. " I should not be nearly so distinguished at Manchester," he wrote to her after a few weeks' residence, " as I shall be at Cambridge. The University has done all it can for me since I have been here. It has (1) allowed me to lecture, (2) made me a ' local centre,' (3) placed me on the Library Syndicate, (4) nominated me to examine for Chancellor's medals. There has been a leading article (favourable) about me in the *Globe*."

With such doubtful beginnings, only encouraged by occasional Press notices, did O. B. commence to lay the foundations of the legend which later on was to flower so luxuriantly. If any reasonably lucrative alternative had presented itself, the Cambridge vocation would have ceased almost before it had begun. Not quite, however, for October saw the inception of his Political Society and the beginnings of that social and intellectual intercourse with the undergraduates which was to be his contribution, a unique contribution, to the Cambridge of his day. This soon effaced the regrets of the schoolmaster for the loss of boyish companionship in which he had delighted. In charm and high spirits the youthful manhood of Cambridge was every whit as fascinating as the boyhood of Eton, whilst in the qualities of mind it was infinitely superior. Before long he is looking back on his work at Eton as being that of a " nursery-governess," and congratulating himself on his escape from such a thraldom.

He became confirmed in his opinion that in returning to Cambridge he had taken the wise and sensible course when he was told by Henry Sidgwick that there was a scheme on foot for giving him a lectureship of £150 a year with fees under the Historical Board. So far his lectures had merely been sanctioned by the University, and he received nothing for them except the fees of those who chose to attend. This, however, would give him an official status, make him, as he explained to his mother, " a sort of professor," and be a very opportune riposte to the ungenerous treatment he had received at Eton. At the end of the term Professor Seeley, the Regius Professor of History, announced it to him officially. In a letter, which must have come as a pleasant contrast to Dr. Hornby's coldly critical communications about his history teaching, Professor Seeley, one of the most distinguished of contemporary historians, explained that a number of persons, either old Etonians, parents of Eton boys, or those engaged in education elsewhere, had made a subscription to show their sympathy with him in the trying circumstances in which he had been placed, and their appreciation of his value as a teacher. They had thought that he would like to receive this sum in the form of an annual payment during the first years which he gave to the University in his new occupation of teaching history, and he proceeded to make the proposal already mentioned, concluding with an expression, in the name of all the teachers of history in Cambridge, of the pleasure they had in welcoming him as a colleague. Henceforth there was no more mention of a return to school-

mastering until, in 1915, at the age of seventy-eight
he offered his services to the Board of Education
as an elementary schoolmaster to replace any man
who had gone into the army, an offer, by the way,
that was not made use of.

III

On the whole he had reason to be satisfied with
the shape his new career was taking. Cambridge
promised him an excellent future, he wrote to his
mother, and he was quite sure that his dismissal
from Eton was now considered by many, and would
come to be considered by more, as an honour.
Dinner-parties and College feasts added to the
amenities of life. He had soon acclimatised himself
to Cambridge customs in the matter of dining late
and drinking wine, too soon in the opinion of his
mother, who reminded him of his former ideals of
spare living and high thinking. She congratulated
him upon his appointment as University lecturer,
a testimony to his honour which she trusted would
be made known to enemies as well as friends.
" But what," she went on to ask, " is become of
the ascetic life you were to lead at Cambridge ?
Where the simple dinners—the early to bed—the
early rising—the daily morning service ? Where ?
I fear you will become gouty, a gourmet, and
cease to care for the simplicity with which your
university career began." If he had ever seriously
intended to lead the ascetic life, easier to follow
perhaps now in the general deterioration of manners
at Oxford and Cambridge than it was in the 'seventies,
a more intimate acquaintance with the ways of the
University must have seconded his own inclinations
in persuading him to give up the attempt.

O. B. delighted in hospitality, whether as host
or guest, and he drew spiritual as well as physical

comfort from the ritual of the table. Man is the only animal that dines; the daily Hall was to him an important function, expressing at once the dignity and the solidarity of their communal life, and he always dressed for it every evening. He and one or two other of the dons tried by the force of their example to make the fashion general at the high table. Outwardly he failed in this, as in so many other things. But who knows whether the vastly greater interest now taken in the art of gastronomy may not be due to his having implanted in the minds of some or other of the intellectual élite of Cambridge a respect for good cooking? When undergraduates used to ask him why he changed for Hall, he would reply : " Because I like to consider the *amour propre* of the cook." The advent of the married don and the plethoric growth of the larger Colleges, as the result of which high tables are a desert of table-cloth and the undergraduates dine in relays, have played havoc with such formal notions, and we may in part trace to these causes the curious paradox that whilst the level of cookery has risen elsewhere it has declined at the older universities. Nevertheless, though the ideal of simple living had become clouded, O. B. had not yet developed into that glorious combination of gourmet and gourmand he was later to achieve, a combination which, as Brillat-Savarin admits, the tenth Muse, the polite Gasterea, reserves for few of her favoured children. But no man can be a schoolmaster for fifteen years and not bear its stigmata, so when his friend E. M. Young, whom he sees at a Rugby meeting of the U. U. during this first term, advises him to live simply, he tells his mother that he means to follow his advice. He even coquets with vegetarianism, a tribute at least to his intellectual curiosity. Even so, one feels, might an enlightened sheikh experiment in the virtues of ham.

IV

Thus he was happy at King's, happier probably than he had expected to be. Though he had no position on the staff of the College, he was a member of a self-governing institution which by his influence, his oratory and his vote he could assist in guiding towards the realisation of the broad, generous conceptions that he, and the other liberal-minded Fellows of King's, had formed as to its future. The rich and splendid foundation of Henry VI had burst its bonds, but the young giant was yet unconscious of its strength. It had been bound to Eton for so long that even men like Augustus Austen Leigh were inclined to pay undue homage to a connection which had proved so deadening to what its Founder had meant to be the more august of the two sister foundations. The days of its old exclusiveness had passed away for ever in 1861 when King's ceased to be the appanage of Eton Collegers. But it was not till 1865 that the first pensioners were admitted, and the first open scholarship was only offered in 1873, in the same year as a non-Etonian for the first time was elected to a Fellowship. Progress had been slow, as was to be expected in an institution which had remained unaltered for five centuries, and in which reform was largely dependent on the good-will of the senior members of a society who had been nurtured in the conservative atmosphere of old King's. The statutes of 1861, which grew out of the Act of Parliament of 1856, soon proved, however, too narrow for the functions which the new King's was to fill in the University, and throughout Oscar Browning's Eton career, the reforming party of which Henry Bradshaw was the intellectual leader, and Augustus Austen Leigh the most effective champion at

College meetings, continued its campaign to make King's worthy of the place it was destined to occupy. This party Oscar Browning, whilst an Eton master, had consistently supported, and many were the letters he received from Austen Leigh and W. R. Churton, keeping him acquainted with the trend of College politics, and not seldom demanding his vote at Congregations. Even at this time, when, as one of the " Eton plutocrats," he had incurred the hostility of the resident Fellows, his own views had not been coloured by any prepossessions in favour of Eton. As a Liberal he wished the portals of King's to be thrown open to all schools. Not unnaturally the harsh and, as he conceived, unjust treatment he himself had received at Eton rather strengthened him in these views.

When he returned into residence the rôle that the College was to play still remained doubtful. It had already been decided in 1873 that only men who intended to read for honours should be admitted. This put a severe strain on the College exchequer, since the fees paid by undergraduates reading for honours were the same as those required of " pass " men, whilst the others obviously required more elaborate and expensive teaching. No other College had passed this self-denying ordinance, and though there was general agreement as to its being desirable, there were some who thought it unpractical. There were stronger differences of opinion as to the type of undergraduate King's should try and attract. Should it require " tone " as well as brains, social as well as intellectual qualities ? This question, whether King's should become the Balliol or the New College of Cambridge, caused some division even amongst the Liberals in the College, many of whom lacked Oscar Browning's robust faith in the ability of King's to carve out a future for itself apart from

Eton. Again there was the question of the size of the College. Should it put no limit to its numbers, or should it lay down decisively a term to its growth? Here again his own view was clear. And here too, some thirty years later, when the College had reached the size he had foreseen, his view was adopted.

A memorandum he circulated in 1877, when the College under the shadow of the intervention of the University Commissioners was framing new statutes, puts forth his views on these matters. Though a radical and a democrat, he begins by observing that a good and prosperous College cannot be called into existence by legislation; it must be of slow, organic growth, the result of deliberate work and thought on the part of the Fellows who control its destinies. "We ought then," he continues, "in framing a body of statutes for ourselves, first to decide what kind of College we most desire and are most likely to produce, and then to construct measures for its government which will at least not interfere with the attainment of this result and will, as far as possible, ensure and hasten its accomplishment. I assume then that we all wish our College to remain a College of honour men. . . . To admit poll-men to the College would be to lay upon ourselves a heavy burden of disagreeable work, to commit ourselves to an unknown future, in which our present connections might be a danger rather than an assistance to us, and to deviate from the lines marked out by our previous history, the maintenance of which is the surest guarantee of stability and prosperity. I have always fancied to myself the King's of the future as a College of about one hundred and fifty undergraduates, reading for honours in the various faculties of the University, provided with the best teaching which the University can afford, which should be given to them to a great extent at the expense of the College, enjoying the stimulus of a very cultivated and energetic society, protected from the temptations of a larger College and directed with a careful and sympathetic attention from the older men which is at present little known in Cambridge, but which is one of the chief advantages of the sister University." Here Oscar Browning must have been thinking of his friend Walter Pater, with whom he often stayed at Brasenose. He proceeds to lay down the reasons " why a young student, hesitating which College he should choose, would prefer King's : (1) Because it would be ready, out of its large resources, to help him in any line of study which he might adopt; (2) Because it would provide him with the companions most congenial to an industrious and able man, and (3) Because it would furnish him in its resident Fellows with a fullness of intellectual experience and encouragement which he would look for in vain elsewhere. A College which chose for itself a task like this would be doing the most valuable work which could be expected of a place of education, however highly endowed. The parallel of the École Normale at Paris has been for many years present to my mind as a model for ourselves." Here was a fine and statesmanlike conception of what King's should be, a conception which has subsequently been realised. And when, as frequently happened, the past threw its shadow over him, he could gain comfort from the reflection that if he had failed to liberalise Eton, where he had been but a " helot," in the self-governing society of King's he was more fortunate and better able to do good.

None the less the task was often hard and thankless. The Provost was an obstacle in the way of reform, and whatever Oscar Browning suggested he was almost sure to frown upon. To prevent future Provosts from being similar obstructionists, O. B. proposed to make the Provostship a terminable office, and to reduce its emoluments. He pointed out that the system at Cambridge by which the College tutors did all the work, whilst the heads of Colleges enjoyed a position of dignity and ease, was an anomaly. They would do well to follow the example of Oxford, which was wiser in this matter. If it had been the rule at King's to elect as Provost someone chosen from outside their own number on the grounds of his attainments in literature or science, the position should then be highly paid in order to attract men of distinction. But it was absurd to select one of themselves and then to pay him with disproportionate generosity for doing very little. Austen Leigh, who was destined to succeed Dr. Okes, supported Oscar Browning, but the Governing Body refused to follow them in making the Provostship an office tenable for a term of years, though the salary attaching to it was reduced for the next occupant to £1200 a year, calculated on the basis of its equivalence to four Fellowships. In the matter of the election to Fellowships he was more fortunate, and his view, which he persistently advocated, that dissertations should be the basis of the electors' choice, was that which has prevailed, to the enrichment of the intellectual life of King's. Under this system the College has chosen men like Rupert Brooke and Mr. E. J. Dent, and others whose achievements in the Triposes would not of themselves have been sufficient to secure their election. The fight over scholarships was harder and the yearly struggle to secure what he considered adequate recognition for his own subject, history, seemed to grow more bitter with the years. He was under the impression that Edmond Warre, himself a Balliol man, sent the ablest Etonians to his own College, and that King's only received the aftermath of Eton talent. And he complained bitterly of those Fellows who believed that it was better for King's to secure an Etonian " almost at any price," an opinion which he lamented grew no weaker as the new regime established itself.

But in his early days, though he did not always get his own way, he and his party generally managed to push their measures through. He records in 1878 having gained two victories at a College meeting, one about the College buildings and the other for the abolition of divinity examinations. He supports the proposal for union with St. Catherine's College : " We decided to settle provisionally to unite ourselves with another smaller College profanely called Cats, but it will take time," he records in the autumn of 1879. (The fusion was in the end opposed by St. Catherine's.) He supported the project of buying the Bull Inn in order to gain the accommodation now rendered absolutely necessary by the growth of the College. This would have become the Provost's Lodge, and the present unsightly Lodge would have then been pulled down to make room for other buildings. But the project came to nothing owing to the veto of the Copyhold Commissioners. College meetings were long and often tedious, only enlivened by the fun of fighting. Almost everything had to be reformed and a thousand details claimed attention. Thus at one meeting the party of progress managed to secure the introduction of Hymns Ancient and Modern into the Chapel services. At another, O. B. had some difficulty in prevailing on the College to allow women to come to the same lectures as the men, a resolution which when first put into effect produced " quite a sensation." He disapproved of the decision to put up a statue of the

Founder and a fountain in the front court, and when it was finished he remarked that he looked " terribly foolish." In his desire, however, not to pull down the screen that fronts the King's Parade he was in agreement with a majority of the Fellows.

All this occupied a good deal of time and helped to distract him from writing the *magnum opus* which was to establish his reputation as a historian. King's had to be re-made, nevertheless, and only by pertinacity and pugnacity could the reformers, who never had a proper working majority, hope to impress their will on the wobbling spirits who loved compromise.

He has sung of one such meeting :

> " Tell me, O Muse, for thou wast there to see,
> How eager Nixon and benign O. B.,
> Trained in a thousand tactics of the fight,
> Defended common-sense and College right.
> How Leigh with mild persistence gently drove
> His flock in those soft accents which they love;
> How Selwyn, boy in years but man in place,
> Frowned with the trenchant sternness of his race.
> Stearn, by conflicting duties hardly pressed,
> Chose the less evil course and acquiesced.
> Meanwhile the Provost, with his master-mind,
> The wavering balance to his will inclined.
> Fickle as woman, Prothero once more,
> Turned the old coat he'd often turned before,
> And Welldon, high above all thoughts of pelf,
> Heaved a deep sigh and voted—for himself."

V

It was good enough fun, helping to mould a new thing, battling against a Conservative Provost, winning over doubtful colleagues. Altogether very different from Eton. Yet his own personal position in the College had no official status to back it. His friends wished to remedy this, and in the summer term of 1877, after he had been in residence seven or eight months, the proposal was brought forward that he should be given a College lectureship in history. It looked as if it were going through, but when it came to the vote it was lost by eleven to ten, the Provost throwing his casting vote in the scale against him. This was the first disappointment he had suffered at King's. He took it, however, philosophically, merely relating the fact to his mother and adding : " Walter Durnford came up from Eton to oppose it, which seems to me a piece of very bad taste." When the post was actually made for him three years later he told her that he thought it very good of the College, an unusual expression of modesty on his part. Thereafter he continued to associate with the history school in King's, first as subordinate to Prothero and subsequently as assistant tutor, until his retirement in 1909. This was destined to be the extent of the authority given him in the management of the College. It was, of course, quite incommensurate with his own ambitions.

But if he was clear-sighted in his views of what King's should be, he was singularly deficient in estimating his position in relation to other members of the Governing Body and careless of those arts by which men climb official ladders. In November 1877, after he had been a little over a year at King's, the Vice-Provostship became vacant, and at first he seemed to have considered that as Henry Bradshaw refused to be a candidate, he had himself a chance of being chosen. But it was soon evident that he had none at all. " I am not a senior Fellow," he wrote to his mother, " till next June, so I don't suppose they will have me." She thought that absurd, and was annoyed with Cornish because when he had come to tea with her he had remarked : " So they are not going to make Oscar Vice-Provost." This looked as if there were a cabal against him.

Why was not his merit recognised? He replies that he does not know what will be settled about the Vice-Provostship. " I try," he says, " as far as possible to abstract my mind from such things. As to my being famous, I fear that you will never see it. I am one of the kind of men whose work is never appreciated till they are dead." There had in reality never been any doubt that Austen Leigh, if his own scruples about accepting the position could be overcome, would be chosen. He was the obvious man for the position, and Oscar Browning, when it came to the point, supported his candidature. Three days before the election he writes: " I am not to be made Vice-Provost, but I believe I shall be made Dean."

His belief, however, was not to be fulfilled. What happened, or at least his view of what happened, is contained in one of his letters: " I had made up my mind not to stand against Churton. He told me with his own lips that he retired in my favour and would nominate me. Nixon went to him and persuaded him to give his consent to a piece of paper saying that he would serve if elected. He then showed this to a number of young Fellows just come up to the meeting who knew nothing about the circumstances, and persuaded them to vote for Churton, who had been Dean so many years. I knew nothing about it till the actual moment of election, and I was beaten by three votes. Everybody is very angry with Nixon, and with good cause. They say that he has done me rather good than harm. It has made a great row in the University. It has been very unfair to me to be dragged into this quarrel against my will." The incident blew over. O. B. did not yet think that he was being persecuted.

At the same time he felt it was decidedly curious that two, or even three attempts to give him recognition and status (for there had been a suggestion that he should undertake the functions of Assistant Librarian, worth £25 a year) should have come to nothing. His mother, too, is uneasy. " What is the prejudice against you ? " she asks. " Why are you always thus treated ? Who are your foes ? " In reply he assures her that the efforts to keep him down could only result in a more complete triumph. The figure of speech at least tickled his vanity, even if it were a little grandiose to apply to a matter of a mere College Deanship. By his own lights he should have had no vanity, no ambition for office, however humble it might be. He tells his mother that he has no wish to emerge from the obscurity into which he has fallen. " My desire is to get control of myself, to work hard, to do my duty, to pay my debts and to let reputation take care of itself." Sentiments worthy of a sage. But, like other philosophers, O. B. had his off days. On these he takes a less serene view of things and forgets the greatest of the Christian virtues. As he grew older his off days increased. For the present, however, he was happy enough at King's and every year becoming more of a personality in the University, which easily counterbalanced such small set-backs as these.

CHAPTER XI

I

WHILE he was helping to create the new King's, to make it "the most distinguished College at either University "—for, as Eton when he was there had been the first of schools, so now King's was to become the first of colleges—while the University Historical Board, of which he was a member, was developing the Historical Tripos into that soft option for intelligent boys who had neglected their classics at school, while these and his numerous other interests, one of them being the training of teachers, all combined to prevent him from making that frontal attack on the citadel of Literary Fame for which he had drawn up plans in his boyhood, and ever since continued to regard lovingly in its pigeon-hole, Oscar Browning was already bearing out in his own experience the truth of his favourite aphorism that reputation cometh not by observation. Though not ceasing to be poor and suffering from a chronic and inexplicable overdraft at his banker's, he was ceasing to be obscure. He was becoming a personality, a figure in the academic world of Cambridge. Everyone knew him. And whereas at Eton his colleagues had smiled whilst his pupils had taken him seriously, at Cambridge his colleagues took him seriously and the undergraduates laughed. Those boys upon whom he had had most influence at Eton, boys with taste for art or letters, boys who were liable to be neglected in the routine of a great school, had repaid him with feelings compounded of admiration and romantic affection. One of them, afterwards to wear the bays of a minor poet, has expressed himself with ingenuous charm :

> " Down the slow, pale-eddied river, down the river
>   slow went we,
>   Till we came to where the rushes,
>   With the tangled alder bushes,
>   Made a bulwark weird to see.
>
> There we rested, there we rested, lying lazily
>   While the evening gnats were humming,
>   And the droning beetle drumming,
>   O'er the river fair to see !
>
> Then the treasured volume read he, very quietly,
>   As the flecks of light were falling
>   And the cuckoo close by calling—
>   Calling to his mate was he."

At Cambridge it was not necessary to present so unyielding a front to the Philistines, and instead of boys he had young men to associate with. It was, we may believe, an agreeable change. For years he had had to try and make his pupils forget that he was a schoolmaster. " Nolo episcopari " had been his motto, yet it was occasionally necessary to speak *ex cathedra pædagogica*. In the greater freedom of his new surroundings there was no need for such distasteful solemnities. He was now able to exercise a lighter touch. He could be as young as the youngest, say whatever came into his head, allow high spirits to carry him where they would. The shadow of a Head Master no longer darkened the path of this mid-Victorian Socrates. In the Liberal atmosphere of Cambridge thought was free and tongues did not wag reprovingly as at Eton. He remained, of course, intensely serious. His vocation, his duty, nay, his pleasure, was to influence and guide young men. And his inner voice supported him, for he too, like Socrates, possessed a singularly encouraging *daimon*, thanks to whom he knew that what he did was good.

Not only his able *daimon* but his colleagues also took him seriously. Here is a serious appreciation of him by a colleague : " Gifted with a deep insight into character and the most catholic power of sympathy, having it perpetually as his one object to further the interests of the young men with whom he came into contact, Oscar Browning exercised an influence wider and more beneficial than any other don, probably in the University, certainly in King's. He saw as if by instinct a man's good qualities and weaknesses, intellectual and moral, and suppressed the one and developed the other with unremitting but unobtrusive skill. Again and again within my own knowledge he discerned latent gifts where the ordinary observer would see little or nothing, and having discovered the potential excellence had not rested till it had become actual. To the performance of such tasks he devoted himself unsparingly. Personal convenience counted for nothing. Thought and time, which from the point of view self-advancement might have been far more profitably employed, were lavished in the interests of others."

II

But such an appreciation, though it underlines his earnestness, cannot convey the vitality, the enormous fund of good-humour, the frankness of speech, the idiosyncrasies of vanity, the enthusiasm, the magnanimity, the vindictiveness, all the strange jumble of qualities which went to lift Oscar Browning into a personality with that touch of absurdity which constitutes a character. From these sprung the O. B. myth, with all its apocrypha of anecdotes and its battery of laughter. It was created almost as soon as he came into residence. J. K. Stephen, who was definitely to give it its Falstaffian quality with his famous quatrain, was still a schoolboy at Eton when the undergraduate papers realised that in this small and stout King's don, with the large head, the rotund body and the short legs, was a subject from which unlimited humour might be extracted. He had not been at Cambridge a year when he found it necessary to assure his mother that University dons were not like schoolmasters, afraid of being chaffed. On the contrary, he basked in banter and revelled in ridicule. It was a tribute to his personal dignity that he was able to join in the laugh against himself.

From the beginning he had determined to know as many undergraduates as possible. Following the example of Henry Bradshaw, the man who impressed Mommsen after an evening's conversation as the ablest living Englishman, his rooms were always open to anyone who wanted to see him. In Victorian phrase he never " sported his oak." And he entertained on a scale unapproached by any other don. As a result no King's undergraduate in his time, and very few of the " beautiful and good " in other Colleges, slipped through the net of his hospitality. " If you were here now," wrote Sir J. J. Thomson, the Master of Trinity, to him in 1918, " you would not find any undergraduates to whom you could have been as hospitable as you were to those of my generation and long after." " Saturday is my day for entertaining," he tells his mother in those early Cambridge days, " and I do what I can to bring promising young men together. It seems to me the best thing I can do here. I do the utmost to make the best use of my time and influence. Whether I succeed or not I cannot say, but I seem to know most people in the University worth knowing."

III

This symposial culture was catholic in its intentions. The old distrust of athletes had even vanished. He has the two College boats to breakfast and takes an interest in the rowing which he never showed at Eton; indeed he follows the fortunes of the College on the river with the keenness of a rowing man. Frequent are his laments at the apparently ineluctable fate of King's to be bumped. " We have been bumped every night," he says of one Lents, " to our great disgust. I am afraid that the College is split up into sets and that there is no proper feeling of patriotism." It is some consolation that King's has done well at football and been in the final of the inter-college cup. The famous 'Varsity Cricket XI of 1882, one of the classic XI's of cricketing annals, he entertains to dinner in honour of the Studds, who were in his house at Eton, and visits Fenner's on all the days of their match against the Australians when they " won a glorious victory." He meets a possible charge of inconsistency by pointing out that athletics are not nearly so demoralising at the University as they are at school, and his old attacks on the Oxford Colleges which foster athleticism and idleness do not rise to refute him. But then there was no Warre at King's. Many others besides athletes, however, sit at his table. Sixteen of his old Eton pupils come to dinner, including Gerald Balfour, Jim Stephen, Selwyn and the Studds, and Leigh and Cornish are able to take back news to Hornby " that he still goes on ' corrupting the youth.' " " They do not seem to mind it," he adds complacently.

As his popularity grew there was hardly a side of University undergraduate life with which he was not identified. At the "Footlights," of which he was President for ten years, he met the gayer and more frivolous spirits. He came into contact at the Union, of which he was Treasurer for more than twice that span, with serious undergraduates who, like himself, had political ambitions. His own interest in what he calls " velocipedes " caused him to be president of the University Bicycle Club, which had a brief existence in the 'eighties, when it attracted the adventurous and mechanically-minded type of undergraduate much as the Aero Club does to-day. At various times he was an officer of the University Swimming Club, the Musical Club and the University Hockey Club—a game he often played.

And besides taking an interest in such varied pursuits as the members of these clubs followed he was for a good many years a keen Freemason. " Can you conceive of my committing such a folly in my old age ? " he writes to his mother after his initiation. A day or two later he adds : " The Freemasons' Lodge here is good and unusually cheap, and I joined it because I always like anything which forms a permanent link between the transient undergraduate and myself. I daresay it was an act of folly, but not a serious one." When he passed to the second degree he found it " more interesting." Mention of Masonic meetings thereafter is frequent for many years in his letters to his mother, and he went through several degrees, including those of the Mark Masters and the Royal Ark Mariner, reaching that of the Excellent Masters. He also held office in his Provincial Grand Lodge.

Whatever his original motive for being initiated, Masonry was clearly congenial to him. Doubtless it appealed to many sides of his nature, to his intellectual curiosity, to his taste for ceremonial, to his love of good-fellowship, even to his vanity, for Masonry offers offices for all who come. Anyhow he gave up a good deal of time to the craft and his rooms were not infrequently the setting of Masonic lodges. But even in Freemasonry he ceased in the end to find those fraternal feelings which the craft is supposed to foster, and in later life he ceased to have any active connection with it. Freemasons, however, keep their controversies, if they have them, to themselves, and over O. B.'s disenchantment, for disenchantment there was, hangs the veil of secrecy. Suffice it to say that he was present when the Duke of Clarence was raised to the degree of a master mason, and recorded the dignified bearing of the young Prince on that occasion, and that he was for many years a popular *ceremoniarius* at the annual Masonic Ball which is one of the events of May week.

IV

Pleasures and duties thus pressed relentlessly on each other's heels. It was indeed impossible to separate the one from the other, the surest sign that he was ordering his life in the right way, that he was making a due contribution in social service for the gifts with which Nature had endowed him. Never before was it so easy for George Eliot to say " Amen " to his gratitude that he had a definite position with unquestionable duty to save him from " vague ambitions." Recognition was coming from all sides. Very soon he is " overwhelmed with correspondence." Societies in provincial towns, Leeds, Birmingham, Newcastle write and ask him to lecture. At Horsham, " a town in Surrey," as he described it with a historian's fine disregard for geography, he has

183

placed it on record that the vicar, a more intelligent man than most of the parochial clergy, introduced him as one who had been a great schoolmaster. Financial reasons induce him to lecture at the College of Preceptors; the passionate desire to educate the masses urges him to give talks to working men in Westminster, talks on the fuller life which Liberalism meant to give to the people. He has often to attend meetings of the Arundel Society or of the Royal Historical Society. He is a regular contributor to the weekly papers and the reviews.

That he manages to keep up with his work in spite of the Cambridge air, which has now grown very relaxing, is something of a miracle. It can only be done indeed by frequent holidays abroad. There only too can he get through "serious writing." Not that his pen at Cambridge is ever idle. One day he has to indite a letter to *The Times* on elementary education, the next to compose a menu in verse for "The Extremes," an undergraduates' dining club in King's. Both he does *con amore*. The letter can remain in its dusty files; the sonnet shows that his gravity could unbend.

> "*Ad Eschatiam.*
>
> Fair Goddess, Hater of the Golden Mean,
> Smile on thy sons Extreme, and as they dine,
> Fill them with juicy meats and joyous wine
> Till Moderation, vanquished, leaves the scene.
> Consummate soup with sherry; and between
> The crispéd smelts infuse the gay Sauterne.
> Stir up the thoughts that breathe and words that burn
> With foaming grape of amber-coloured sheen,
> Bottled by good Count Robert of Avize.
> Grant us a Gallic entrèe, sure to please,
> A haunch of venison from the haunts of Herne.
> Through icy creams and devilled savouries.
> Guide us, till half inspired and half distraught,
> Like storm-tossed mariners we reach our port."

A man who could write such amusing trifles could hardly escape being a favourite with the undergraduates, specially when he would follow up this effort by replying for the toast of " The Crowned Heads of Europe."

There was indeed but one thing wanting to make his social gifts complete—to learn to waltz. He went to balls and danced till the early hours. The polka and the lancers he could manage; but the waltz was less easy to master, and he wished that he had more aptitude for this " sensuous yet difficult measure." His regrets, which seem to have been soon forgotten, had been aroused, one may add, by his failure with Miss Stephen, a partner " of commanding stature " with whose feet his own were unable to keep rhythm. In other respects he flatters himself that he is growing more truly master of his environment than perhaps he had ever been. In 1879 he and Whitting had given a garden party in the Fellows' garden to the newly-made LL.D.'s, the " aristocracy of Cambridge," and it had been a great success. This prompts him to write : " I think I am feeling more than I have ever yet done that my Cambridge work is beginning to tell. Kegan Paul told me that someone had spoken to him of my splendid work here. . . . How lucky I was to have left Eton, where I was working single-handed, and to have come here, where I had a fair field. These feelings will, I think, increase rather than diminish as time goes on." He adds immediately after this : " I have a man called Oscar Wilde staying with me who is also named after the King of Sweden."

V

Here was another of the hindrances to work. His friends, old and new, were constantly coming to stay with him. O. B. was no provincial and he did not exclude Oxford from his purview of the civilised world. He had first met Oscar Wilde at Oxford when staying with Walter Pater. Nothing could be more natural than that he should become friends with this clever, if affected, young man. " Oscar Wylde, an Oxford man, also called after the King of Sweden," is the way he described him to his mother on his second visit some months later. On this occasion Oscar Wilde came for the A.D.C. performance which he and O. B. went to together, O. B. afterwards having a supper-party in his rooms at which most of the caste were present. Wilde's " affectation " amused him. He was " really very clever and amusing and full of interesting conversation." Some years later, when he is staying with him again, this time a self-invited but not the less welcome guest, O. B. observes that he has " lost a lot of his affectation and is much improved." Oscar Wilde returns his hospitality by suppers at the Café Royal, when O. B., leading the life of a man about Town, has been to see his friends the Bancrofts in their latest play at the Haymarket, or has gone to the last Savoy opera for which Arthur Sullivan has given him a box.

O. B., who loved all new things, from religions to mechanical inventions, was pleased to trip about with the æsthetes " in short-skirted epigrams and pink-tight phrases." They were beginning to invade King's in the 'eighties and found their finest expression in Robert Ross, for whom he had particular affection. He regarded them with the same beneficent and catholic eye that he turned on Nonconformists, who were " the salt of Cambridge," on Indians, on Jews, whose demand for exemption from the paper in the Little-Go on Paley's *Evidences of Christianity* he championed, on those Cinderellas

186

of the University, the non-Collegiate students, and lastly on the Newnhamites and Girtonites, who, if gawky, yet stood for the cause of women's education, in which he had already been actively interested at Eton, that cause of which his friend Henry Sidgwick was "the high priest." Nevertheless in this he was an ungallant Liberal and was wont to declare that the impression left on his mind, after looking over any set of examination papers, was that, irrespective of the marks he might give, the best woman was intellectually the inferior of the worst man. On the other hand, they were much more regular at lectures than the men, and O. B. liked his lectures to be well attended.

Though his rooms were very comfortable and confirmed him in the view that marriage would add nothing to the usefulness of his life, guests in College were difficult to escape from and encroached on his working hours. All the same they were very welcome, especially Curzon and his old Eton pupils. Curzon was a frequent visitor. "George is as delightful as ever," he wrote in 1878, "and those who do not think well of him are quite wrong." Wolley-Dod was no longer his tutor, but Stone also appears to have lacked O. B.'s breezy confidence in Curzon's talents and character. One letter from Curzon on his return to Eton, where he was now in the Sixth Form, concludes :

> "Horngog is mild and apologetic,
> Dod is bluff and good-humoured,
> Stone querulous and doubting,
> Myself your most affectionate friend."

O. B. repeats this to his mother with evident amusement. The don smiles at the foibles of the schoolmaster, the indulgent tutor at the wit of his pupil.

Another visitor was Vassall, now Father Vassall-

Phillips, the well-known Redemptorist. "Owing to the overlapping of the Oxford and Cambridge terms," he writes, "I was able to go and stay with him for two or three days at the end of each Oxford term before Cambridge went down (at least I think that is how I managed what were certainly frequent visits). I shall never forget the position he held in the University. He was at the height of his powers and his Sunday evenings were the most brilliant things imaginable. Everyone was there. I call to mind especially Henry Bradshaw, the learned don, and J. H. Stephen, my beloved school-friend, who was held to be, as his brass in King's Chapel testifies, beyond compare the most brilliant of undergraduates." To O. B. the news of Vassall's conversion gave the satisfaction which his sympathy with spiritual experiences engendered. But soon Vassall took orders, and the old intimacy was broken in the new life upon which his young friend of other days had entered.

There were many others who kept up the link with Eton or prevented him from becoming a "mere provincial." Knatchbull-Hugessen, now Lord Brabourne, is his guest upon occasion. Emil Sauer, already a virtuoso of international reputation, stays with him and plays at a concert in the College Hall, having to retire after playing Schumann to a place of solitude in order that he may put himself in the proper state of emotion for the Chopin that is to follow—a gesture which much impressed O. B. at the time. And there were nephews—some of them idle, and worse still borrowers, young men for whom Canada was obviously intended—to persuade him that nepotism was not one of his vices. All these helped to make Cambridge "into a whirl, but a pleasant whirl," and to draw laments from him that he is a "poor, weak, miserable wretch in not being able to stand a little racket."

Life was certainly very enjoyable. Yet vague ambitions still haunted him. "I oscillate between love of solitude and desire of society," he writes to his mother when he has been ten years at Cambridge, "and I am as unreasonable as most human beings. When I am alone I wish for companionship, and when I have people with me I wish to be alone. If only I could produce more *writing*."

VI

Those who only knew Oscar Browning as a vigorous septuagenarian would be surprised how unsatisfactory was his health until he was well advanced in middle age. It took him all that time to outgrow the debility of his youth. During these earlier years at Cambridge he was a martyr to colds, to which he believes that his baldness made him peculiarly susceptible. He suffered from bronchitis, from shingles and more or less chronically from insomnia. A homœopathic doctor, "who assists rather than fights against Nature," does him good. And he derives benefit from giving up wine. "I drink none for lunch," he tells his mother, "a little sherry and water for dinner. Last night I indulged in a glass of port. I shan't cut myself off altogether." She tries to strengthen her favourite son in an abstemiousness which was hardly less foreign to her nature than to his. She assures him that he is growing fat and losing all the good looks with which Nature and his parents had endowed him. He admits the charges to be true. But he had just been told by a first-rate doctor of his acquaintance "not to mind being stout and to let Nature have her way." Did not the Bible say that we were to enjoy the fruits of the earth? And whatever the state of his health, his appetite was voracious. He often " feels a sense of hunger in the night " and comes to breakfast ravenous. In order that this meal shall possess a daily sense of novelty, he draws up fifteen different menus and has them arranged in a mathematical series of which the cook has the key, so that no conjecture on his part can forecast which is coming next.

" Languor " was the constant enemy, which good food and wine often had the effect of driving away. For instance, he has been feeling run down for several days, when rather against his inclinations, he has to go and dine in remote Downing to celebrate the appointment of a new master. He tells his mother about it. " The undergraduates were present, and after toasts were over there were loud shouts of Browning, O. B., Oscar, and I had to make a speech. It appears that I am very popular with the under-graduates, though I should have thought that those of Downing had never heard my name. I drank a great deal of champagne, and this morning feel quite vigorous again. It does credit to the wine." But although he worries about his ail-ments, which he excuses on the ground of its being an inherited trait, and he has become very fat, and it gives him no pleasure to contemplate himself in the glass, and although—a fact still more in-disputable—he is growing old, he is not at all shocked at his advancing years. For he makes it a rule to anticipate in imagination the age he has arrived at, and he always considers himself two or three years older than he really is. Most important of all, he does not find that age makes it more difficult for him to " associate with young men."

VII

Happily there was no clash here between pleasure and work. If he had an influence over young men, so did they over him. If they learnt from him, so did he from them. "The month we have spent together," he observes of his holiday abroad with Curzon in the summer of 1880 at Oberammergau and elsewhere, "will, I hope, have been of great service to both of us." The master of novices, who could be domineering with colleagues, was humble before the shrine of youth. To his mother he seemed perhaps to pursue such companionships with excessive, almost undignified, zeal. Even when he visited her at Windsor he was accompanied by one or more undergraduates. "If I spend any time with you at Christmas," he writes to his mother, who was then an old lady of eighty-six, "I must have my friends to stay with me. Of course I will pay for their board as I did last year. It is necessary not only for reasons of companionship but of education. Your house is the only house I have, and much advantage is done by asking under-graduates for a few days. I quite understand that you do not wish to have any excitement, but I am sure that this can be easily reconciled with what I propose." His mother agreed, but one suspects from the tone of her acquiescence that she thought Oscar might give his vocation a holiday on the infrequent occasions that he stayed with her.

Often she advised him to marry. She was anxious for his health, of which she considered he was careless. It was foolhardy for a man of fifty to bathe in the Cam in the month of February and two days later to take a Turkish bath. Besides, she was a woman, and mistrusted bachelorhood as she loved grandchildren. But she met with little encourage-ment. On one occasion when she was more emphatic than usual, he replied that he had "no qualm of affection of any kind." Not even his friends' felicity could stir his envy. He stays with E. M. Young, who has just been appointed Head

Master of Sherborne, where in his fight against evil he too was to have difficulties as Oscar Browning had had at Eton, and records that he is not less pleased to see his friends Head Masters than to see them married.

Such flirtations as befell him were exceedingly mild. One summer on the Rigi he meets a young lady " who is very delightful, good-looking, clever, bright, graceful, of a distinguished family." All the people in the hotel declare that he has been smitten. The train is laid, but the fuse fails to ignite. " I shan't tell you her name," he says to his mother. " However, you need not be alarmed. I saw very little of her and she is now gone away. It would be very hard if, after failing to fall in love during the many years in which I could have married, I should do so now that I have to be single." The young lady and other members of the party go to Felsen Egg, and write from there to ask him to join them. He cannot, however, manage this " without inconvenience " and gives up the idea. Occasionally the ennui of a bachelor's life overpowers him and he " really begins to wish " that he was married. " Would it not be delightful," he writes from Cannes, " if an eligible heiress turned up in these regions ? " But such wishes are transitory. And however fortunate he may have been in his friendships, in that " pure, passionate, devoted friendship, love without his wings," which he had sighed for as a boy at Eton, he never succumbed to the shafts of the full-fledged Cupid.

Only two women had any influence in his life, George Eliot and his mother. With George Eliot he was for fifteen years on terms of intimacy. For her mind and character he always felt " a deep and unswerving devotion." She on her side doubtless directed towards Oscar Browning some of the " maternal feeling towards both men and

women " younger than herself which, as she
assured him, she experienced the more fully as she
grew older. He looked upon her as his Priestess
of Delphi. During his Eton mastership he was
continually submitting his doubts and anxieties
to her judgment. His letters sometimes made her
" serious, if not sermonising," for they contained
" such sad glimpses of the world." She was
troubled by " those wretched boys of nineteen who
are among the myriad causes helping to make all
the more hasty and damaging the inevitable revolution that should be beneficently slow." And she
strengthened him in his hatred, which she shared,
" of negative destructive teaching given to the
young. Superstition of almost any sort," she
once wrote to him, " is better, and has more
moral truth in it, than an attitude of contemptuous
superiority to the hard-earned experience of the
generations." He saw less of her in the last few
years of her life, but welcomed her marriage with
John Cross, who, as he tells his mother in commenting upon the news, had been devoted to Mrs.
Lewes for a long time. But his reverence for her
personality never waned, and over his writing desk
at Cambridge hung her portrait, gazing on which
he used to draw some portion of that spiritual
strength for which he was so deeply indebted to her
during her life.

To his mother he was a kind, if self-indulgent,
son; she towards her son was fond and indulgent,
but not uncritical. He wrote to her regularly every
Sunday, and when she was ill, as was not infrequently the case, every day. Her beauty, grace
and wit had helped to give distinction to his house
at Eton, as her mordant tongue had helped to make
wider those rifts which so often gaped across his
path. To her he communicated all his doubts and
controversies, and she like most mothers who have

clever sons, took him very seriously. At Eton she had continually to be impressing on him that he was not wasting his abilities as a schoolmaster, and that the comforts and blessings of everyday life were worth appreciating if only because he would feel their loss grievously. When he went to Cambridge she tried to act as a spur to his ambition, so that he should achieve that fame to which his character and talents entitled him. And she did not mince her words. Never, for instance, did he seem to have any money, not even when his income was £3000 a year. And at the end of one Eton half he had said that he was looked upon by his family as a milch-cow. Other masters saved, he was always more or less in debt. His mother did not let the petulant remark pass. " Such a thought," she assures him, " is unworthy of you, such an act would be most unworthy of me. You are dissatisfied with the arrangements. Let them cease. Between this and election you can look out for a housekeeper. At my age I am not inclined to be tutored either by Mrs. Cornish, her matron, Mrs. Warre or any other person. I have done my best, and the result, so far as I can see, has been eminently successful. I shall leave you in the full tide of prosperity. . . . And now I must add one word more. You do not save money. Why? Not because your mother and sisters cost you so much, but because your personal expenses are so enormous. You travelled 10,000 miles last year. Reckon the expense at a shilling a mile—and it cost more I am sure—that alone would be £500. Then your horse, boats, books, music. . . . You ought not to blame the person who manages the current expenditure when the great extravagance is not under control. . . . I write more in sorrow than in anger." As with so many persons with a reputation for generosity, there was a side from which it did not appear quite so commendable. The answer is not extant, but we may be sure that it was a soft one. To his mother O. B. was always piously contrite.

Sometimes this old lady with the gift of self-expression is mildly ironical. Eight years of Cambridge had not produced the expected great work. Oscar was always busy and yet nothing seemed to come of it. Then at the Eton and Winchester match George Curzon had met her daughter and played the candid friend. He had told her that Oscar was surrounded by friends and immersed in dissipation, that it was a pity he frittered away his talents on primers, that he was a money-grubber, and that he ought to be writing a big book to hand down to posterity. His mother passed on Curzon's remarks faithfully, and added that she supposed he was " taking Gibbon for a precedent, who considered his *Decline and Fall* for seven years before putting his pen to paper." Neither was she very sympathetic with his " money difficulties." " If you borrow £500 from a friend to pay old debts," she observes, " the loan and the debt cannot both exist." Nor did she believe that staying in London during June at the height of the season was good either for his health or his pocket. Her candour was inspired by the purest motives of maternal devotion. His recklessness about his personal expenditure reacted on his powers of work, for it prevented him, she was sure, from taking those frequent foreign holidays necessary to counteract the relaxing air of Cambridge. Only if he kept his health could he produce something worthy of himself and her ambitions for him. She wanted above everything to see him famous, famous " beyond the jealousies of soi-distant friends and the spite of enemies." The precious years were slipping by and still he delayed. She was almost impatient in giving her approval of the many projects for the great work which was to establish once for all his literary reputation.

Like a dutiful son he accepted her criticisms, her irony and her encouragement with equal complacency. For his poverty he could not quite account. It was always unpleasant to contemplate, and the matter became serious when the bank refused to cash any more of his cheques. He was " poorer than St. Anthony," for he had not even his temptations. " I try to be economical," he says, " but you know that for me it is very difficult." But he reflected that there are two ways of being rich, by earning much or spending little, and " those who do not do the one must be content with the other." As for his position in letters, the impression continued to grow upon him that he had a style, and if only he could give more time to writing, recognition would assuredly follow. There indeed was the rub. It was impossible to do much of his own work at Cambridge. If he could retire like his friend John Addington Symonds to the Alps every summer . . .

But mother and son only referred to these questions incidentally. Their letters as a rule are compounded of those petty details which in their sum make up the tale of human life, and they are illuminated by a deep devotion, which on his side stood revealed in her not infrequent illnesses. " I should be sorry," he writes on one such occasion, " if a day were to pass without your hearing from me, or my hearing from you. There is always an excitement when the post arrives. Mrs. Spinks " (his bed-maker) " rushes into my bedroom at 7.30 and waits whilst I read the morning bulletin. She is quite as excited as I am. Indeed there is great interest about you in the whole College. I cannot tell how constantly I am thinking about you." She

MARGARET MARIANA BROWNING, OSCAR'S
MOTHER, AT THE AGE OF 84

suffered much towards the end of her life from the damp and cold of the English winters. George Eliot sends her a foot-warmer which she has found " most efficacious against the distressing malady of cold feet." And Oscar Browning is constantly advising her to keep large fires, advice he himself followed in his rooms at Cambridge even at mid-summer. The cold makes him shudder, but on her account. " This horrid wind cuts me like a knife." " This weather is most cruel and you cannot imagine how angry I feel at the biting wind."

This intimacy between mother and son, which had been cemented by fifteen years' work together at Eton, lasted unimpaired to the end of her life. Sometimes the high-spirited and tenacious old lady was depressed. She saw so little of him, even in the vacations, and her plans for their spending them together so rarely came to anything. Old age was a burden too heavy to be borne. It was time she passed from a scene where her work was done. On such occasions he consoles her. " I cannot think," he says, " how you can suppose that you have ' lived too long ! Is not your society the greatest delight to your children, and would not your death be the greatest blow they could receive ? I assure you that any illness you have goes like a pang to my heart, and I hope for fine weather chiefly because it is good for you. What could be done for you this summer ? If we had gone together, where could we have gone to ? Any place which would have suited you would have done me no good." When in extreme old age she paid the universal debt to Nature, his words were verified. Not a day, not a night passed on which his thoughts did not lend her a vicarious existence in the world from which she had passed. Oscar Browning never seems to have had any doubts,

not even when he dallied with Positivism in the
'sixties, in the immortality of the human soul.
He was as convinced in the reality of the life of the
spirit as he often was in the unreality of that which
men lead in the flesh.   And his mother to the end
remained very close to him :

> " Whene'er at night I lie awake,
> Faces possession of me take,
> And clustering round from out the gloom,
> Beset me in my little room.
> Mother, with voice and manner mild,
> Keeps watch upon her darling child,
> And, loving both, in serious mood,
> Arrests the bad and stirs the good."

Thus begin some lines which he wrote when he was
eighty.   Whatever the merit of the poem there is
no question of its sincerity.   But though he had
the consolations that religion and philosophy could
afford, her loss was in a very real sense to him
irreparable, and her death in 1889 left a gap in his
life which nothing could fill.   There was no one
now with kindly hand, " to arrest the bad and stir
the good," no woman, no member of the sex
which, as he himself observed in the wisdom of
his age, is the more sensible in the ordinary affairs
of existence, to prune him of his foibles, to urge
him to the endeavour which the occupations of
the moment continually hindered.

May 12. 1863.

My dear Mamma

I do not see
why after the great experience
of death it should still be
so terrible one. If we believe
at all in a future state death
is merely the passing to another
life, probably a better one. As
are the state of life and the state
of death seem indissolubly connected,
one passing insensibly into the other,
it being very difficult to say which

is the reality and which the shadow. I had a college meeting also yesterday which did you not [improve?] my [shattered?] nerves. [However?] today I am better so that I dare say be myself in a day or two. Many thanks for your [letter?]. My plans are very uncertain, depending on my work so I look forward to [?] being cured [?] little as possible.

is very kind and sympathetic
... you sent your ... long
letter.

Believe me
yr very affec.ly
Oscar Browning

CHAPTER XII

TOWARDS THE IDEAL

I

THE occupations of the moment, however, were not unimportant. Two of these, which were never absent from his thoughts, interested him vitally and professionally. They were the history school at Cambridge and the training of teachers. Both were essential to the cultured, democratic England which his philosophic radicalism postulated. The Cambridge history school was to be the intellectual palæstra of young statesmen. It was to train the neophyte to take a broad and unprejudiced view of human affairs, to learn to weigh truth in the rough balance of human action, to realise how traditionalism and idealism, the instinct of order and the love of liberty, were the twin blades of the shears with which man's destiny on our planet has been carved out. Nourished with this feeling for the past and this reverence for the future, their knowledge and enthusiasm seasoned with a lively interest in the politics of the day, the men who read for the Historical Tripos would become fitted to take their place in the ranks of the governing class, either at home or in the Empire.

Equally practical was his other interest, the training of teachers, which ultimately came to dominate his work at Cambridge. The key to the future lay in education. England, already threatened by young rivals among the nations, could only continue to hold her place by its means, and through it alone could the people achieve true freedom and the culture inseparable from it. But we could only enjoy a better system of education if we had the teachers to impart it. The ideal schoolmaster, and Oscar Browning was not thinking in this matter of any particular class, should have a mind which responded to the intellectual influences of the time, and he should know the technique of teaching. This was an art that had to be learnt, a science that should be taught in the University. It was important, of course, that men going to staff the great public schools should know something about the theory and practice of their profession, instead of always remaining ignorant of the one and learning the other at the expense of their pupils. But it was much more important that the older Universities, and more especially Cambridge with its traditional leanings towards Liberalism, should send out its graduates into the elementary schools. Only in this way could there be built up a complete educational system with a real interdependence between its various branches. In his conception of the true end of historical study he was the disciple of Seeley. But as regards the need for the training of teachers, and more especially for providing a University education for elementary school teachers, he was a pioneer in Cambridge. The struggle was long, the issue often in doubt. After sixteen years a measure of victory was achieved by the creation of a Day Training College, an institution born into the world of Cambridge without a home and almost without funds. It was not, however, until the present century was well on its way that the full importance of the movement which he and Henry Sidgwick had initiated was generally recognised in the University.

II

In both these questions he was perfectly clear as to what he wanted, and was always ready for battle in support of his views. Thus on the question of the Historical Tripos he came into conflict with G. W. Prothero, whose subordinate colleague he then was on the teaching staff of King's. Prothero wished to alter the Tripos in the direction of making it more purely historical. Oscar Browning was anxious to keep it as it was, " a school of the political sciences," and the fact that for once he was a Conservative did not detract from the fun of the controversy. He adopted the congenial rôle of pamphleteer and dragged in Henry VIII and George I. "The Professorship of Modern History and Modern Languages was founded by George I to train public servants for the service of the State. It was to be analogous to the schools which flourished during the last century at Göttingen and at Strassburg, to the École des Sciences Politiques in Paris, to the Schools of Political Science in America. This high endeavour, imagined by Henry VIII on the dissolution of the monasteries, set on foot by the genius of Sir Robert Walpole, neglected by the apathy of succeeding generations, has been realised in the Cambridge of our own day by the creation of the Triposes of History and of Modern Languages and ought not to be lightly thrown away." His championship for the " clear-headed thinker," such as the Historical Tripos turned out, as against " the laborious sciolist whose mind was a mere magazine of facts and who twittered like a sparrow on the house-tops," was successful. "Our great debate about the Historical Tripos," he says, " has come off and my opinion has prevailed over that of Prothero. What is

more important, the Tripos remains an excellent
examination."

III

When Oscar Browning returned to Cambridge
in 1876 the University ignored its responsibilities
in the matter of the training of teachers. Almost
at once he began preparing memorials on the
question, and when in 1879 the Teachers' Training
Syndicate was established at a yearly cost to the
University Chest of £100, his efforts were recognised
by his being made Secretary. The Syndicate
arranged courses of lectures on the Theory, the
Practice and the History of Education, and examinations were held once or twice yearly. When the
lectures began in the October term of 1879 they
were a great success, being attended by nearly a
hundred students, though women were in a very
large majority. But when in the following year
these were no longer free and a fee of a guinea was
charged, the numbers dropped away at once. So
we find R. H. Quick, who had given the scheme his
blessing from the start, writing on its difficulties
three years later in an unhopeful strain : " The
Cambridge scheme seems on the point of falling
through; and this is surely not to be wondered at.
The British public is ignorant and indifferent. . . .
The great bulk of the teaching profession is satisfied.
The ordinary Head Master can see little amiss in
the system which has produced *him*. So it is only
just a few of the most active-minded of our schoolmasters who see that things can't remain as they
are. . . . Still, when a few active-minded men keep
hammering away on the same nail, the same nail
does show a tendency to intrude, and so at Cambridge and elsewhere they have got people to assent
to the proposition that ' something should be

done!'" Now, said Quick, that the whole thing had been pronounced a failure, the Syndicate would very likely not be reappointed and the thing would be given up altogether.

But he underrated the persistence and determination of the *esprits remuants* in this question of the training of teachers. The Syndicate continued a modest existence, the number of its examinees gradually grew, and ultimately it was able to report to the University on the desirability of establishing a Training College for Teachers.

IV

Throughout the 'eighties O. B. fought the battle of education with passionate sincerity. To the ordinary Englishman it is a dull, if not a tiresome, subject, and this may be the reason why his efforts never met with fuller appreciation. He did nevertheless manage to create something of a sensation with his presidential address to the Education Section at the Birmingham Social Science Congress in 1884. People overwhelmed him with " compliments and kindness." He was told that he was the "one member of the Congress who had impressed his individuality on the town," he was pursued by autograph hunters, and indeed began to think himself " a sort of Gladstone on a small scale." One can understand that to an industrial centre like Birmingham his address went home with special force. " England," he said, " still maintains her position at the head of the industrial world. But the progress made by the continental nations during the past half-century has been immense. When less than half a century ago continental mechanics began to construct railways and to erect modern mills and mechanical workshops, they found themselves face to face with an industrial organisation existing in England which was almost a sealed book to those who could not obtain access to our own factories." He went on to point out that in the production of synthetic dyes and in the development of electricity Germany was already ahead of us. This economic progress was due to special training based upon a substratum of sound secondary education. "The sceptre is still in our hands, although its possession is claimed by our rivals. We can only retain it by learning their arts and by setting our house in order without loss of time."

He did not, however, confine himself to the commercial aspect of the question. It was especially important that a nation on whom had fallen the mantle of imperial Rome should do its very best with the material it possessed. He drew a picture of the facilities of self-improvement offered to a clever German boy, who could pass through all the stages to the University "with no more expense than a modest household could afford or than could be easily supplied by charitable or public funds." In England it was otherwise. "An English boy similarly born has none of these advantages. It is not every town that has a grammar school, and the entrance is often barred to the poor." Chance charity occasionally helped a promising boy, but it was uncertain and capricious. Men did attain distinction in different walks of life after starting from the humblest origins. This was often urged as a justification for the existing system. To him it did not appear in that light. "The instances of which I have investigated the details have been such accidents, and yet their success has been so marked, that I have been drawn to think rather of the tens who have failed than of the units who have succeeded, and of the ore which lies buried in our social strata rather than of the bright coins which circulate from hand to hand. If a field of coal, or of some other mineral, lies unworked and unused, yet it is always there. It may be kept for some future age when its wealth will be more needed, and posterity will bless the prescience and parsimony of their ancestors who refrained from using it. But the human mind is born and lives and perishes. If it is unenlightened it passes away into its native darkness. We lose not only all that it might have given us of itself, but the enlightenment of other minds which would have drawn illumination from its brightness. By not educating our masses according to the measure of their capacity we squander both principal and interest. We cast the ' one talent which 'tis death to hide into the depths of the ocean ' and cannot produce it when called upon for an account."

Then he sketched the plan of the system of secondary education such as England, in his opinion, ought to possess. It included the establishment of local educational councils, the provision of three times the existing number of secondary schools, the State inspection of all schools, security of tenure for schoolmasters and their registration after compulsory training, the transfer of the power of appointing Head Masters from Governing Bodies to an official board of educational experts. " The time will come," he said, "when the amount contributed by the Budget to the expense of national education will be considered as an index of the national prosperity. The organisation, I might say the creation, of secondary education is the most pressing question in the whole political horizon : it is connected with social questions of the most momentous character. The depopulation of our villages, the dull routine of our country labourers, who have improved very little in the last half-century, the backwardness of our agriculture and its inability to cope with new conditions, the absence of the higher pleasures, the addiction to vulgar merry-making which is the parent of lust and crime, the estrangement of classes, the idle luxury of the rich side by side with the ignorant toil of the poor, the strife between capital and labour, bred in ignorance, nurtured in prejudice, do not all these things show us that the mass of our nation requires a great intellectual lift, which shall form a solid foundation for special instruction, make rational enjoyments possible for the multitude, and knit the bonds of sympathy between man and man ? "

V

Such was the ideal. But progress towards it was to be guided by statesmanlike principles. There were to be no shibboleths, no quack remedies. The talk, for instance, of free education " made him sick." " It is strange to find," he says in a letter to the Press, " free education lifted to the rank of a political maxim. . . . As one who regards the present condition of education in England as deplorable, as the cause of most of our grievances and discontents, as producing a vague *malaise* that we are every year losing ground to the better trained foreigner, the only importance of this political movement is whether it will help or not in the great cause, whether it will help us to obtain an efficiently organised system of education. Free education might, or might not, do this. Let us not ask now for free education but for more education."

In the meantime at Cambridge the causes which he had at heart prospered, or at least were kept alive. History continued to attract men from classics, law and moral sciences, till in the end its numbers became an embarrassment, and history dons, though not O. B., winced under the imputation of their school being a Lotus land for lazy young men who wanted an honours degree on the easiest terms. And year by year the University training of teachers grew more of a practical question. The Royal Commission of 1886, presided over by Sir R. A. Cross, one of the members being Cardinal Manning, brought the matter into the arena of public discussion, making the position of the *intransigeants*, amongst whom was, of course, Dr. Hornby, less possible of defence than before. Did not even Matthew Arnold, whom the Liberal educationalists had never trusted, declare that to teach teaching was difficult, but that it ought to be done?

The evidence before the Commission showed, however, that there was no unanimity upon the desirability of elementary school teachers graduating at the Universities.. On the contrary, the Principals of existing Training Colleges were rather inclined to be suspicious of a policy which if successful might detract from their own importance, and Conservatives generally were irritated by what they considered a piece of Utopian nonsense. The only reason, they thought, why University graduates were to be encouraged to become teachers in elementary schools was that these " should be raised to the level of Eton and Harrow." P. Cumin, however, the Permanent Secretary to the Board of Education, questioned by one member of the Commission on the point, denied that this was " the theory of it." He pointed out that the better the class of teacher, the better his teaching was likely to be and the better his influence over children, and instanced Scotland as a country where there was a close connection between the elementary schools and the Universities. Thus with the support of Whitehall the prospect became much more hopeful, and it is noteworthy that the Teachers' Training Syndicate

Report two years later, in which Oscar Browning as secretary was the moving spirit, recommended the continuation of the £100 a year grant on the ground that maintaining lectures on educational subjects in the University had a material effect in developing public opinion in favour of the professional training of teachers generally.

Finally, in 1890, a new Code of Regulations issued by the Board of Education with Parliamentary sanction made the way clear for the establishment of a Day Training College in Cambridge. The Syndicate in its Report in the following February called attention to this, and stated that in its opinion the University should avail itself of the offer of the Education Department to give grants to students of Universities who were attached to Day Training Colleges by the establishment of a College in Cambridge. This would form a link between the University and the elementary education of the country, and would tend to raise the character and status of elementary teachers. The scheme had the advantage of entailing no expenditure on the University. The Syndicate then made two recommendations : (1) that the Teachers' Training Syndicate should be empowered to make application on behalf of the University to the Committee of the Council of Education to allow the establishment of a Day Training College for Men to be attached to the University, and (2) that the College should be managed by a local Committee, partly of members of the Syndicate and partly of others appointed by it, the whole remaining under the control of the Syndicate. Amongst those who signed this Report were two intimate friends of Oscar Browning, Montagu Butler, who was Vice-Chancellor at the time, and Henry Sidgwick.

It met with plenty of criticism. It was said that it would be impossible for students to carry on the two branches of work side by side, either their University work or their professional training would suffer, and most probably indeed it would be both. How too could there be a College without the expenditure of a large capital sum to provide buildings and without the provision of an annual income to pay for teachers ? And if the students really attended to their job and justified their Government grant, they would only be sham University men, living by themselves, not belonging to Colleges and taking no part in the ordinary University undergraduate life. Oscar Browning did not allow himself to be influenced by these specious and plausible arguments. He was convinced that he and those who shared his view were right and that all these prophecies would prove to be wrong. His prescience was justified, thanks largely to the singleness of purpose with which he strove to make the venture a success. As with the future of the new King's, so with that of the yet unborn Day Training College, he had no doubts, or if he had them he never let them appear. Even supporters like Sedley Taylor, when the Report came up before the Senate, grew frightened and, expressing all sorts of fears, that the Government examinations might prove too difficult and that Cambridge could not provide teachers for them, suggested that the project should be dropped till October. Though the Report was non-placeted, it was carried and nothing remained but to negotiate with the Department of Education. The University was represented in these pourparlers by Oscar Browning, Henry Sidgwick and Professor James Ward, and by August 1891 they were complete. Official sanction was then given to the opening of the College. Oscar Browning and Henry Sidgwick met in London and discussed whether they could open the College without the final orders of the University to that effect. They overcame their hesitations, and although they did not escape criticism for thus taking the law into their own hands, the *fait accompli* was recognised and Cambridge had the satisfaction of obtaining a year's start over Oxford in this new phase of University activity.

VI

At last Oscar Browning, when he was fifty-four, found himself in a position where he could be something of an autocrat, and in his rule over the newly-established College show those powers of leadership and administration which hitherto he had had no power of displaying. Everything had to be created. The College was formless and homeless. It had no funds and the Principal's salary was £10 a year. But if it lacked everything else it was not without idealism, and Mr. H. G. Wilson, the first student to enter his name on the College books, has remarked how O. B. was " indefatigable " in everything appertaining to the College, of which the head-quarters were his rooms in King's. Here he coached the three students, who for the first year of the existence of the College made up the number of its pupils, in elementary classics and history for the General, their knowledge of Greek and Latin being small. It was a new experience for him to be brought into contact with undergraduates who had worked their way through the elementary schools to become pupil-teachers, and he has recorded the pleasure their " virile and self-denying " qualities gave him in comparison with Etonian and other public-school boys. The students were naturally poor—many of them passed through the University on £60 and £70 a year—and their force of character and strong individuality impressed this connoisseur of young men.

If there were only three entries the first year, the second there were ten, most of these joining Colleges, as O. B. had prophesied they would. Eight of them, to his "delight and dismay," stated their intention of reading for honours; to his delight because it showed that the men meant to get the most out of their University career, to his dismay because the arrangements with the Board of Education had not foreseen such a contingency. These difficulties were easily overcome, and the students belied the croakers in showing that it was quite possible to read for honours whilst undergoing their training and taking their diplomas as teachers. They proved to be immensely hard workers, and O. B., in the last year of his reign as Principal, was able to point out that the percentage of first and second classes was higher than that of any College at Oxford or Cambridge, whilst on the professional side the students were stated to have done better than those of any other Training College entering for the examination. As the numbers grew the staff was gradually increased. Permanent premises were found in Warkworth Street, and Warkworth House remains its head-quarters to-day, when with 150 students the College is as flourishing as the optimism of its first Principal ever imagined.

As Principal O. B. had many difficulties to overcome. On the one side was an apathetic Committee, the members of which were extremely slack in attending its meetings, and on one occasion at least he and the Chairman had to transact the business alone. When the College grew to be an important institution and to be recognised as such outside Cambridge, the tune changed, and the Committee, from taking too little, began to take too much interest and often prevented the Principal from having his own way. There is a good deal of truth in what he used to say, that when he had

succeeded in obtaining the recognition of the training of teachers " as a work worthy of man and not
as a mere fad, other people came in to try and
collect the kudos." But in the earlier years he had
no difficulties of this kind, and he was able, on the
very important question of establishing a secondary
department, to secure the adoption by the University
of his view, that it should be attached to the existing
institution and should not be an entirely separate
venture, as at Oxford.

The Board of Education, too, though sympathetic on the whole, was guided by its regulations,
and Oscar Browning had never found it easy to
observe regulations. Sometimes these were quite
inapplicable to the special conditions of Cambridge,
where the students were living the normal undergraduate life. Tradition has it how on one occasion
a visit was paid to the College by an inspector of
physical training, a subject which at Cambridge,
where physical fitness is in no need of artificial
stimulants, was tacitly ignored. The announcement
caused some consternation, but O. B. declared himself equal to dealing with the emergency. He met
H.M.'s inspector at the station and proceeded to
show him the sights of the University, not failing,
as they sauntered from Trinity to King's, to call his
attention to the fine physique of the undergraduates.
Luncheon in his rooms followed and O. B., with
that ingratiating gastronomic background, con-
versed as one man of the world to another. Then
came the business of the day and he accompanied his
guest to his inspection. It happened that afternoon
that a lecture was being given by a member of the
staff who was a tall and slender and by no means
an athletic-looking individual. They entered the
class, and O. B. followed the usual introductions
by laying his hand upon his assistant's shoulder
and saying : " There, did you ever see a finer

type of physical manhood ? " And the inspector, being a wise man, held his peace. But things were not always so amenable, and as age grew upon him his irritation with the Board of Education and its permanent officials increased, till to hear him talk one would have thought them the products of some Tsarist regime. The only education Minister who had earned his unqualified esteem was Sir John Gorst, who held that office, of course, in a Conservative Government.

To his staff he was an autocrat. When in 1902 the growth of the College necessitated the appointment of a Lecturer in Education, he secured the services of Dr. S. S. F. Fletcher, whom he brought from Germany to fill this post. To him he resigned most of the actual teaching and the details of administration, though he kept the threads in his own hands. He did not disguise, indeed, the pleasure he took in the exercise of his authority, which was all part of the creative process moulding a new institution. One of his rules was that every member of the staff should make him a detailed weekly report on the work of his pupils. Once during a prolonged illness of Dr. Fletcher this proved an onerous burden, and one of them suggested that the practice might be temporarily suspended. " Certainly not, my dear fellow," was O. B.'s answer, " When I get your reports I feel like Napoleon reading the reports of his marshals." Like other autocrats he sometimes interfered in what seemed trifling details. Thus when the head-quarters of the College were moved to Warkworth House, the resident members of the staff, who, unlike most University teachers, were occupied during the afternoons and were thus unable to take the usual forms of exercise, decided to use a small backyard, otherwise neglected, for badminton, and for this purpose put wire netting round the walls at their own expense. When O. B. discovered it he was put out, observing that badminton was a "most undignified game" and that he ought to have been consulted before anything of the kind had been done. The staff, conscious in their rectitude of purpose, continued to enjoy occasional games until the end of the term. When they returned after the vacation they found that the wire netting round the court had been removed by the orders of the Principal. The appearance, too, of a new clock in Warkworth House caused him much uneasiness that was only allayed by his own presentation of another and the disappearance of the offending timepiece. But if in little things his interference was apt to irritate, there was no limit to the paternal kindness he would show to any of his subordinates, with all of whom he cultivated the closest social relations, which were emphasised by his entertaining them all to dinner every year on his birthday.

The students, or at least a good many of them, found him something of an enigma. They came to Cambridge without experience of the graces of social intercourse, and his absence of pose and his geniality rather nonplussed them. But those who presumed to take liberties soon learnt to their cost that this ease and bonhomie were the result of a sophisticated and highly developed culture of which the sense of dignity was an important ingredient. Oscar Browning was not a man to be "ragged." On his side he did not attempt to cultivate those intimacies with the students which lifted education to poetic heights. The note of inquiry, however, in which he so profoundly believed, he introduced into the work of the College by holding a weekly "Seminar" in his rooms at which educational subjects were brought to the bar of discussion, though the difference between this and the Political Society, where the members sat about informally and the President lay back in his easy-chair and affected sleep, was marked by its being held round his dining-room table, with himself seated at one end and Dr. Fletcher at the other. Like the Political Society, the " Seminar " has outlived its founder and is very much alive in the Training College to-day.

His personal interest in the students never flagged, and he followed their subsequent careers with a pride which was inspired by his belief in the work that the College was doing. He records his admiration for one old student who, after taking a second class in the Tripos, went to teach little children of the first standard at a Board School in the Waterloo Road, and reminded him there of Pestalozzi amongst the orphans of Stanz; or his appreciation of another who turned from the atmosphere of high thinking and hard work which surrounded the College to go to a racing centre where he found that his pupils were making books instead of reading them. O. B., in spite of his Epicurean desire to taste of all the things in which humanity delights, never reacted to the excitement of horse-racing, and the few visits he paid to New-market seem to have been inspired by purely social incentives. In his middle age he learnt to play poker, and he was not above a mild gamble on the tables of Monte Carlo. But though he placed fox-hunting with mountaineering and standing for Parliament as the three most exciting things within the range of his experience, racing lay well outside his interests.

Thus it was that from modest beginnings and in the face of much scepticism Oscar Browning built up an institution which he firmly believed would in time set a new tone to English elementary educa-tion. From the time when he returned to Cam-bridge labouring under the discredit of his dismissal from Eton, he worked steadily and almost alone towards the ends which he had in view. It is true that these became clarified through the contact with elementary education which he gained from being Secretary of the Teachers' Training Syndicate. But his vision had already enabled him to conceive, in its main outlines, the end to be attained, and for thirty years he worked steadily for its realisation. In Cambridge his contribution to English education was never recognised, as indeed the incidents connected with his forced resignation in 1909 sufficiently prove. Reasons may be found for this. The training of teachers, for one thing, is not of itself an inspiring subject, whilst the material it added to Cambridge undergraduate life was rather sound than brilliant. And for another, O. B.'s belief that colleagues conspired to ignore his work, irritated his contemporaries not altogether unjustifiably. It resulted in this sort of attitude : " You have seen my doings in the papers," he writes to his mother somewhere in the middle of the 'eighties, " and apropos of this I had an amusing conversation with an undergraduate yesterday. He said : ' I never open the paper without seeing your name in it.' I said : ' Are you surprised ? ' He then said : ' But I never see any other University names.' I again said : ' Are you surprised ? ' I then explained that no one is a prophet in his own country and that it is better to have a reputation outside one's country than in it."

The honour with which he met " outside his own country " had led to his being decorated by the French Government for his work in education and to his being President in 1898 of the Association of Principals and Lecturer in Training Colleges under Government Inspection, when for his presidential address he took the subject of his favourite child, the Day Training College. Its excellence was freely recognised. "I think you know," writes one who had already attained distinction in the same field, "that I have a habit of speaking my mind and am not given to flattery, and that when I say that no other Training College approaches that at Cambridge, I mean what I say. . . . I have been round to the four London residential Colleges, and even at Westminster, where the normal work— under Mr. Cowham—is admittedly a great feature, I saw nothing in my opinion to better the work I saw at Cambridge; and the men I saw there were good Senior students, not freshers. Warkworth House has sprung up with the unexpectedness of an Aladdin's Palace. It is imposing, yet it does not dominate the Day Training College men to the exclusion of their College and University interests, which is as it should be."

CHAPTER XIII

MUSIC AND CONTROVERSY

I

BUT the prophetic rôle has its drawbacks. Amidst Oscar Browning's battling for unpopular or despised causes one notices a growing embitterment with colleagues. These cease to be as "kind and affectionate" as before. Not only do they seem to him determined not to recognise the place he was winning in the world; they give him the impression that they would like to get rid of him, that to this end they mean to "starve him out." It was, of course, absurd. He was helping to democratise Cambridge, to infuse a new spirit into education. And in consequence of his other occupations the great literary work which was to set the seal on his reputation had yet to be written. But outside the University he was recognised as a person of distinction. During the London season he was overwhelmed with invitations from the great world which necessitated tiring journeys to London by a late afternoon train and an equally early return to Cambridge the next morning. He was in request too as a speaker at Liberal meetings, where his jingoism on occasion refuted the Tories' claim to a "monopoly of patriotism," and had he only possessed a private income the political career after which he hankered would have been waiting for him almost ready made. If the illustrated Christmas number of the *World* was any criterion he was "among the fifty most distinguished persons in England," who appeared in silhouette grouped under their Christian names. In that procession he brought up the rear of the trio of Oscars, of which the van was led by Wilde, not a little to the irritation of his mother, who expressed her " dislike of the man." Small things, however, sometimes indicated that the tide might turn. One night, for example, he dreams of an earthquake, which he believes is very lucky, and sure enough the following morning's post brings him requests to examine for the Indian Civil Service and to lecture at the Birmingham Midland Institute, both of which are " honourable and lucrative."

Not always was he so fortunate. Sometimes he missed by an accident the thing which he would have liked greatly. A tutor, for instance, had to be found for Prince Eddie, and the post was given to Jim Stephen because, as O. B. believed, the member of the Prince of Wales's entourage who came up to Cambridge to arrange about it failed to find him in his rooms. To train the future King of England, to follow in the footsteps of Aristotle, Seneca, Bossuet and Hobbes would have been the most congenial of occupations, would have rounded off his work as an educator of statesmen in an incomparable manner. For that it would have been worth while to leave, for a year or two, Cambridge and his schemes. A chance which came at about the same time of going round the world with a young man of less exalted rank he resigned to a Fellow of All Souls', for he considered that thus to cut a year out of his life would have been a waste of time. But the Ulysses strain in O. B., the strain which gave him his passion for travel and made him say that to the true tourist it was worth while going to a place to know that there was nothing worth seeing there, caused his mouth to water at this chance of visiting the

Antipodes, which he had " always longed to do."
More seriously in 1890, under the strain of the
starving-out process, he considered standing for
the Professorship of History in Sydney, being
dissuaded by Lord Latymer, who, to other arguments, added the opportune gift of an allowance
of £100 a year, which enabled O. B. to economise
on his frequent visits to Town by taking chambers
at the bottom of St. James's Street, above the
Post Office.

The year before Provost Okes had died at an
advanced age, and Oscar Browning had received
another proof that he had no following amongst
the King's dons. The claims of Austen-Leigh to
succeed to the Provostship were pre-eminent and
O. B. was amongst his supporters. Not even when
Nixon, whom ever since the incident in connection
with the election to the office of Dean he had
regarded with distrust, led a party in favour of
Henry Sidgwick did he for an instant waver.
Sidgwick might be his most intimate friend. But
he was " an unbeliever "; besides, promotion,
O. B. considered, should remain in the regiment,
and Sidgwick was a Fellow of Trinity. So that
although Austen-Leigh, knowing their friendship,
magnanimously wrote to O. B. to release him from
any promise of support, O. B. never hesitated and
was one of the considerable majority which voted
for Austen-Leigh. His election caused the Vice-
Provostship to become vacant, and it really did
look as if he might be chosen to fill the second
position in the College. But it slipped away.
" The young Liberals," he writes, " are very anxious
for me, but the Tories and the weak-kneed people,
amongst whom I am afraid I must reckon Prothero,
seem to prefer Whitting." Whitting was elected
without opposition, much to O. B.'s disgust, for
the time when he and Whitting used to give parties

together to the élite had passed beyond recall.
Oscar tells his mother about it and adds: "I
thought that I should feel it, but now it has happened I do not do so in the least. I am not one
of those to whom the prizes of the world fall."
In the same week he had the pleasure of emphasising those unpopular Liberal principles which had
stood in his way ever since he went to Eton by
presiding at a Liberal meeting at which George
Trevelyan was the principal speaker. It was
followed by a large breakfast party the next morning
in his rooms, " with much Liberal talk," and George
Trevelyan, who had been his guest for the night,
declared when he left that he had never spent a
more pleasant twelve hours.

Why indeed should he worry about his fellow-
dons when life was such an exciting business?
Every day there was something new. Either
King's won their hockey match and O. B. nearly
scored a goal; or he played fives, or carpentered,
or took a Turkish bath, or rode eight miles on his
tricycle in the hour. And the evenings were
always full. He dined out, perhaps, at the
Sidgwicks " with a distinguished party," and after
dinner they abused Carlyle, " agreeing that he was
a snob and could not forgive his wife for being
a lady." Or the " Ghost Club " (the Society
for Psychical Research) met in his rooms, and
the cat, which lived on his staircase and under
ordinary circumstances would never cross his
threshold, surveyed the proceedings " in solemn
and mysterious grandeur" from the round table
that stood in the middle of his drawing-room.
He had always been interested in psychical research.
"Thanks for the apparition story," writes Tennyson
to him on one occasion. O. B. had " hundreds
of ghost stories in his possession with which to
convert the unbelievers," stories that, alas! are

not to be found amongst his papers. But ghosts in that academic atmosphere sometimes lost their power to thrill, and he used to think that the lady members of the Society read papers too full of facts to be entertaining.

And if ghosts were dull he preferred to be amused by humans, notwithstanding that there was in the world much folly which was anything but amusing. He himself was not blameless. For he confesses once that he has played whist at the Athenæum and lost 15s. But he excuses himself on the ground that it was the first time and he dared say the last that he would ever enter the card-room at the club which is not associated, in the public mind, with the vice of gambling; "a piece of astounding folly" indeed. In a different category is the misfortune which happens to Robbie Ross, who had been ducked in the Fountain at King's for being an æsthete, and this although he had rowed in the College boat, which, contrary to all the traditions of King's rowing, had gone up two places. "Poor dear Ross," he writes to his mother in March '89, "has been seized with a violent brain attack, the result of the outrage preying upon his mind. He was taken suddenly ill on Friday night and was so bad that I was not allowed to see him. They were afraid that he would kill himself. However, his brother came down and was able to take him to London. Poor fellow! I was afraid that something of the kind would happen. He is terribly sensitive, and though he bore the thing itself bravely, yet it was always preying upon his mind. I do not know what will become of him. I cannot tell you how distressed we all are about it. His friends are devoted to him." It should be added that those who were responsible for the incident were not the least pained at its unfortunate consequences, and expressed their regret to O. B. in a letter which brought it to an honourable, if not a satisfactory, conclusion.

II

Naturally in a community where one had to be continually fighting on matters of principle with colleagues who were conservative, reactionary, or merely obtuse, it was often necessary to use hard words. Those, too, who lead a communal life often get on each other's nerves. Oscar Browning noted with satisfaction that the shock of Henry Bradshaw's sudden death had made them all more kindly and forbearing with one another. But it wore off and things became worse than before. He himself was drawn into passionate disputes. A scholarship candidate, for instance, had put down Caius as his first choice, by a clerical error as O. B. maintained. He was a clever youth and O. B. was accused of trying to filch him for King's. It was a monstrous charge and to make the matter still more monstrous the Tutor of King's appeared to give it credence. " My grievance against you," O. B. writes to him, " is that on November 17 last " (the letter is dated the following March) " you treated me with injustice, with cruelty and with ingratitude. . . . You exposed me to the vulgar insolence of Nixon and R. . . ." (Nixon, as the many who knew and loved him will be aware, was the mildest of men.) There follows a résumé, covering thirteen type-written pages, of the differences which have interfered with their personal relations. " When I was talking to you about these matters on November 30th, I remarked that I had been very badly treated, and you replied : ' You have done a great deal of harm to the College,' and walked away. I had not the least idea what you meant." After all Eton, as O. B. pointed out, had its advantages. " The great merit of Eton, with all its faults, lay in the fact that there existed the fullest and freest intercourse between the masters with regard to their pupils and their work. We met the Head Master every day in Chambers for that purpose, and for that purpose only. I have always desiderated something of the kind at King's. As a body we know little of each other in this respect, and I hope at any rate that between you and myself the confidence which once existed may be restored."

The difficulty was that when peace was restored and one bone of contention had been decently buried, he stumbled over another. It was not his fault and it was always perfectly clear that he was in no way to blame. Others had been hasty or inconsiderate; he had acted with entire singleness of purpose. His mother had suggested long ago that he was hyper-sensitive and that he " imagined what was never intended," that he expected from others more than they were capable of. But such explanations he set aside. For it was his belief that, since his fellow-dons could not prevent him from carrying through the schemes which he had at heart (so plain was the reasonableness of his policy and so potent his advocacy), they were determined to make life as difficult for him as they could.

O. B.'s views were set out in a letter which he wrote to Montagu Butler in 1894 apropos of his candidature for the Professorship of History in Glasgow : " I was particularly gratified," he says, " by your remarks about my beloved College. Its success is nearer to my heart than anything else. During the last eighteen years nine-tenths of my work and thought have been given to the practical administration and the development of

King's, a fact which is known to very few outside the place itself. During that time I have had no really efficient helper in the *development* of the College except Welldon during the short time he was here, although there have been several good *workers*. When I came here in 1876 I had an advantage over my colleagues that I had conceived very clearly what sort of an institution the College ought to be. That has been very nearly worked out, except that I have not altogether succeeded in getting the Provost, as he ought to be, the working Head. Every step in the development had to be won by conflict. For many years opinion was so equally divided on fundamental questions that I never dared absent myself from a meeting, however apparently insignificant, for fear of an important division turning the wrong way. Also frequently I had to choose between getting a post and money or getting my own way. My opponents could prevent the first, but with a democratic constitution they could not prevent the second. Consequently my average stipend from the College during the last eighteen years has been £133 6s. 8d. The battle has now been won and there is no chance of things not going on rightly. If this were not so, nothing would induce me to leave. But, as you know, I rather like a struggle, and one of the attractions of Glasgow is that everything is to make." In spite of an imposing collection of testimonials, however, Oscar Browning failed to secure the vacant Professorship.

III

King's had established its place in the University. Statistics showed it. It was a consolation, when he reflected on the folly of the Conservative dons in his own College who would go on " buying " classical scholars from Eton, and on the jealousy that the success of King's was arousing in the imperial heart of Trinity, to demonstrate by tables of figures that over the period 1883–1892 the percentage of first classes in King's was 37·9 per cent., or 23·7 per cent. more than the next highest College, St. John's. And of these firsts, classics, in spite of the shower of gold with which the classical scholars were corrupted, only took a little over half of the grand total. A pamphlet, which he had printed at his own expense, set out the figures so that all could see. With the passing of Jowett and the inevitable decline of Balliol, King's would soon be the first College in either University. And Oscar Browning unquestionably was the first man in King's.

IV

When he could derive consolation from statistics, it was not likely that rebuffs from colleagues, or charges—absurdly unjust charges—of dishonourable conduct in the matter of a scholarship examination, would affect his exuberant vitality. Besides, if he were a prophet without honour, always he was O. B., a man of the world amongst recluses, a celebrity amongst dons; a visit to whose rooms had become a necessary part of the itinerary of every distinguished visitor to Cambridge.

One morning he had a letter from the Princess Mary, afterwards to become the first lady in the land, saying that she and her brother were visiting Cambridge that very day and would be delighted to lunch with him. Time pressed, but O. B. acted with Napoleonic promptitude. Private carriages were borrowed, guests representative of Cambridge life, the Master of Trinity, the President of the Union and others, were hastily bidden. Luckily

226

King's had a cook, trained in the royal kitchens at Windsor, who could confection regal dishes— before then his art had received the homage of O. B.'s muse—and luckily too, as he flattered himself, his own wine-cellar was that of a connoisseur. By midday all was ready, including the red carpet, though the amount required for the two flights of " A " staircase, at the top of which stood his rooms, put a strain on the resources of Cambridge. And the luncheon party of twelve passed off without any suggestion of improvisation, the conversation, thanks largely to Dr. and Mrs. Butler, flowing with the ordered ease which royalty appreciate. Afterwards they drove round Cambridge, and O. B., as cicerone, sat in the first carriage with his august guests. And when they passed a barrel-organ which was playing " The Man that Broke the Bank at Monte Carlo," the Prince began singing that popular song and the Princess joined, and O. B., throwing etiquette to the winds, sang it too. A red-letter day.

He had entertained royalty before this with less formality. When Prince Eddie had been in residence at Trinity, O. B. one morning awoke an undergraduate friend who slept on the same staircase. " Jimmy," he said, " what do you think happened to me last night ? " The James thus disturbed from slumber grunted sleepily. " I was given a bath by the future King of England." And O. B. then recounted how he had been showing the Prince the bath which he had had installed in his rooms, and how the Prince had suggested to the other undergraduate present that they should then and there initiate him into the Order of the Bath in the mediæval style. " Wasn't that an honour, Jimmy ? " And with that question O. B. half trotted and half rolled off to early Chapel or to early shopping, for it was the early shopper who

227

secured the best lobster, satisfied—who knows?—
that he had for once succeeded in rousing a sluggard
under a decent veil of camouflage.

Yet it is detestable thus to read motives into
human conduct. O. B. followed the gleam—that
is all that can be said. As when climbing his
staircase one morning with a basket under his
arm he espied through an open door the present
Librarian of the Foreign Office, then an undergraduate, still rejoicing in his bed. It was natural
that O. B. should show a fellow-epicure a magnificent lobster he had just secured at the fishmonger's
in Petty Cury—now, alas, a multiple shop—that he
should sit on the end of the bed, and whilst talking
proceed to consume it, claw by claw. Still O. B.
was not without the fanaticism of those who rise
early.

"Non sit vobis vanum mane surgere ante lucem,
quia promisit dominus coronam vigilantibus," was
the text that ran like a frieze round the room
which served both for sleep and dining, and O. B.
was always anxious to assist others to obtain a lien
on the same crown. For an undergraduate whom
he used to chaff on his habit of reading history in
bed of a morning he composed the following
epitaph :

Non Resurgam.
Hic Jacet
Uti Vivus Jacebat
Spe Tardæ Resurrectionis
REGINALDUS LESLEIUS BROWN *
Qui Res Olim Dissociabiles
Otium ac Laborem
Ita Conjunxit ut Dignosci non Possent.

He was immune from the fear-of-giving-himself-
away disease, for which medical science has so far

* The name here inserted is a fictitious one.

provided no prophylactic, an immunity that he extended to others. The future King Constantine of Greece, whose intelligence for royalty he rated highly, was lunching with him. Upon his dining-table there always stood a plate of the biscuits known as ginger-bread nuts, which at once stimulate thirst and deaden the palate. The Prince, engaged in eager conversation, munched the biscuits and sipped the sherry until both plate and decanter were empty. " A very excellent wine, Mr. Browning," he observed. " I'm glad you like it, Sir. It's Gilbey's shilling sherry," was the too truthful answer.

" If you dine with O. B.," said a Fellow of King's who belonged to the old school, " beware of his wines." O. B. was perhaps too much of a theorist, too good a European, too little in sympathy with the French genius, too much a Radical, too ready to see good in every vintage, to be an orthodox connoiseur of wine. The memory of his Rhine and Moselle wines, which alone he was able to drink in later life, of his Schloss Johannisberg and his Berncasteler Docteur, still caress the palate after twenty years. But he might prove that the only sherry worth drinking in England was that usually put in soups, precisely because this alone was innocent of brandy, or burnt sugar, or other ingredients to make it suitable for the English palate, without dispelling the conviction that he appreciated it not least for the fact that it cost a shilling the bottle.

V

Oscar Browning's talk was, like himself, rotund, exuberant, ample, with a certain bland naïveté which hovered between the deliberate and the unconscious, and was equally valuable in disarming an opponent or in helping him to modulate into the Rabelaisian, the malicious, or the egotistical, the last of these being a key which always had a compelling fascination for him. His conversation moved in a broad and ample stream, too full in later life to sparkle, bearing upon its waters the anecdotage, the *chroniques scandaleuses* of half a century. General ideas it brought to the touchstone of personal experience and thus easily led back all subjects to himself. *Quoi qu'on fasse, on ne sort jamais de soi-même*—to O. B. this was not a bitter, but a glorious, truth. The idiosyncrasy of egotism grew upon him as his contemporaries dropped away, as they died, or married, or became absorbed in interests which were not his, and he had to turn more and more to the companionship of younger men. If in later life his conversational supremacy were challenged he was apt to relapse into silence, to close his eyes, inflate his cheeks and set his knees in tremulous motion. Even so he might intervene with disastrous effect to anyone who was holding the table. Thus at one of his Sunday luncheon parties a newly-created Liberal peer, who had once for a short time held an office of Cabinet rank, was explaining how he had recently been through the list of his Division at Eton, and how he had found that it contained three future bishops, a judge or two and various generals. "But," he added triumphantly, "only one boy became a Cabinet Minister." "Really," said O. B., suddenly opening his eyes, "and who was that?"

He was quick in repartee. A friend was complaining of the coldness of his wife and saying that he might as well be living with a deal board. "Take care," he replied, "or you'll find that you'll soon be living with someone a deal bawdier."

One day a discussion arose in his rooms about

the Botticelli picture of Venus rising from the sea, of which an Arundel print hung upon his walls. A would-be connoisseur asserted that the figure of Venus was out of drawing and turned to O. B. for confirmation. " It's no good asking me, my dear fellow," he answered blandly, " I've never seen a naked woman."

When he was contesting one of the Liverpool divisions in 1895 a heckler got up at a meeting and asked whether it was not true that he was Oscar Wilde's uncle. " No, sir," he replied without a second's hesitation, " there is not the slightest truth in the rumour, and even if there were I have yet to learn that the sins of the nephews should be visited upon the uncles." And the laugh was turned against the heckler.

For the female don he used another method. A lecturer at Girton, who was his colleague upon some University examination board and was irritated with him for giving indifferent marks to the women candidates, wondered sweetly how he had managed to look over all the papers so quickly. He replied equally sweetly : " Genius, madam, sheer genius."

Sometimes when argument was difficult and going against him, he knocked his opponent down in the true Johnsonian manner. To another don, who refused to agree with his point of view and upheld his own in language which betrayed his American-German origin, he remarked at length : " My dear X., I can understand every language in Europe except yours."

One of the younger Fellows complained to him one day that a third had been to him and said that he would not give him his vote for some College Committee because he had not got a first-class mind. " What should I have said ? " the young man asked. " What should you have said ? "

repeated O. B. in a deeper bass than usual. "Why, you should have said that if you had not got a first-class mind he had got a first-class bottom, and that you would have much pleasure in kicking it unless he cleared out of your rooms."

VI

If O. B., like his hero Napoleon, *aimait beaucoup à causer et à se faire écouter*, he was not a talker born, for he was always ready to exchange conversation for music. Of all the arts music charmed him the most, and of all composers Mozart held the first place in his affections. As a boy at Eton he recorded his loyalty in his diary; in 1922 he wrote to Mr. Percy Scholes from Rome: "My Mozart concerts go on splendidly every Monday at 5.30. We are now doing (for the second time) the quartets dedicated to Haydn and the performers are enthusiastic. Beethoven has not a chance beside him."

Within this seventy years' interval O. B. was always the most zealous of amateurs. He belonged to a type now growing rare, the type which likes listening to music much but making it even more. With magnificent, and, as his neighbours in King's used sometimes to think, with misguided courage, he struggled against his shortcomings as a pianist, continuing to take lessons even when he was eighty-three. But in this respect, at least, he was under no delusions as to his own capacity, and he confided to Lord Latymer, towards the end of his life, that he remains the worst pianist in the world. A hard judgment, though indeed it must be admitted that as an executant he was ill-equipped. His touch was ponderous, his fingers anything but nimble, and once his foot found the damper pedal, which from the shortness of his legs it did not always do at once, it rarely let it go.

These shortcomings, however, were as little compared with the enthusiasm that underlay them, an enthusiasm which made him the prince of duettists. He played duets all his life, sometimes in distinguished company. "I wish you and Parry wouldn't thump so," said his mother to him on one recorded occasion at Eton, using an expression which has now a pleasant Victorian flavour. Though Hubert Parry was not one of O. B.'s pupils, his taste for music had attracted his notice and he was among the boys bidden to those water-parties which excited the ire of Dr. Hornby. Parry went on one of them when they took train to Pangbourne, where they embarked, dined at Maidenhead *en route* and sculled home afterwards to the singing of songs. Oscar Browning, however, had little to do with Parry's musical or intellectual development, and the only book, so far as we know, which he ever lent him was *The Bible in the Church*.

As O. B. grew older and stouter the difficulties of those who were his partners *à quatre mains* increased and only bold spirits attempted to extend their empire higher than F or G in the bass clef (O. B. always liked to play the treble part), for encounters around the no-man's land of middle C were apt to be painful to the intruder. When a Beethoven Overture or Symphony unfolded its beauties on his expansive soul, he swayed from his middle upwards like a Dervish inspired, singing in the rapture of his spirit and repeatedly asking his partner whether he did not think it awfully jolly. At such times his hands descended with the fortissimo of the full orchestra and with a fine disregard for meticulous accuracy or for any unwary fingers which might be dutifully trying to play the notes on the score. "For God's sake, woman, play a

wrong note," Hans von Bülow is reported to have
said to a painstaking, but dull, pupil. Such an
adjuration could never have been addressed to O. B.
As the years went by his ambitions and girth combined to make him satisfied with nothing less than
a whole piano to himself, so that his four-handed
excursions through the realms of the classics became,
on two keyboards, still more sonorous than before.

For the performance of chamber music he possessed a number of *orchestrine di camera*, familiarly
known as "obeophones," which represented the
wood-wind, or even supplemented the strings.
O. B. was very partial to taking the horn, or
oboe, part in a Divertimento, or some more formal
work, of Mozart's on one of these instruments. If
the pedalling was uneven they were apt to produce
the most amazing grunts and squeaks, and many a
young composer of to-day who wished to shock
our ears with the boldness of his timbres would
have been enraptured at the effects which not
infrequently resulted. But O. B. was not of those
who suffer from an over-refinement of musical
culture. He did not sigh after the perfect performance. He knew that *le mieux est l'ennemi du
bien*, and was content if the final cadence found
him not last amidst the throng. With very little
pressing also he would sing "Non piu andrai," or
"La vendetta" from his beloved *Figaro*, and since
there was nothing in the least high-brow about him
he would, if his audience called for it, interpret
comic songs of another kind, such as "The Baby
on the Shore," which for years was one of the
most successful things in his repertoire. Nevertheless, though he loved to assist in making music,
or even to entertain a room-full as a soloist, he
was not a stranger to modesty. He did not venture
to sing after, or even before, his friend Jenny
Lind, and when Otto Goldschmidt and Arthur

Sullivan sat down together at the piano, his stout duettist's heart resigned itself to listening with at least apparent content.

But it is unfair to write thus, for he was in reality the best type of amateur, the type who loves music and wants others to share his enjoyment of the art. With the help of Edward Dannreuther, most scholarly of pianists, he gave his Saturday evening concerts at Eton, which Dr. Hornby frowned upon (Dannreuther refers to him after Oscar Browning's dismissal as "that idiot of a parson—the head, or rather tail, of Eton"), an atmosphere of real musical distinction. Dannreuther took much pains to arrange suitable programmes and to secure rehearsals. Sometimes he thought O. B.'s suggestions too bold. He was nervous, for instance, on one occasion about the possible impression a Bach Violin and Piano Sonata might produce on the audience. But O. B. had no fears, for he knew that the less musical boys would anyhow find their way to his library, which was always thrown open on these occasions, whilst he at least would enjoy Bach, even though the particular work was in the same key as the Beethoven trio which had preceded it. He worried less than Dannreuther about avoiding in the programmes "a monotony of key and colour." Pezze, the 'cellist, A. D. Coleridge, the founder of the Bach Choir, and Le Marchant Gosselin, an Eton boy who, if he had not subsequently chosen to attain distinction as a diplomat, might have done so as a pianist, were amongst those who helped at these musical evenings—evenings which were occasionally honoured by the presence of one of the royal princesses when the Court was at Windsor.

Music was one of the many things which Oscar Browning wanted to reform at Eton. In his opinion the appointment of Dr. Hayne as Succentor and Musical Director in 1868 did little to improve things. As a boy he had reacted against "the organ-loft school" which had dominated English music since the death of Arne and brought it to a level of almost unredeemed provinciality. The Succentor and the Musical Director at Eton, O. B. considered, should be different persons. The organist could be an old-fashioned Mus. Doc., composing his anthems, his hymn tunes, his double chants. The Musical Director should be a live musician, who for choice had studied in Germany. He had talked the matter over with George Grove, and Grove had agreed with his views. So it happened that when Dr. Hayne, after four not very fruitful years, was about to leave, Grove produced the ideal candidate, and sent him down to Eton with an introduction to O. B. "All I want to do is to ensure him a favourable reception from you," Grove wrote. "I feel quite sure that he has more genius, more geniality, more tact, more power of teaching and attracting fellows, more practical gifts than any other musician I have ever met. I know that if any change in music is made at Eton, your knowledge of music and weight in the College will give you greater influence than anyone else." Luckily Sir George Grove was unaware of the inner politics of Eton, since had O. B. succeeded in securing the post for Arthur Sullivan—for it was he who was Grove's candidate—the Savoy operas would probably never have been born. In the event the place was given to a nonentity, a certain Dr. Maclean. But the incident marked the beginning of a friendship between Sullivan and O. B., which was to secure for him many free tickets for the Savoy operas, the merits of which his knowledge of Mozart, Rossini and Offenbach prevented him from exaggerating.

236

Arthur Sullivan influenced him in his curious dislike of the Royal Academy of Music and caused him to give enthusiastic support to the Royal College of Music from the moment when he was present, as a representative of Cambridge, at the meeting at Marlborough House in 1882, when the project for its establishment was formally launched. It was there that he ran across Barnby and asked him how he was getting on with music at Eton. "Oh," said Barnby, who had been there since 1875, "I am just beginning to learn what sort of a place Eton is." "And I," replied O. B., "am just beginning to forget."

VII

In those days the musical world was split asunder by the mighty genius of Wagner. Oscar Browning was never a passionate Wagnerite—a true Mozartian could hardly be that. But Dannreuther, who fought the battle for Wagner in England, secured his allegiance and his subscriptions for the Bayreuth Theatre. O. B. paid and hoped he would see or hear something for his money some day. As years went by the prospect grew more doubtful. There were rumours sometimes in the German papers that the Festival was really to be held, or that Wagner was to visit London with an opera troupe in order to raise money for his great scheme. But Dannreuther, when asked, could only give denials. There was nothing as yet, he wrote in 1874, to announce about the Bayreuth Theatre, and as for Wagner coming to London it was a ridiculous canard. "W. would as soon go to Timbuctoo." But the patience of the subscribers was at length rewarded. "Knowing that you have years ago expended vast sums on the Wagner Theatre," wrote Le Marchant Gosselin to O. B. from Berlin in March 1875, "and having been told that you mean to explore Nova Zembla in the summer of 1876, I think it only fair to warn you that the Festival is announced for the August of that year, when you will be expected to appear at Bayreuth and hear the four operas." Though a Wagnerite, Gosselin could not approve of Wagner's methods. "No means are left untried, no stone unturned, to collect the necessary means. The wretched Sultan has been made to buy ten tickets of *Patronatscheine*— on the understanding that such an outlay would go far to cement Turco-German alliance; whereupon the Khedive immediately invested in fifteen to show that he was just as good as his suzerain, if not better. All of which I think indecent and *artful*." O. B. expressed no opinion on Wagner's methods. He went as a matter of course to the first performance of the *Ring* in 1876. He tried to obtain admission to the rehearsals, for it would thus have been possible to become better acquainted with the music. But Dannreuther had assured him on a post-card that all rehearsals were strictly private. " B——" (the name is illegible, but it looks like Brahms) "wrote to Bayreuth for admission and was refused!" However, the Committee had assured Dannreuther that all his wishes about Oscar Browning securing a good seat should be carried out. And arrangements would also be made for his young friend.

It was a historic occasion. O. B. realised its significance and wrote to *The Times* to advise "English lovers of music not to neglect an opportunity of hearing the perfect execution of a work of art such as will not occur again in the present generation." The only other English people present besides himself were professional musicians or music critics. Nevertheless he found the *Ring* a little long. This North German was heavy-handed.

He button-holed you, was either an *exalté* or a bore. And during the *longueurs* which are not absent even from *Siegfried*, O. B.'s mind, one may imagine, more than once left the theatre amidst the pine trees on the hill, left Bayreuth and the contemplation of human ills as they are presented in Wagner's trilogy, to hover over the pinnacles and trees of Eton and to revolve again the injustice which he had suffered the year before. To his mother always he came nearest to revealing his inmost thoughts. And in his letter to her from Bayreuth there is only a passing reference to the *Ring*. He is revolving not the fate of Siegfried or Wotan, but of Oscar Browning. He has been talking to people about Eton, and is quite sure that his dismissal was now considered by many, and would come to be considered by more, not as a disgrace but as an honour.

Nevertheless, though he came away from Bayreuth without having been in any way hypnotised by the new art and unshaken in his belief that the appeal of music was to the intellect rather than to the emotions, he remained a supporter, if not a disciple. When Richard Wagner came to London in the spring of 1877, O. B. was among the few bidden to hear the latest message. " Will you come in on Thursday evening," Mrs. Dannreuther wrote, " to meet the *Meister*? He promises to read his new work, *Parsival*, to us at 8.30, so do not come later please." Whether the poem made any impression on him, one does not know, but when he saw the work at Bayreuth in 1883 it affected him deeply. " The second performance," he wrote, " fascinated me more than the first, and the after-taste, the recollection of both words and music, has been dwelling in my mind ever since." In later years, however, whilst Rossini, Pergolesi and of course Mozart maintained their place in his heart, Wagner, except for *Die Meistersinger*, had altogether ceased to interest him.

VIII

Even music sometimes gave an opportunity to sniff the delicious air of controversy. That he had been unsuccessful in getting Arthur Sullivan to Eton did not discourage him from organising the Cambridge vote amongst the Eton masters on behalf of Dr. Macfarren's candidature for the Professorship of Music. It was preceded by an immense deal of wire-pulling. To use a phrase of a contemporary statesman, O. B. and the party of reform wanted to see music get a square deal, and they were anxious that the new Professor should be a commanding personality. Since the production of *St. John the Baptist* musicians had come to believe that Macfarren had a message, that he might indeed be the new Purcell of our music. True, some good judges were of opinion that the young Stanford, then in the early twenties, was the long-awaited genius. But he was still too youthful to be elected Professor. In any case Macfarren was a far more suitable candidate than Garrett of St. John's, the elegance of whose services and double chants was more than counterbalanced by his " faults of temper," or than Dr. Henry Wylde. Dr. Wylde may have been a musical nonentity, though he was a prolific composer in his day, but he possessed a great deal of social influence amongst non-resident electors in Town, where his London Academy, as it was pointed out, " had been for years the fashionable resort of young, aristocratic ladies to learn piano playing under Benedict." Nowadays few young ladies have time to spare for such dull and profitless pursuits as learning the piano. Then they not only learnt, but canvassed furiously for

Dr. Wylde, who showed that he was a "vulgar fellow"—as Dr. Macfarren's supporters thought— by offering to pay the expenses of all who went down to Cambridge to vote for him. G. F. Cobb, of Trinity, who led the Macfarren party, pointed out to O. B. that the risk was "appalling" and that they mu&t "poll *all* their &trength to their uttermo&t inconvenience."

O. B. shared in the pleasure which the ele&ion of Macfarren gave to those who considered that they had made the cause of music their own. He did the same at the ele&ion of C. V. Stanford to the same position twelve years later. Stanford, however, proved not unlike what many had thought Garrett to be, and he and O. B. managed to quarrel very easily. He did that composer the compliment of considering him among his mo&t particular enemies, attributing to Stanford's influence a curious incident when a King's don of learning and blame-less life, whom O.B. had proposed for the Athenæum, was blackballed. On the top of this affront O. B. received an anonymous telegram informing him that the same measure would be dealt out to any other candidate whom he might propose. A vigorous canvass secured the ele&ion of his next candidate. The correspondence which this affair produced O. B. had handsomely bound and he used to keep it on his drawing-room table. The volume now reposes in the Brassey Memorial Library at Ha&tings, where it remains as a memento of ani-mosities that once di&turbed the London home of Pallas Athene.

This, however, is by the way. Oscar Browning was not the only don taking an intere&t in music with whom Stanford quarrelled, nor did such per-sonal disagreements prevent him from upholding the claims of the art, which has gained the reputa-tion of exciting the spirit of cantankerousness in its devotees, to a recognised place in a liberal education. Apart from the music which he made at other times, including even the sacred hours of the morning when undergraduates' pianos perforce are dumb, his Mozart Club met in his rooms regularly for years. And every Saturday night he attended the concert of the University Musical Club, where the arm-chair by the fire was reserved for him. Comfortably disposed in one of the few warm spots in that cold and repellently ugly room, he used to read his *Westminster Gazette*, then an organ flourishing in its liberalism and viridity, to the strains of Mozart and Beethoven, sometimes looking over his spectacles and the top of his paper to remark at the beginning of a Quartet or a Pianoforte Trio, " Too fast, too fast," and rarely omitting to add his own coda of " How awfully jolly," or " Very good indeed," at the end. There was nothing finnicking or hyper-sensitive or over-refined in O. B.'s attitude towards the noblest of the arts.

CHAPTER XIV

HUMANITAS

I

On a drizzling winter evening O. B. was once walking with an undergraduate through one of the narrow and draughty passages which abound in Cambridge when the sight of a piece of childhood crying on a doorstep stopped his rolling gait and he stood "hove-to" like a steamer in a choppy sea. "What is your name, my boy?" he asked, swaying uneasily, and it was long before he could get any intelligible answer. "Poor boy, he's hungry," said O. B. at length. "Let's get him something to eat." With some difficulty the boy was haled off to a cook-shop, where O. B. purchased various comestibles and had them wrapped up in newspaper. By this time he had extracted his entire family history, even down to the names of his brothers and sisters, and was lamenting that there was not more propaganda for the Navy. "Wouldn't you like to be a jolly sailor-boy, Fred?" he asked the urchin whilst engaged in buying him a pair of boots—for his own were disgraceful—a question answered by a non-committal and sheepish smile. "You know," he remarked to the undergraduate as they resumed their course (with O. B. some ten shillings the poorer), "when I walk about Cambridge, I look upon myself as a sort of knight-errant, and I nearly always find some dragon to spear—or some windmill to tilt at," he added with a laugh.

II

One of the many soft spots in his heart he kept for sailors, and for many years he took an active interest in the Cambridge Branch of the Navy League. He was never happier than when he had secured a Cambridge boy for the Royal Navy. Mr. A. B. Hyde, now gymnastic instructor at Dulwich College, relates how in his early 'teens he was fired with the ambition of going to sea, and one day went to ask Oscar Browning to help him. O. B. was enchanted and arranged for him to join the *Impregnable* at Plymouth. Mr. Hyde's reminiscences of O. B. in a nautical environment are best related in his own words : " During my naval training in the *Impregnable* I was one day being instructed by a petty officer in the art of making knots and splices. My chums and I were in a circle around the instructor, apparently much interested, when to my surprise on turning round, whom should I see but my dear old friend O. B., who had brought my brother from Cambridge as a surprise to myself and the other bluejackets from my native town, who had always had a hearty welcome at his rooms when on leave, with plenty of good cheer and singing of nautical songs by them and many a rollicking song by our host. Sometimes he played on a grand piano, at others on a harmonium. How he used to let rip on ' On the Road to Mandalay.' I can see his dear, kind, jolly old face now in my mind's eye.

" During the evening the quarter-deck was decorated with flags and an entertainment was given by the ship's company. O. B. and Commander Somerset admired the sailors' hornpipes and sand dances, etc., and at the end of the show I made my way to O. B., when the Commander shouted to me with a voice like a fog-horn : ' Boy, tell that gentleman he's to have my steam launch to go ashore in.' When we got ashore, what luxury at the Duke of Cornwall Hotel! What a contrast for your humble boots to be cleaned and for a maid to bring a cup of tea. Surely this was a dream. The next day a trip to H.M.S. *Lion* in a shore boat which was kept waiting so long that the man demanded £3. However, O. B. didn't mind so long as he saw the other Cantabs on board, and incidentally dined with the Commander, who also had all hands on deck for a march past and after that a gymnastic display.

" A few weeks after this we had summer leave and we were all invited to O. B.'s rooms at St. James's Street. He took us to see a play called *Flying Colours*, and left orders with his landlady to provide a feed for us on our return. She made a large roly-poly jam pudding. We called this a steerage hammock, and O. B. simply writhed with laughter. After the feed O. B. saw us all off at Liverpool Street Station *en route* for Cambridge. This was quite a hobby of O. B.'s when in London. He would tackle a group of lads, give them a ' blow-out,' as he called it, and then vanish like a fairy godfather.

" When at Plymouth a reverend gentleman, an old King's man, wrote to me to come to tea every Sunday I was ashore, and sent me on board with a bundle of food, such as cakes and oranges. Also on Thursdays another King's man in rather a small way (his people kept a sweet-shop) wrote to me to say that O. B. had arranged for me to have tea at his place and a half-crown to be given me for pocket-money. By the way, the King's man at the shop told me that O. B. had paid a lot for his education, as his people were hard up."

Oscar Browning corresponded with Mr. Hyde, and later with Mr. Hyde's children, and followed his fortunes and those of his family with unabated interest, till the very end of his life.

> " As I sit, before me stand,
> Exile in a foreign land,
> Faces which recall to me
> Days of mirth and jollity. . . ."

Thus begin some verses he sent him, inspired by a photograph of Mr. Hyde with his wife and children, of Mr. Hyde,

> " Who for forty years on end
> Has been, and is, my dearest friend."

But it was not all O. B.'s protégés who had the sterling qualities of Mr. A. B. Hyde.

III

" People used to say that O. B. took up with young men either because it flattered his vanity to detect unsuspected genius—the same sort of pleasure as some people get in backing an outsider— or because their youth and good looks attracted him. But you can't explain him on such simple egotistical grounds." It was a friend and one-time colleague who was speaking. " I remember, for instance, going to see him in his rooms one evening when he had just returned from Paris, and there on the sofa in his dining-room reposed a shabbily dressed and apparently exhausted youth. He was a mere skeleton, his cheeks were cavernous and sallow, his teeth were black, and he did not appear to have the full use of his limbs. Altogether he was a terrible-looking object. I went in and talked to O. B., who was in his inner room. As I was leaving I asked him who his visitor was. ' Oh,' he said, ' that's Arthur ' (or some other Christian name). ' He's been a stable boy at Chantilly and was shamefully misused. They starved him to get his weight down and then beat him because he lost his strength. Finally, they threw him out. I found him destitute in Paris, and the only thing I could do was to bring him back with me. He's a dear boy really and most high-minded.' That was a quality, by the way, which O. B. usually discovered in the youths he took up with. And then he asked me if I knew anyone who could give the boy a job. That sort of incident can't be squared with any of the explanations many people give of O. B.'s motives in things of this kind. There was nothing about it that could possibly bring him any kudos, and what inspired him, I think, was a sort of Franciscan feeling for humanity at large. It embraced all classes, from emperors to clowns, and he talked just as freely about his friendships with the one as with the other. Only people remembered the royalties and forgot the rest."

His charges multiplied, as was to be expected. " This evening I received the visits of several boys who are protégés of mine," he writes to his mother during a busy Lent term, " a young blacksmith, a young printer and a young instrument maker. The last plays the flute very well for his age." After the death of Henry Bradshaw, which gave him a great shock—not lessened by the fact that as O. B. was on his way to morning Chapel the gyp met him and told him that he had just found Mr. Bradshaw dead at his table, and O. B. had therefore gone back with the College servant to discover that it was as the gyp had said—O. B. never liked being alone in his rooms at night, when if he were seized by sudden illness it might be impossible to summon help. From that time on he always had a personal servant who slept in his rooms. And like the Austrian nobles of the eighteenth century, he valued their services the more if they could play a musical instrument.

" I recall," says another Fellow of King's, " how years ago when I was an undergraduate I had to see O. B. one afternoon at about tea-time. He had been playing some game, tennis probably, for he liked its historical associations, and I found him just emerged from his bath, wrapped in an enormous towel and looking more like a Roman emperor than ever. There were two youths in the room— one was giving him tea, which he was drinking out of the saucer, a universal fashion in Russia, he assured me, the other was playing the violin. O. B. received me without the least embarrassment, and continued his conversation whilst the one youth dried him and the other played—extremely badly, it appeared to me. He told me that afternoon that he had once had his horoscope cast, and that he had been born when Saturn was in Capricorn. Capricorn was a propitious influence, but Saturn was, of course, a depressing one. The result was that when he had a bad time he knew Saturn was ' having a go at him, and when fortune smiled he said : ' Good old Capricorn.' There was something humorous but charming in seeing a man of a certain age and more than a certain stoutness sitting in his arm-chair, wrapped in a towel, and discoursing with apparently complete gravity to me on the influence of the stars in their courses on his private affairs, whilst one servant drew harsh strains from the fiddle and the other pummelled his back with the towel."

Nothing delighted O. B. more than to discover musical talent in anyone around him, and in at least one case he defrayed the expenses of education at the Royal College of Music for a young man who had been his personal servant. For such the claims of music occasionally conflicted with more prosaic duties, and his anger overflowed on one occasion when he returned to his chambers in St. James's Street and found that his valet, instead of preparing tea for two as he had been bidden, was so busy composing that the debris of lunch remained still on the table. But the storm was soon over, and whilst the crestfallen young genius was out of the room, he took up the manuscript from the side table and offered it to the critical approval of his visitor, observing that Harry was really a very remarkable boy.

Secretarial duties were another means of assisting talent to overcome the disabilities of poverty. "I feel sure," he says, "that I was made to have a number of clerks under me. I can imagine myself in a room dictating to five at once. My regular secretary (Willie Thomas) comes from 8.30 to ten and does all kinds of things for me. Another youth whom I have engaged to help me in arranging the Auckland papers arrives at ten and works till two, and again from five to seven. I pay him ten shillings a week, but of course he is only retained for a special service. Besides this, I have discovered a clever young shorthand writer whom I have engaged to come from 7.30 till 9.30 every evening for three shillings a week. I can never write myself after dinner, but I think that I might be able to dictate." At another time he is teaching German to a young man in the University Library, or again he is learning Russian from a youthful barber, and is astonished when the Slav, whom he provides with tea, also requires a money payment.

IV

He was naturally the prey of rogues, and generally an easy prey, for he used to say that he derived a certain spiritual satisfaction from the knowledge that he was being taken in. But he bore no ill-will to those whom Providence chose to be the agents in this matter, though sometimes there was an underlying malice in the way he granted their petitions. Thus to the young man who went to him and complained that he was stranded and begged for the loan of a pound to pay his ticket to Liverpool, where he asserted that he lived, O. B. was more than sympathetic. He listened to his story, then took him to the station, bought his ticket and did not leave him till the train for Liverpool steamed out of the station. "Yet," said O. B. in recounting this incident afterwards, "such are the unaccountable workings of the human mind that the expression on his face showed rather disgust than gratitude." Of this class, the only one whom he considered to have really abused his good-nature was the undergraduate of his own College, to whom, as the result of a tale of woe, he lent £5, which the worthless young man proceeded to spend that same night at the Empire.

V

His humanity was not confined to the youthful male. When there was any possibility of injustice being done he sacrificed his own time and convenience without a thought. Thus he writes to his mother in June 1885 : " Last Monday morning my barber told me that some Italians who had been going about singing had got into a terrible mess through using knives. I had felt much interested in them when I saw them about the place, and I hurried off to the police court, knowing that there would be no one to interpret and that they would require assistance. It is lucky that I went. One man was completely innocent, and two of the unfortunate prisoners had been knocked about and half killed while in the custody of the police, when they were handcuffed and not able to defend themselves. There were four poor women in terrible distress with no one to look after them. The prisoners were remanded for a week, and when they were being driven away the mob surrounded the fly and nearly lynched them. We got the women out by a back door. One undergraduate got inside and another on the box whilst I protected them from the mob. There is a very wealthy Russian family living at Audley End. We asked them to take them in and give them a room over their stables. They have been very comfortable there. The case comes up again on Monday. I shall do all I can to get the innocent man off and the other two punished as leniently as possible, for there was great provocation. This had occupied me a good deal."

VI

If Oscar Browning considered himself a knight-errant in Cambridge, in the village of Barton, which lies some two or three miles outside the town, he looked upon himself in the light of the squire. For King's has, or had, estates there, and O. B., although he had never had any connection with the bursarial duties of the College, held decided views about the duties of the Fellows towards those resident upon the College properties. He used to tricycle there frequently, and got to know most of the villagers. Some twenty odd years ago, when an effort was made to organise such social work on the College estates, he put his views on record. " The first object is to cultivate friendly relations of a private nature between the inhabitants of the village and the College, so that the villagers may feel that the College knows about them and cares for them and that the College may feel the same. Considering the circumstances of a college, it is best to begin with the young men and boys, those who have left school and gone to work, which I am sorry to say they do at the early age of twelve. A complete list should be drawn up of all these, and care should be taken that they should all be known in a quiet, unobtrusive way by various members of the College. It would then be found out who are the best of them and what they are fit for. Acquaintance with the young men would lead to acquaintance with the families, which should be utilised but not pushed to the degree of interference, as of almsgiving. Members of the College cycling through the village would naturally speak to those whom they knew, or go and see them at work. The lads could be invited to tea and made friends of. This would be the first step.

" We might then proceed in the summer to invite people from the village to visit Cambridge and give them lunch or tea in Hall. Many of them are, I daresay, imperfectly acquainted with the University. Also, as in Germany and Switzerland, the schoolmaster might bring the children over to see the place. I ought to have said that things should be done, if possible, through the schoolmaster with the approval of the clergyman. He should be made a friend of and encouraged to come in and see us and made generally interested in the University." He then goes on to outline in detail what should be done on the physical side, and also on the intellectual. Cricket, football and swimming clubs, village reading rooms, village orchestras, lectures, the encouragement of home industries, as he had seen done already in one or two Cambridgeshire villages —these would help to counteract the monotony of village life as it existed in rural England. And finally, for one must always remember the possibility, " if a genius were to rise up in any of our villages (some mute, inglorious Milton), we might give him a chance."

To allow everyone a chance for self-expression, that was the basis of his radical creed. A study of village graffiti showed that under the bucolic surface of country life there ran a vein of frankness and indeed of coarseness which had an Elizabethan flavour. In one of the most racy and obscene of these writings he found such a power over words that he translated them into Greek iambics, and when in the vein he would declaim both original and translation. They went to show also that in social environment very different from any to which he had been accustomed there were the same problems of ethics to make the social reformer pause and think. To O. B. morality was based on love. Assuredly he would not have subscribed to the motto of the Abbé Barthélemy, " Aimez et faites ce que vous plaira," though this is only a paradoxical paraphrase of the Gentile Apostle's classification of the Christian virtues. But time brought in its train for O. B. an un-Pauline tolerance of human weaknesses, and if the middle-aged don of sixty was not less interested in those questions of morals which had stirred the zeal of the young schoolmaster, he came to regard such problems with greater detachment, and more perhaps in the spirit of the inquirer and less in that of the reformer.

VII

One could do good in many ways, but the greatest and best was by striving to enthrone wisdom as arbiter in human affairs. Oscar Browning the philosopher wished only to create the atmosphere in which the " statesman-mind " could develop, and was indifferent which party his pupils, or the young men who came under his influence, embraced. The most distinguished of them, Mr. Gerald Balfour, Sir Austen Chamberlain (who though at Trinity had been a member of his Political Society), Lord Curzon, Alfred Lyttelton, became members of the Conservative Party.

But Oscar Browning the citizen was a lifelong Liberal. More indeed, for he belonged to that left wing of the Party which, led by John Morley, went to the root of things and gloried in the name of Radical. Everything combined to make him a mid-Victorian extremist. The teaching of John Stuart Mill, his friendship with those advanced thinkers of the time, George Eliot and Frederic Harrison, his belief in human nature, his sympathy with the under-dog, his antipathy to those in authority at Eton and King's—doubtless all these things were factors in determining his views. The Radical too, though he might suffer socially for his creed, derived the comfort of spiritual pride from the reflection that he was guided by Principle where others were led by Prejudice. To a young and unknown correspondent, who was about to embrace a political career and was doubtful whether he had been born a little Liberal or a little Conservative, O. B. was able to explain the true beauty of Radical-ism. " I have been a Radical all my life and I have found that Radicals are almost uniformly guided by principle, much more so than Tories, partly because, having to attack in many cases existing institutions, they have to consider what in these institutions is vital and eventual and what is merely transitory and unimportant, whereas Tories uphold old institutions simply because they are old and very often surrender the most important substance in order to grasp the shadow. Of course a Radical is a democrat. He does not therefore consider the Demos as a monster at all, but as having a complete right to manage its own affairs. A democratic statesman will try to ascertain popular sentiment quite as much as to guide it—certainly in most cases he will be led by it. We are not afraid of the Demos; if we were we should not be Radicals but Tories." But the young man should not decide hastily. He should read Sydney Buxton's *Political Questions of the Day*; O. B.'s own *Modern England* might be useful. It was more difficult to arrive at a decision by the study of recent legislation. " If you will sound your own heart and feelings," he added, " and ascertain on which side your strongest sympathies lie and on which you are prepared to throw your influence, you will, I think, arrive at a better conclusion than in any other way." Could anything be further from the spirit of the doctrinaire ?

His first encounter with the Demos which he trusted was not particularly encouraging. When he appeared at the hustings in favour of Roger Eykyn, who stood as Liberal candidate for the Borough of Windsor in the election of 1868, his speech was accompanied by howls from the Tory candidate's supporters of " Pay your butcher's bills," presumably a plausible cry to use against an Eton master. It was followed by interviews with both Provost and Head Master, who professed astonishment that an Eton master should take an active part in an election. To the one O. B. pointed out that his own Lodge was plastered with Conservative posters (" Put up by my daughters in play," said the Provost irritably) and that he considered it his duty to counteract such propaganda as far as lay in his power, whilst to the Head Master he observed that his friend, Dr. Ridding of Winchester, had not only marched through that city in a procession of Liberals, but that the procession had been headed by a brass band. Roger Eykyn got in and a friendship sprang up between them which led to Oscar Browning making the acquaintance of many Liberal politicians and to the sharpening of his own political ambitions.

When he left Eton nothing except the want of means stood in the way of these being realised, and soon after his return to Cambridge we find him discussing the idea of his standing for Parliament with Henry Fawcett, the leading Liberal don in the University, whose triumph over blindness forms one of the romances of the Victorian era. On the conditions which he then laid down—that he should not have to pay his election expenses—he contested Norwood in 1887, East Worcestershire in 1892, and one of the Liverpool divisions in 1895. All were forlorn hopes and in no case did he come near success. But his campaign at Birmingham, in its avoidance of personalities and its concentration upon principles, made some impression upon that city, then under the domination of Joseph Chamberlain, in spite of the fact that O. B. was neither a teetotaler nor a Sunday school teacher, both essential qualifications for a Birmingham Liberal. " It may be just of passing interest to know," writes a correspondent, " that some thirty-five years ago, as a young many in Birmingham, I was deeply impressed by Mr. Oscar Browning, who came there as Parliamentary candidate, opposing Mr. Austen Chamberlain at a time when party feelings were very strong. It was an extraordinary candidature, for Mr. Chamberlain had only recently been a pupil of Mr. Browning's at Cambridge, and his public references to his erstwhile scholar were peculiarly felicitous and kindly. His meetings were most truly educational, and I remember how I used to think that instead of taking part in a heated election campaign, I was privileged to listen to a series of instructive lectures from an eminent scholar and gentleman. I never saw him again, but in those few days he influenced me in a way that few public men have done."

In a less Conservative country a seat might have been found for him in the Upper House, where as a Senator he could have placed his gifts as a political philosopher at the service of the people. He was too independent ever to have made a good Party man. His views were full of antinomies. He believed in the House of Lords as a " fine democratic instrument." " A Home Ruler before Gladstone," he disapproved in the 'eighties of his leader's South African policy and made jingo speeches; he was a Pro-Boer in 1900 and kept Kruger's photograph on his mantelpiece, yet five years later he could feel no enthusiasm for Free Trade nor indignation at " Chinese slavery." A Liberal who believed that the Tsarist Government was at least better than any probable substitute—the attitude of the Liberal papers on this subject " made him sick "—an imperialist who believed in Cromer's work in Egypt and Curzon's in India, Oscar Browning held opinions which were not those of a sound party politician. So to prevent further trouble, Liberal Head-quarters employed him to lead forlorn hopes. The most notable of these would have been his standing against Joseph Chamberlain in 1895, but for once O. B.'s courage, or his energy, failed him, and he refused, which was the more remarkable because he had transferred to Joseph Chamberlain those deep-seated animosities which he had once felt for Dizzy. Afterwards he regretted having missed so glorious and hopeless a battle, and explained it by his having acted on reflection instead of impulse.

And naturally enough the undergraduates laughed, and their laughter pleased both themselves and

O. B. " ' What I think about it is this. We must consider the poor, the way they are housed; the luxury of the upper classes and well-to-do is disgusting—disgusting, I repeat.' (And here he orders one of his Arab boys to bring a little Cyprus wine, which he drinks himself but does not offer one a glass. He addresses the boy in Arabic, for it is one of the languages which he speaks fluently.) ' I am a Radical almost—simplicity of existence is all I plead for.' " Thus the Osc=r Br=wn=ng of myth spoke to an anonymous Robert Ross, then the representative of the *Gadfly*, one of the many Cambridge mirrors of " morals, men and matters " which time has smashed.

Above all things, though a Radical, he was proud of his country. He was no pessimist, not even in the difficult time after the war. The wealthy classes perhaps lived too much for pleasure, but what else could one expect with the tone set by Eton to its youth ? His robust faith is shown in the message which he penned in the first year of the present reign : " An Englishman has good reason to be proud of his country, and of the Empire which it rules, in the Coronation year. No other portion of the world is so happy, none is so free, none so prosperous. There is indeed a danger that we may rest upon our laurels and forget the exertions which won them. There are signs of an exaggerated devotion to sport, of a tendency to enjoy what we have gained instead of extending our conquests. But if this is to be found in the wealthy and governing classes, the heart of the democracy is sound and the energy of the people unabated. Above all we have a King who sets us the best example and a Queen who supports him in every good work. He not only bids England to wake up, but he exhibits for our instruction an active life and a self-sacrificing devo-

tion to duty. His reign will probably be long, and
there is no fear that during it and during that of his
son, whom he brings up after his own model, the
highest standard of the strenuous life which he sets
before his subjects will be in any way lowered or
impaired." O. B., as I have already remarked,
had a Johnsonian respect for the Throne.

CHAPTER XV

I

THE century drew to its end and O. B.'s liaison with fame stood on its old unsatisfactory footing. He had given no work to the world to regularise the union. The book, the great book, had never been written, and his claims as a historian consequently lacked an academic foundation. Yet his pen had not been idle. Besides the "money-grubbing" primers, which had annoyed his mother, he had edited despatches and political memoranda, published histories of mediæval Italy, produced a *Life of George Eliot*. He had written too an introduction to a book on his own subject of political science by a certain American Professor of the name of Woodrow Wilson. And he felt himself every year "getting more and more of a man of letters." If only he had the time, if only his health permitted him to spend the vacations in Cambridge instead of driving him to Italy, to Switzerland, or to the Riviera, he would have been in a better position to produce something which would make his name live. In the meantime enemies could scoff at a reputation which seemed to repose on its own idiosyncrasies, and even friends at the mention of his name could smile and say "Dear O. B." One may suspect that Oscar Browning never found his true medium in the broad fields of authorship. The *métier* of professional historian was unsuited to his temperament. He had little

260

inclination for what is called original research, and his historical books embodied none of that sort of knowledge which comes from studying and collating the documents which are the dry bones of history. Thus when he applied for the degree of Litt.D. it was refused him on these grounds. At the same time his plain and austere style—his High Roman style, as Matthew Arnold once called it—lacked the warmth, the glow of sentiment which attracts the wider public and wins the respect of publishers. It had, at its best, the virtues of *justesse, facilité* and *clarté*, which Mme. du Deffand postulated as three of the essential qualities of good prose. But it lacked the warmth, the *chaleur*, that is created by the inspiration of a congenial theme. Even when writing about himself he did not allow his pen the time, or his personality the freedom, for true self-expression. Those who have read his *Memories of Sixty Years*—which O. B. used to describe as a standard work on education— and knew the original, are aware how inadequate a portrait it contains. There were friends who urged him to explore the wider questions of ethics and morals in which he took so keen an interest. John Addington Symonds wished that he would turn his attention to that particular branch of ethics which he himself had investigated. A year or two before his death Symonds wrote explaining that he had written two treatises, which he had " diffused very sparely and cautiously," and that it was of some importance to him to know into how many persons' hands they had fallen. " I am sure," he remarked, " you could add a great amount of information and critical matter. I wish you would write this sort of stuff." One very important point, for instance, on which O. B.'s opinion would be valuable was whether the study of the classics by boys in the impressionable years of their adolescence was

261

harmful. The views of the ancient world on the question of homosexuality were so different from those held in the England of the Victorian era. Yet to regard the phenomenon as pathological was beset with difficulties. Assuredly much more light, as Symonds observed, was required on all these matters. But O. B. did not yield to Symonds's persuasiveness, and though he was always ready to discuss such questions with a strange mixture of pagan enthusiasm and moral fervour, he refrained from writing about them.

Had he possessed more detachment, had he been more of an artist and less of a moralist and teacher, one likes to imagine that he might in his own way have produced another such epic of intellectual youth as Walter Pater, who during the years that *Marius the Epicurean* was conceived and written was on terms of considerable intimacy with O. B. In the "pure and disinterested friendship of schoolmates," which is the central event of Marius's adolescence, one can detect more than traces of O. B.'s philosophy, and maybe of his influence. It was, however, not decreed that O. B. should trace the flowering of the human soul, that his imagination should create a world where all the problems that beset his craft as master of novices were resolved in the ideal regions of art. There were so many living Mariuses, so many young men faced with difficulties no different from his, and what weaving of words could compare with the delight of working on the living clay?

II

Since he was driven neither by a passionate love for literature nor by the desire to explore the past in the spirit which historians had borrowed from the scientists, his reputation was supported by no corresponding position of dignity in the University. On the death of Seeley, Lord Rosebery gave the Regius Professorship to Lord Acton, and O. B.'s congratulations to the Premier on his " courageous appointment " were as generously acknowledged. It was still more evident that the fact of being one who had done much to develop the History School in Cambridge was no claim to the Professorship when Mr. Arthur Balfour in 1905 had to go to Trinity College, Dublin, to find a successor to Lord Acton. O. B. had hoped it would be otherwise. He had asked Campbell-Bannerman whether he would be wise to bring his claims to the Premier's notice, and Campbell-Bannerman had replied that, if he were Prime Minister, such a proceeding would be fatal to the person adopting it. O. B. welcomed Professor Bury none the less cordially, and was a regular attendant at his professorial lectures on the intricate subject of Balkan politics ten centuries go.

Sometimes rumour, silent in Cambridge, was busy elsewhere. In 1902 he took the Lent Term off and went on a visit to Lord Curzon in India, then in the most brilliant period of his Viceroyalty. He had not been there a month when there was a report, which even reached the London papers, that the post of Minister of Education to the Government of India was to be made for him. It was flattering and opened up romantic possibilities. To exchange Cambridge for India, to set his hand to one of the greatest problems which the present age has to face, the education of the East by the methods of the West, all this would not have been too heavy a task for his sixty-five years. Of course there was nothing in the rumour. He knew that. Nevertheless Lord Curzon thought it worth while to write specially about it. " My dear O. B.," he said, " I don't know who started that hare about your being Education Minister. Of course, as you know, we are not going to have such a man."

III

Thus, as he moved towards old age, no prizes came to cheer his lot and he remained a Fellow of King's, dependent on the good-will of the other Fellows for continuing to hold office in the College. With seeing the prizes fall to others O. B. could put up; he could not endure quietly the obstinacy that refused to realise the importance and excellence of the History School of King's in which he was the head. The College pampered the classical scholars, it ignored the historians. King's was well known outside its own walls as *par excellence* the Historical College of the University. Yet after a year of " exceptional brilliancy " there was not a single Historical student in King's who was a foundation scholar. The thing was a scandal, and he said so in a circular letter to the other Fellows. " I am not in favour," this concluded, " of extravagant rewards for academical successes. I am of opinion that the classical students of the College suffer from the Danaë shower of gold which too often corrupts their virtue. But this disregard of the claims of Historical students transcends all decency and is tainted with gross injustice."

This was in 1904. In 1905 the Provost, Austen-Leigh, died, and the fact that Oscar Browning, notwithstanding his seniority, was never even considered as *papabile* at the election of his successor, showed plainly enough that he had no party amongst the Fellows. And he did not command very much good-will. For one of the first duties that fell to the new Provost, Dr. M. R. James, who tried to make things as easy as he could for O. B., was to tell him that the Council had only reappointed

him to his post of History Tutor for three years—
the usual term being seven—and that at the end of
that period, since he would then be over seventy,
an age at which the Council considered it was time
to give way to younger men, he would probably
be superannuated. O. B. was deeply shocked at
this news, which he regarded as an intrigue of his
enemies to get rid of him. He had never been
stronger, never felt more vigorous. The King's
History School was known all over the Kingdom.
At that moment boys in all the great schools were
looking forward to entering it, were working with
that end in view. The College ought to be proud
of it, instead of taking a step that would weaken its
efficiency, or even endanger its existence. If he
ceased to be head, who would succeed him ? He
looked round and could see no one. All his old
pupils, thanks to his training, were absorbed in
their own pursuits. Obviously the real interests
of the College lay in keeping him head of the school
as long as possible. These and other points he
exposed in a letter to the Provost. " The proper
course, in his opinion, for the College to take,"
he wrote, " is to reappoint me for the full term of
seven years, giving me to understand at the same
time that I am getting on in years and that if my
power of doing work properly fails I ought to
resign."

Over the controversies of those years one need
not linger. O. B. thought that the Council of the
College, from the moment that it had put a term to
his tenure of office, was doing everything in its
power to weaken his authority. He fought every
point, was as always indefatigable in exposing the
errors that he saw around him, errors which, he
believed, had sprung from the jealousy that follows
upon success. The classical and mathematical dons
were jealous of history. Trinity and the other

Colleges were jealous of King's. That was why Trinity had refused to continue the Inter-Collegiate May Examination, in which a King's man had been top in 1904. True, O. B. had given him 100 per cent. for his Essay, but its merits deserved no less. He had read it to a Leeds Professor, who had said that Robert Louis Stevenson might have written it—if he had been given six weeks to do it in. And this brilliant young King's-man had done it in three hours !

" All I can see clearly," he writes to a colleague on another occasion round about this time, " is that the Council has sacrificed the vital interests of the College because I am supposed to be rather a difficult person to argue with. Where did you ever find a man with strong convictions and character who was not difficult to argue with, and what is to become of an institution which is administered by weaklings ? I find you a difficult person to argue with, because you so often come to talk over matters at an inconvenient time, and when I begin to state my case you look at your watch and run away. How could I have built up the History School here, held countless communications with undergraduates, founded the Day Training College and carried it to its present state of efficiency if I had been a hopeless man to get on with. . . . Do you really prefer discussing matters with R., who has earned the contempt of undergraduates by climbing up their staircases and asking them if they liked my lectures ? "

IV

Amidst these gathering clouds O. B. found solace during the vacations—though his travels during these years took him as far afield as Russia and South Africa—at Bexhill. There in a " vulgar little

house " he lived almoſt next door to his unmarried
siſter, and enjoyed once again after many years'
interval the pleasure of having a home of his own.
Bexhill, then in its callow youth, at once laid its
spell on his ardent spirit.   It had the moſt bracing
air, the moſt sunshine of any town in England.
The music at the Kursaal was delightful, the bathing
everything that could be desired.   The local papers
printed his letters with three head-lines and called
him " Professor."   He gave leĉtures himself and
presided at the leĉtures of others.   He was the moſt
important person in Bexhill.   And he was popular
everywhere except on the golf links.   For he played
that game without moral earneſtness and at the
same time with solemn deliberation that was often
intensified by conversation with the caddy ; his red
coat and cap (of the St. Andrew's Club, as he was
fond of explaining) set off by enormous white
sand-shoes, soon became a familiar danger signal
to all those following him.   A danger signal, since
he was true to himself in never giving way unless
obliged, and when it came to bandying repartee
there were few who scored off this elderly and
benevolent figure.   At Bexhill he could forget
Cambridge and the dons who wanted to get rid of
him, he could begin work at six-thirty in the
morning and continue till luncheon time free from
interruption, he could enjoy the society of his
friends who came to ſtay, and at his siſter's he
could find an agreeable contraſt to his own bachelor
eſtablishment, where his housekeeper's autocracy
was unqueſtioned so long as she gave him " a good
dinner every night and a specially good one on
Sundays."   The Sunday evening cold supper O. B.
held in utter horror.   And that belief in himself
which was the mark of his genius embraced the
whole of the dull and ugly little town, from the
livid sea, the pebbly beach and the respeĉtable

Esplanade to the yellow plush coverings on his drawing-room chairs—the suite having been bought *en bloc* from the local furniture dealer—and imbued them with the romantic qualities that had adorned everything with which he had been connected during his whole adult life.

Yet he could not always forget, and often as he sat in his beach hut " Tilsit "—so called from the floating pavilion on the Memel in which Napoleon had signed his treaty with Alexander of Russia— he suffered the old torture of unrealised hopes and ambitions, emotions which prose was inadequate to express :

> " The tide is out, the rocks are bare,
>   The beach is lone and lorn,
> And in my heart a cankering care,
>   And all my life outworn."

And again :

> " Closed are the windows of the hut
> And every aperture is shut,
> Save where the Cabin's open door
> Surveys the ocean's restless roar.
> Closed are the windows of my heart
> To thought and fancy, love and art,
> And still the door of life gapes wide
> To stormy passion's restless tide."

These Byronic effusions he dashed off to his friends, often to lady friends, for they were more sympathetic and appreciated their literary quality with finer judgment.

He was not always in such dark moods. His " Seaside Musings by our Own Poet," sent daily one long vacation on picture post-cards to a con- valescing undergraduate who wanted cheering up, were in a lighter vein :

> " Everything is calm and placid,
> But the little busy ants,

Eager to supply their wants,
Creep o'er cake and bread-and-butter,
And never heed the curse you utter.
Then they seek your ankles bare,
Penetrate the clothes you wear;
There the lively little things
Flutter their transparent wings
And while everything is placid
Gently drop their formic acid."

Even tragic things then had something of the comic spirit :

" Darling little Freddy's dead,
The sea has closed above his head,
He will come back no more.
His tiny little wooden spade,
And the unlovely hole he made,
Are left upon the shore.
Alas ! "

Or in his arm-chair after dinner, when he had no one with whom to play duets or whist, which he preferred to auction bridge—" a game for stock-brokers "—it passed the time to smile at himself :

" Others, whene'er they read a book,
Or on the face of nature look,
Of knowledge standing on the brink
To gain a deeper insight, think.
But I, more wisely, when I find
Things somewhat arduous for my mind,
Reclining, all voluptuous, share
The comforts of an easy-chair,
Into my inner nature slink,
And, when I should be thinking, blink."

V

And above all there was the spiritual comfort which comes from trust and belief in a higher power. Oscar Browning in his own way was a deeply religious man, one of those men to whom all religions, as being the strivings of the race towards the ideal, had a deep and abiding appeal. Sir Atul Chatterjee, who showed him the temples at Benares, has remarked on the reverential spirit, rare in a European, with which he approached those holy places of Hindoism. For Islam, in its contempt of death and its belief in prayer, he had a profound respect; the sight of a Beduin saying his prayers on the desert sand filled him, as he said, with a holy awe. The rites and ceremonies of the Roman Church stirred his imagination no less than " the awfulness of Jehovah." His faith indeed, though all his life he was a regular communicant of the Church of England, transcended creeds and continents. Even the heroes of history became circled with an aureole, and he used to declare, with the utmost solemnity and in the gravest tones, that where others took Jesus Christ for their guide in the daily difficulties of life, he, when in doubt whether he were following the path of right, would ask himself what Napoleon would have done under such circumstances as were perplexing him at the moment. Yet that he found a humanity in Christianity which other subtler or simpler religions lack can be seen in his religious verses.

These, for instance, have caught the very breath of Catholic devotion. They might have been written by a Catholic child, or a Catholic saint :

> " A Hunter went a-hunting,
>   From Heaven's Holy Throne.
> What met him as he hunted ?
>   A maiden all alone.
>
> The Hunter, him I sing of,
>   Is known to endless fame.
> There went with Him an Angel,
>   And Gabriel was his name.
>
> The Angel blew his clarion,
>   Which sounded o'er the place :
> ' Hail to Thee, Maid Maria,
>   For Thou art full of grace.

' Hail to Thee, Maid Maria,
    Thou Virgin pure and mild,
Thy blessed womb shall bear Thee
    A little tiny child.

' Thy blessed womb shall bear Thee
    A Child of wondrous birth,
Shall hold in His dominion
    The Heaven and the Earth.'

Maria, pure and lowly,
    Sank down upon her knee.
She said : ' Lord God in Heaven,
    Thy will be done in me.

' Thy will be done in me, Lord,
    No sorrow, pain or smart.'
Thus Jesus Christ was kindled
    Beneath her Virgin heart."

Yet these verses date from 1906, from about the time when through the agency of Mr. Daniel Mayer, still a well-known figure in the concert-world, he became converted to Christian Science. It happened in the strangely fortuitous way by which momentous events are often brought to pass. He met Mr. Mayer in the train to Bexhill and, in answer to Mr. Mayer's conventional " How are you ? " remarked that he was worried. Mr. Mayer observed that since he had become a Christian Scientist he had known no worry, and O. B. listened with delighted interest to his talk about this new and wonder-working religion. On the next day, a Sunday, O. B. went to the service which Mr. Mayer was in the habit of holding at his house in Bexhill. From that time he became a regular attendant at the services of the Churches of Christ Scientist, and he made the Rev. Mary G. Baker Eddy's *Science and Health with a Key to the Scriptures* his bedside book. He loved the services, which, unlike Matins, " never bored him," he approved of the employment of women as readers, and particularly enjoyed the five minutes which is allowed during the service for private

meditation. There was indeed something profoundly impressive in the way that O. B., during
that period, would close his eyes and with bowed
head indulge in his characteristic gesture of slowly
inflating his cheeks and then of gently blowing
through his half-parted lips, like an elderly cherub,
till his breath failed him.

Though he presided at lectures on Christian
Science, though he wrote and talked about it in
terms of the most glowing enthusiasm, he was not,
one may imagine, an orthodox member of that
sect. In his opinion Christian Science came not to
supplant but to fulfil, and its practice was in no
way inconsistent with membership of the Church
of England, nor with the service of medicine. He
continued to be a communicant and to call in
doctors when he was sick, without considering
that in so doing he was less good a Christian
Scientist. Indeed his belief was justified in the
most striking way, by nothing less than a miraculous
cure from death when his life had been given up
by the doctors. He was suffering from double
pneumonia, a complaint which at the age of
seventy-two one imagines is usually fatal. It had
been complicated in his case by having been
preceded by bronchitis. One evening the illness
was at its climax, and from the extravagant way in
which the nurse shovelled coals on the fire he
realised that he was not expected to live through
the night. He turned his face to the wall, and after
reviewing his past life, which his *daimon* in that
extreme hour whispered to him was good, looked
into the next world, derived joy from the reflection
that he would awake in the morning in the presence
of his mother, and repeated continually, " God is
Love." He did awake in the morning—but in a
profuse perspiration and with the fever gone. It
was something very like a miracle, and he had been

cured by Christian Science. The only disadvantage was " that he would have the trouble of dying all over again." But his illness marked the term of his Cambridge career.

V

This, however, is to anticipate. For he was never more active than in those last years at Cambridge. The Training College was always growing, as was too the interference of the Board of Education on the one hand and that of the Governing Body the Teachers' Training Syndicate on the other. Both had to be fought if he meant to have his own way, which was the right way. The necessity of this made less distasteful the thought of giving up his history work in King's, for he would then have more time to devote to his beloved College, which he had promised his not less beloved friend, Henry Sidgwick, that he would never desert, a promise which the force of circumstance was to prevent him from keeping.

The longer he lived and the more he saw of the world, the more interesting he found it. His visit to South Africa in 1905 had strengthened his optimism in the future of the white race in that continent, as Johannesburg had strengthened his " dislike of money." He had too for the first time learnt to love flowers in the gardens of Cape Town. At St. Helena Napoleon had appeared more of a hero than ever, our treatment of him more despicable. The great Liberal victory at the end of that year was another and more promising 1868, and the fact that the new Government showed no inclination to recognise his lifelong services to Liberalism did not diminish his zeal for the cause, as every morning after breakfast he read the *Daily News* and smoked his Boer calabash. The world was getting better and better and reason at last was triumphing over prejudice.

One of the forces that would mould the new Europe was Esperanto. He studied it, his fortieth language, and took part in the Esperanto Congress held at Cambridge in August 1907, playing the part of Pickwick in an Esperanto version of the Trial Scene at the New Theatre, in which, however, his silent rôle offered him no opportunity of showing his proficiency in the tongue of Dr. Zamenhof's invention. Another reason for optimism was the foreign policy of Sir Edward Grey and the *rapprochement* with Russia. O. B. firmly believed that the Tsarist Government was better than any possible alternative which Russia could supply, and spoke with disgust of those fellow Liberals who reviled it. A third was the Kaiser. Here O. B.'s wrath overflowed on the Tory Press, and he was moved in 1908 to write a letter to that potentate expressing his outraged feelings. "Mr. Oscar Browning presents his humble duty to your Majesty and wishes to express his deep sympathy with and admiration for your Majesty, and his indignation at the manner in which your Majesty is being treated by a portion of the English Press at the present time. Mr. Browning believes that England has no better or more sincere friend than your Majesty and that there is no sovereign in Europe who is more earnestly desirous of ensuring the peace of the world. When Mr. Browning was in Berlin last August attending the Historical Congress as delegate of the University of Cambridge, he was assured by influential statesmen that it was not likely, nor indeed possible, that there should be a war between England and Germany." Even so do men mix error and truth in their anticipations of the future.

VI

With Liberalism thus victorious it was natural that University Reform should once again come under discussion and that O. B. should give his views on the question which had been uppermost in his mind for a third of a century. Reform, he said, should come from within, not from without. It should be decided by the free suffrages of graduates, not by the interference of Royal Commissions. The University should be brought into closer touch with the democracy, it should be made cheaper and more efficient. But let them beware of following the German ideal of a university.

"We no longer look with admiration upon a place which makes the University consist of Professors, who are masters of their subjects, chiefly engaged in writing books, of students left entirely to themselves, free to attend any lectures they please, and to spend the rest of their time as they like, a system which may stimulate a few but does not educate the many, which addresses the mind but leaves the character and the heart untouched, a system in which whenever a professor happens to come into personal contact with an undergraduate he calls it a 'seminar.' We will have our young men looked after, and for this purpose we must provide tutors and Deans, Chapels and Halls, and a system of College life which allows the lecturers to become the intimate friends of the pupils entrusted to their charge. The German system of the first half of the last century may have been better than the English system of the same epoch, but since 1850 we have made great advances, and our system of to-day is justly admired by our Teutonic neighbours who are striving to imitate it."

275

In another paragraph he gives the essence of his views on Education :

" We must determine whether we desire our University to be mainly a place of education or a place of research. We have never come to a definite conclusion upon this matter. Education as a science is scarcely recognised by the University, but if we regard the University as a place of Eduction we shall have to recognise it. What is meant by Education ? It is not only the giving of information which can be reproduced in examinations, but the imparting of this information in a scientific manner, and further the training of the mind, the character, the habits, and indeed the whole man. Education regarded from this point of view is a modern discovery. It began with the work of Pestalozzi at Stanz in 1798, it was continued by Froebel, and systematised by Herbart. These men have as forerunners Comenius, Locke and Rousseau, but their principles only found practical expression in later times. At Stanz a teacher of genius came for the first time into close connection with little children, so that he might study them minutely. He lived with them, slept with them, starved and suffered with them, and thus he discovered the hidden secrets of child nature. The system thus begun, and since formulated, has become the basis of our training of teachers, has improved our elementary schools, and made some way into our secondary schools, but has as yet scarcely affected our Universities. In them Education has been confused with ' coaching,' a very inferior occupation justly looked down upon by Professors and Educational reformers. Some lecturers do nothing but coach, they prepare a careful set of lectures where the subjects to be studied are tabulated and cut up into digestible morsels. The lecture is read out clearly, so that every word of it may be taken down.

It is then learned by heart, and when reproduced in an examination is certain to gain marks. The lecturer of a higher type will do no work for his pupils which they have not earned by an equal amount of work done by themselves. He appeals not to their memory but to their intelligence. He thinks not of their success in the Tripos, but of their grasp and understanding of the subject; he trains not only their minds but their characters, and fills them not only with knowledge but with principles which are to govern them in life. Some Professors do the same, but complete success in their endeavours can only be attained by complete contact, by an intimacy which reproduces in the society of young men the intimacy which was the keynote of the reform at Stanz. For this we must have Colleges, small classes, discussion societies, essay writing, and above all individual friendship. These things are only possible in Colleges, and a reform which neglects this ideal and substitutes for it a mechanical arrangement for the imparting and testing of knowledge would, if established, be found to be a delusive failure."

After going into the items of an undergraduate's expenditure and recommending, as one obvious economy, that students should be allowed to live in a single room, he entered a plea, a wise plea, against the belief that all that was wanted was money. "There is a widespread belief that what the University principally requires for its fuller development is more money. . . . But the need of money has been exaggerated. It is not certain that the money which we have received from benefactors has been wisely spent. There has certainly been too much building. Men are the life of institutions—buildings, unless they are kept within due limits, are often the heralds of decay. In my thirty years' work at Cambridge I have been closely associated with three institutions, which have been extremely, even notoriously, successful : the first is King's College, the second is the Historical School of the University, and the third is the Cambridge University Day Training College, and all of these have been conspicuous for their poverty and have had little or no assistance from outside. The Fellowships at King's, which it was expected would never fall below £250 a year, have in recent years been generally less than £100; all that the University has contributed to the teaching of history is five University Lectureships of £50 a year each, as of the two Professorships the Regius Professor, appointed by the Crown, is an institution quite independent of the existence of an Historical Tripos ; and the Professorship of Ecclesiastical History, besides being partly theological, is a private endowment connected with Emmanuel College. The Day Training College, which now numbers eighty students, has received but little assistance from the University, and if a secondary department had not been attached to it, it would have cost the University nothing at all. It is not money that we want so much as devoted workers and intelligent methods."

He ended this academic testament with a warning against the state of the Public Schools :

" The reform of our Universities is closely connected with a deeper question, the reform of our public schools. They cannot be said to be in a satisfactory condition, they have been corrupted by habits of idleness and extravagance, and by the abnormal development of athletic worship, which is nothing short of a national calamity. In the long catena of theories framed for the improvement of education, there is none which has proposed to reform education by establishing it upon a basis of athletic distinction, and that is what our public schools avowedly and undeniably do. They are,

as Professor Thompson has said, excellent places
to spend the holidays in, but very unfit for the hard
labour of a term's study. If the culture and energy
of England depended upon them, the outlook for
our country would be dark indeed, but the mass of
our people is probably sound, and the intellectual
habit which the public schools fail to impart is to be
found in our elementary schools. Only those who
have had the opportunity of becoming acquainted
with them are aware of the standard reached by the
pupils of these institutions, even under our present
untoward conditions, and of the high merit to be
found in their teachers. The business of the
University is to make the highest education available
for even the lowest social strata, by the training of
its teachers, by the inculcation of sound principles
of education as distinguished from instruction and
from research, and by reducing the expense of
University life, so as to bring it within the reach
of a humble purse; Cambridge, at least, is doing
this; for this it needs no external Commission, it
is quite competent to control its own destinies. All
that is needed is a clear vision of the objects to be
attained, and a strenuous determination to carry
the struggle for improvement to a successful issue."

VII

O. B. had resigned the duties of history tutor,
not without much good advice to the successor
whom the College had appointed from amongst
his old pupils. He had been persuaded not to
continue to lecture, or rather his proposal to do so
had been received so coldly that he perforce
abandoned it. His work in King's was at an end,
and at a dinner given to him by his Political Society
he bestowed his formal blessing on those who were

taking the torch from his none too ready hand, and he received the affectionate compliments of Sir Austen Chamberlain on having reaped the finest reward that life can offer, the gratitude of many generations of young men.

His historical work in King's was at an end. But not his work in the University. Once more the chance of occupying a professorial chair, this time the Whewell Professorship of International Law, passed before him. True, in international jurisprudence—supposing such a thing existed—he was not learned. But, as he pointed out in his letter of candidature to the Vice-Chancellor, one of the specific duties of the Whewell Professor was to give lectures which might lead to the diminution or extinction of war, and this might be done as effectively by the historical investigation of the causes which led to war. Since he had studied and written on the War of the Spanish Succession, the Seven Years' War and the foreign policy of William Pitt, he was well qualified to speak with authority on this aspect of the subject. The electors, however, were unconvinced, and Oscar Browning was not given the chance of lecturing on international law from the historical standpoint.

But there was always the Day Training College, to which he meant to devote the remainder of his health and strength. In the ruling of that flourishing institution, which he had built up almost unaided in the face of scepticism or indifference, his genius could still find scope. Every year he was strengthening the ties between the elementary schools and the University, sowing the seeds of culture in the demos, building up something that would in the end take the place of the public schools, which had become little more than breeding-grounds of snobbery and athleticism. It was all the more necessary to give much time to the

College because, now that the principle had been won, the battle gained, others were coming in to reap the kudos or to interfere with his benevolent autocracy. No longer, as before, was he left free to take what he considered the best course. The members of the Teachers' Training Syndicate, the Governing Body of the College, who at one time could with difficulty be persuaded to attend the meetings, now came, criticised, opposed. They were specially tiresome in finance, which had never been O. B.'s strong point. A sub-committee of the Syndicate had been investigating the accounts of the D.T.C., and had found that it was difficult to " disentangle the items," and that the balances in hand were " artificial." The appointment of a Treasurer was recommended. Matters came to a head at a meeting of the Syndics on one of the days when O. B. was lying dangerously ill of double pneumonia and was, of course, unable to attend. Under the chairmanship of Walter Durnford, who had succeeded to his house at Eton and was now destined to succeed him at the Training College, they carried certain resolutions which caused O. B., when convalescent, to write a letter of protest. " I consider," he said, after making his objections, " that I have been treated by the Syndicate " (he had been Secretary of this since 1878) " with injury and insult—injury by being deprived of my covenanted stipend, and insult by the Syndics dealing directly with a member of my staff without consulting me. This has caused me great annoyance and distress of mind. I sincerely hope that you will not approve of this action of the Syndicate in these matters. If you do, you must be very different to the Walter Durnford whom I knew as a colleague at Eton many years ago."

Instead of O. B. receiving satisfaction for his pride or his pocket, there came a little later a letter from

the Vice-Chancellor, a carefully, indeed a grace-
fully worded letter, in which he was asked to commit hari-kari. It dwelt on his past services, " the
energy and resourcefulness, the knowledge based
upon large experience, the unstinting diligence "
with which he had administered the College. But
changes had to be made, and the Governing Body
did not feel it easy to carry them through whilst
he was Principal of the College and Secretary of
the Syndicate, and the Vice-Chancellor ventured
" most reluctantly to ask " whether O. B. did not
think that the time had come when he might pass
on into other hands work which had now to be done
under other conditions than those to which he was
accustomed. The purport of the letter was quite
unmistakable, but O. B., whilst describing it in his
reply as " very kind and considerate," asked for a
few days in which to make a decision that would
change the whole course of his life—for without the
Training College there would be no work for him
at Cambridge, and he would not remain in residence
as a mere Fellow of King's, with nothing to do
except eat his dinner in Hall, with no occupation
to disguise how unnatural was the life of a don.
The few days were given. No one would wish to
hurry him. Dr. Mason was anxious that O. B.
should be given time. Still hari-kari is an unpleasant
business for the principal actor, and it was necessary
to remind him that he should take the knife so
courteously offered. " The more I consider the
matter," said Dr. Mason in a second letter, " the
more I feel that it would be a relief to both sides if
you were disposed to say that you did not propose
to seek re-election. I should be deeply grieved if
you were to seek reappointment and not be reappointed." So without more ado O. B. ended
his Cambridge career in Samurai fashion, resigning
both offices in a letter which, as the Vice-Chancellor

observed, was marked by the dignity and kindliness to be expected from him.

Thus every tie which bound him to Cambridge was severed, and O. B. was angrier than he had been at any time since his dismissal from Eton. When later he had a letter from the Vice-Chancellor to tell him that the Syndics had agreed to appoint Mr. W. G. Bell as Secretary of the Syndicate and Walter Durnford as Acting Principal of the College, the two members of the Syndicate whom O. B. considered as being responsible for the movement to force his resignation, he could only find relief for his feelings in describing this as having been brought about by the vilest tissue of treachery and intrigue which ever stained the annals of the University. "It was bad enough," he wrote to a friend, "to have been driven from Cambridge at ten days' notice. To feel that my work might perish in incompetent hands was an additional pang."

It was irritating too that people should believe he had resigned owing to ill health. Copies of the correspondence, which he circulated industriously, showed that this was not so. For "they smelt of intrigue," and friends and sympathisers agreed that they left a bad impression. It was another case, remarked the General Secretary of the National Union of Teachers, who had sent O. B. a message of thanks from his Executive for the way he had consistently honoured and upheld the democratic movement for the well-being of the people by improved education, and for his equally consistent support of the Union—"it was another case of that pushing from stools which was too common on the part of pushing people." Lord Curzon was of opinion that the story did not read pleasantly and that there was an evident motive behind, which not even the skill of the Vice-Chancellor could conceal. Letters flowed in, letters of regret from students, from colleagues, from friends. Everyone, even the members of the Syndicate, seemed ready to record their appreciation of his work. But these did not sweeten the bitterness which he felt at being separated from his favourite child. His life at Cambridge had suddenly snapped and he could never go back there again after the way he had been treated. In spite of Christian Science he worried; he dreamt of Durnford, as his diary records. Only on the condition that no dons were present could he be induced to revisit Cambridge for a night in order to be present at a farewell dinner by the students of the College. Even amongst his own subordinates there had been disloyalty. Nothing but gross misconduct, he said, could have justified the treatment which had been dealt out to him, " and all done at ten days' notice when I was recovering from a dangerous illness which nearly cost me my life." It was with such resentment that the best known don of our time shook the dust of Cambridge from off his feet.

VIII

Lastly, as a pendant to this story of his Cambridge career, is a picture of him by an old pupil * who has been able to write unhampered by the responsibility that attends the biographer :

" I first met O. B. in December 1901, the week of my scholarship examination. He asked me to dine with him in his rooms, to consume an Italian turkey which he had raised on his water-logged chicken farm near the swimming sheds. I was somewhat shocked to find that he ate in his bedroom, and I peeped furtively at him during dinner,

* Professor C. R. Fay, of the University of Toronto.

arrested by the way in which he rubbed his hands, now on the edge of the table and now on his knees, in prandial satisfaction. The next afternoon, in cap and gown, he stumped into the old Dining Hall at Caius, where I was unloading my slender store of Aristotle and his politics, and whispered to me : ' How do you like the paper ? I set it.' But I did not reply, fearing that the retiring vigilator would expel me for breach of rules. He wired ecstatically the news of my election, and followed it up with a letter almost illegible, in which he advised me to read Gibbon before coming up in October, and averred that I would have been a foundation instead of a Laurence Sanders scholar but for the outrageous favouritism invariably shown to the classics. He suited a raw but enthusiastic young person perfectly. That is to say, he did not teach me at all. But he slept inspiringly under a red handkerchief while Phillips and I read him our weekly essays; he advised me to consult ' Mickie,' my predecessor at school and College, about my reading (for he said that he never read any books in English himself), and as I too possessed Houssaye's volume on 1813–1815, I had his permission to cut the lectures in which he read out translations therefrom.

" He dropped in on me and the other scholars in King's Lane now and then, and one day bought some prints to cover the naked walls of Page, our thrifty mathematician. To Keynes, a fellow Etonian, he was somewhat cool. I was surprised that he took no interest in my football exploits, but I had not then heard the oft-told tale of himself and Culture versus Warre and Muscle. These somewhat unusual methods of education he crowned by taking me to Italy for my first Easter vacation. He gave me to understand that I was not nearly so bright as George Curzon, whom he had taken years ago, but allowed that I was more interesting than a certain pious pupil who had cycled with him to the Tyrol with a Family Bible on his carrier and who, on crossing the border from Bavaria, had asked him what language they spoke in Austria.

"I took with me £5, hidden away in an inside pocket; and as we neared Milan, I buttoned up my coat for safety. 'Why do you look so green?' he said. 'These Italians are perfectly delightful people. You should say "Buon giorno" to them,' and he proceeded to 'Buon giorno' two neatly dressed gentlemen in our first-class carriage. On alighting he put his hand into his breast pocket for the luggage ticket (he had paid £5 2s. 6d. at Victoria), and then exclaimed : ' My pocket-book has gone.' We hurried to the Administration, and pushing a straw-pierced cigar through the wicket in order to expedite attention, he proceeded to unfold his calamity. But the Administration desired only to know the name of his father and when he died, and wrote down these two facts in a large book. However, the O. B. was a thorough sportsman and decided to laugh at his misfortune and to make the best of it. This took the form of omitting Venice from our route and calling on the various newspaper correspondents, to whom he told our loss, adding a short story in which he and Victor Hugo figured together. About a fortnight later the Press clippings began to come along with the news of the robbery and the Victor Hugo tale. We had adjoining rooms, and he burbled through the door : ' Fay, isn't it extraordinary what an interest the British public takes in me ? ' I was tired with gazing all day at pictures and statutes and muttered back : ' No wonder, considering the trouble we took to let them know.' ' That's a most foolish remark,' he snorted. ' It sounds as though I advertised myself.' But that was the only unpleasant episode in four weeks of sunshine and to me (for I had never been abroad before) passionate enjoyment.

" We were in Florence on Good Friday, and that morning, returning from early service, he met a pleasant young Englishman in the street, and shaking him by the hand invited him to lunch. ' Who is it ? ' I asked. ' I haven't the least idea,' said O. B. ' I never set eyes on him before in my life, *jamais de ma vie.*' But an extra sense must have helped him, for he too was a newspaper correspondent. On the evening of St. Joseph's Day (I think it was) we went to a picture show, and later on reserved for an hour a whole merry-go-round, to which O. B. treated all the male ragamuffins within sight. He secured an ostrich and I a dragon, and I can still see him on his ostrich, his coat-tails flying, his square black hat on the back of his head, exclaiming between the bleats of the organ : ' I say, ain't it awfully jolly ? ' It being Easter week we could get no hotel in advance in Rome, but a wire to Count Ugo Balzani produced a lodging with a certain Madame Cifarielli, the wife of an architect (so she told us), Via Aurora 43. The manner of our leaving was remarkable ; for she made monstrous overcharges on the bill (40 baths— 40 francs, referring to as many pails of cold water), and she pinched most of O. B.'s washing. She lived up one side of the porchway and we up the other. On the last day I stood in the porch and, aided by a policeman, parleyed for linen. Out at last she flung the O. B.'s properties, pairs of boots and collars and shirts. When I clamoured for the three shirts still missing, she dramatically seized a pink chemise and flung it through the door at my feet. We left in such a tension that the O. B. forgot his silk hat, which was under the bed, and I had to dismount from the carriage (for he refused to look upon her again) and creep back for it on foot. I should explain that the O. B. packed, or rather Fritz (his valet) packed for him, by the dozen, a dozen pair of boots, a dozen shirts, and of all things a dozen pairs of braces !

"One hot day we climbed to the top of St. Peter's. I got inside the copper dome, and the O. B., who would never own himself beaten, got his head and shoulders through the aperture. Almost suffocating, I besought him to yield, and finally pushed him back by his bald head. He refused to call upon the Pope as he had so often done so, but he paid a visit of respect to the widowed Queen Margherita. She was out, but a fancy drain-pipe, which served as a receptacle for cards, was indicated to us, and into it he dropped his. I was about to do the same when he checked me, saying : ' My dear boy, she's never heard of you.' Riding back in our cardinal's carriage I fell asleep, to be aroused by the movements of the O. B., who suddenly leaped from his seat and bowed many times. The Queen turned towards him, and O. B. said : ' Did you notice what attention she paid to me ? ' I thought it not surprising, but being wiser by this time said nothing.

"However, it was for the International Historical Congress that we had come to Rome; and O. B., Professor at Cambridge as he told everyone, was convinced that James Bryce was conspiring to deprive him of the recognition he deserved. It was my job to neutralise Bryce by going round the section rooms and finding out if any section lacked a president. On one afternoon I bagged the section on Byzantine Music. For the lawful president, a German, had overstayed the luncheon hour, and when he returned was too shy to dethrone the O. B., who, having magnificently dismissed the interpreters, delivered greetings and summaries of each paper in all the languages permitted at the

Congress. But even greater satisfaction came on the last day. Bryce was to deliver a farewell address, and he was just under weigh, when near to us a black-bearded gentleman climbed upon a table and said that his Municipality had sent him to sing the praises of its local poet, Cesare Cantos, and that with or without the permission of the chair he would read an extract from his writings. The chairman banged his bell, the audience hissed. But all in vain. The O. B. and I cheered lustily, and while the meeting was disbanding in confusion, the orator's bodyguard dragged him from the table and saluted him with kisses on the cheek.

" We used to dine at a small café in one of the Piazzas. While we waited for our food, it was in O. B.'s fancy to write doggerel Latin verses, which he could do at the rate of about two a minute. I never was much of a classic, but as far as I could judge he knew most of the Latin poets by heart and would quote Horace and Virgil as we went to this place or that. I admit that O. B. was not a scientific historian, but it is foolish to use the word charlatan of a man whose conversational range was enormous. He told me that he wrote the article on Florentine Art for one of the guide-books sitting in a hotel lounge at Lucerne without looking at a single catalogue. Things sometimes went wrong. ' I didn't know, O. B.," said a friend once, ' that Charles XII campaigned in Siberia '—as he did throughout the whole of one of O. B.'s books. ' Oh ! ' said O. B., ' merely a misprint for Silesia. I never read proofs.' And speaking of books I am reminded of *Guelphs and Ghibellines*. We wandered through Florence to see which book-shops stocked that immortal work. In one it was remaindered, to the O. B.'s indignation, and we discussed the expediency of paying the bookseller the difference if he would mark it up again.

" My affection for the O. B. increased as the years went on. I never had a row with him and could never see why anyone junior to him ever had. His Political Society was as good as any in the University, then or later, and he was one of the most interesting members of it. Moreover, he had a healthy prejudice in favour of King's men. He examined me in Part I of the Tripos and obligingly told me my marks afterwards. I understand that his co-examiners threatened to resign if ever he was appointed again. But, as he said to me : ' You can't keep too close an eye on Laurence : he is always fond of his own men.' The O. B. had many dislikes, but of three men he never spoke ill—Henry Sidgwick his idol, and two King's men of the next generation, Lowes Dickinson and Wedd. He assured me that they were, like him, inspired as teachers by a Socratic daîmon.

" I corresponded regularly with him till the year of his death. All his letters were full of Italy and his latest book and congratulations on this and that and the other thing. I had made all plans to visit him in the Easter of 1921, but family illness prevented me; so the last time I saw him was at Temperley's wedding, when he and Laurence, stranded outside the same church, jumped into the same hansom.

" As a formal teacher O. B. was elusive, but so (in a different sense) was my other great hero, Alfred Marshall. The O. B. enthused you with the importance of history and the inevitability of getting a first if you were at King's—this he illustrated after his retirement by statistics and charts. But he talked to you about Napoleon, Dante, George Eliot and the latest language he was learning. One paid sometimes in silent listenings to the endless epic of his Training College. But it was worth it. Who will ever forget the sight of him as he splashed into the river, flopping like a porpoise and incredibly round ? Not I. For in that same term he put me, a Freshman, in the way of earning three guineas by coaching another King's man in the Fall of Napoleon. I didn't know much about it yet myself, but, as he truly said, ' That's the easiest way of getting to know it.'

" And then there was Tripos week, when he kept open house for all his men, feeding us on cream cheeses, lettuces, great round cakes and hock. I understand that he once took hock and oysters at bedtime as a cure for indigestion and found it very effective. But at that time he was not a Christian Scientist. When things were getting a bit difficult in later days, Macaulay (who was Tutor then) once came round to me, now a B.A., and asked me frankly what I thought of O. B.'s work. I stood up for him then as I stand up for him now. He was a hopeless lecturer, but there never was a better place for a young historian than King's in the days of O. B.

" In his dining-room at Bexhill there were two, and only two, portraits, Napoleon and himself. Was Napoleon a fraud ? It's easy to say so, but only the fools say it."

PART III
OLD AGE

CHAPTER XVI

ROME

I

WITH his retirement from Cambridge O. B., now in his seventy-third year, definitely crossed the threshold of old age.

> " Life cannot run as runs a silken thread
>   Through soft caressing fingers; we must strive,
>   We men, with wrathful smile and clamour fell;
> But when the fight is o'er, the hot words said,
>   Nought, nought but gracious memories survive
>   Of him who fights unflinching, and fights well."

Thus ran the sestet of a sonnet which A. C. Benson had addressed to O. B. on his seventieth birthday. Since then many more hot words had been said; during the past year or two life had run anything but a caressing course. And now that the fight seemed to be over, the memories which survived, on O. B.'s part, were by no means gracious. He was, on the contrary, sore and angry, as men are apt to become when they have laboured without recognition. The serenity and calm wisdom which are supposed to be the appanage of the years did not adorn O. B.'s old age, perhaps because he never grew old, but then in one sense O. B. was never young. How could he have been when at the age of four the doctrine of the relativity of sensation had been perfectly clear to him? He himself doubted " whether there was any essential growth in human faculty from the cradle to the grave." So now when he should have been already preparing to depart, loosening one by one the ties which bound him to life, he was, on the contrary, preparing at last to begin his career—the career which he had longed for as a boy, the career which he had sacrificed to the claims of duty. His youthful imagination had been warmed by the radiance of the glory which Shelley, Byron, Keats had won thirty years before. It was late, perhaps, at seventy-two " to succeed in winning a serious literary reputation." But he would try, and he was encouraged by Lord Latymer, most loyal and devoted of friends, who once again generously helped him over his financial difficulties, this time occasioned by his retirement from Cambridge.

In deciding thus not only would he be following his own inclinations and the advice of his most intimate friend, he would be heeding more august intimations. For in June 1909, when he had resigned from the Training College and was necessarily somewhat at a loss, as is every man when he finds his occupation suddenly and unexpectedly gone, God said to him : " You have done enough teaching. You must give it up and write." With such zeal did he follow this order from above, that within the space of five years he had written and seen published the formidable amount of 1,100,000 words or the equivalent of eight novels of average length. And since he had received no intimation to the contrary, he went on writing for another seven years, until the total of words had risen to some two millions. Then at the age of eighty-four he lost the use of his right hand. O. B. thought at first that it must be a slight stroke. But the doctors, who diagnosed it as writer's cramp, were for once not mistaken. Anyhow, as O. B. wrote to Lord Curzon, it did not worry him. God had told him to write. He had done so and had made £840.

" Now He said : ' You mu&t give up writing and only read and think.' I obey Him and am quite comfortable and perfeɛtly well." And obedience was the less irksome since, owing to the war, the la&t seven or eight hundred thousand words had not found a publisher.

Though O. B. wrote assiduously he was no slave to his craft. He wrote much but he wrote very easily. It sometimes occurred to him that he wrote too easily. After recording in his diary that during the week he had added another 20,000 words to his *Memories of Sixty Years*, upon which he was then engaged, he adds the que&tion : " Too much ? " Still he could not do otherwise. Neither his diary nor his private papers, which at his death amounted to about one hundred thousand pieces, were as good a quarry as his own memory, and his &tyle was not of the kind that would submit to polishing. In consequence he had plenty of time to enjoy the pleasures of the world. Finding a *pied-à-terre* in Town " a necessity rather than a luxury," he e&tablished himself in Hill Street, Knightsbridge, conveniently close to the Serpentine, where he liked to bathe before breakfa&t. If entries in his diary are to be believed, he was a frequent visitor to its chilly banks in the February of 1910, when he had been three years a septuagenarian. It is a hi&torical faɛt that he offered a cup to be competed for by the hardy Londoners who take their morning bath in its broad waters.

He was free too to travel as the inclination took him, and in the spring of the same year he went on a tour of the Near Ea&t, visiting Athens, Con&tantinople and Jerusalem, and spending some months in Egypt, Cyprus and Syria. Everywhere he was received with courtesy, treated with di&tinɛtion, invited to dine or leɛture. Only at Alexandria, which, unlike mo&t touri&ts, he found

the most romantic city in Egypt, with the spirit of
Cleopatra still brooding over its quays, was he
annoyed by the manners of the British Consul-
General, himself a historian, who took the chair at
a lecture in French he delivered upon Napoleon
and yawned whilst it was in progress. In Egypt
O. B. visited schools, found the young Egyptians
intelligent and pleasant-mannered, though he discovered that their morals left much to be desired.
He was glad also to be able to confirm at first hand
his belief that the British Occupation had been a
brilliant success, a belief that did not prevent him
from writing a sonnet, inspired by the quiet of
Helwan, adjuring Egypt to sleep on

> " Till God, in His full purpose, from the skies
> To teach the West, shall bid the East arise."

After exploring the Gothic and Byzantine memorials
which attest the greatness of Cyprus's past, he went
on to Syria, and in spite of his disgust with Turkish
misrule discovered there the Italy and the Italians
of the East.

When he returned to London he found that he
had no money and no work to do. However, he did
not worry. " I leave my plans to Almighty God,"
he wrote, " who I am sure can arrange for me far
better than I can arrange for myself, and if when I
go to bed I have spent a happy and useful day, I
am content and expect that the next will be similar."
His faith was justified; for Lord Curzon lent him
£100, his bank another £100, and a publisher
suggested that he should write a history of the
world in eight large volumes. At once O. B.
started on a synopsis of this work which had been
so opportunely proposed to him, and in a couple
of months had produced a scheme complete in
four sections (Ancient, Mediæval, Modern and
Recent) and 360 chapters. It promised to be an

immense affair, such as might tax the capacity of any man. But he was confident of his powers and felt, as he surveyed its majestic proportions, that he " could have lectured on any chapter with half an hour's preparation." The publishers, however, grew doubtful about the public interest in ancient history, and ultimately they commissioned him to write only the last section. It was accordingly to this that he addressed himself, and with such assiduity that it was published less than two years later under the title of *A History of the Modern World*. The whole of these two bulky volumes, running altogether to 400,000 words, were written in about sixteen months between the hours of five and eight in the mornings.

II

A large part of every year he spent in Italy. He felt happier under Italian skies, found living cheaper there than in England. Rome, where he made his head-quarters, offered him " the best and most intellectual society in Europe." But he lost none of his interest in the things with which his life had been occupied. His Liberalism burnt with as sure and steady a flame as ever, and when asked by one of the papers to say what he hoped for the world in the new year of 1913 which was about to begin, he replied, the continued triumph of the Liberal Party and the expulsion of the Turks from Europe. It was too a satisfaction, if a melancholy one, to feel that the Tory Party was reaping the fruits of the injustice with which he himself had been treated. The future of the House of Lords, one of the political questions which Englishmen thought important in the spring of 1914, drew from him a long letter to Lord Curzon. " You know," he wrote, " that I am a partisan of the democracy to the marrow of my bones. When I went to Eton in 1860 I was well aware of the political situation. I knew that the revolution must come. I felt that the only chance of avoiding a catastrophe lay in the education of the governing classes, not to prevent the revolution but to make it more gradual, and I believe that I did some good in that direction. I have not forgotten that the first time you introduced me to your wife at Marlborough House, you said, apropos of our conversation : ' Whatever I am, my dear, I owe it all to Mr. Browning.' This was, of course, not true, but it was some acknowledgment of what I had tried to do. I was head of the intellectual party, which consisted of Wayte, Stone, Luxmoore and Cornish. Warre was the head of the other party; Warre who had ' a passionate hatred of the intellect.' Hornby, a hopeless idiot, instead of holding the balance, took Warre's side and out-Warre'd Warre. So I was dismissed and my party dispersed. Stupidity and reaction went on unchecked and all chance of the governing classes receiving an education to fit it for its duties was lost. The test came in 1910, when the aristocracy was on its trial. The peers came on to the platform and were laughed at. *You were the only peer who drew an audience comparable to that drawn by the leaders of the Commons.* The country found that the peers were worth nothing, that they had bartered their duties for self-indulgence, and the Parliament Act was passed. . . . The aristocracy is responsible for its own downfall, and in many it is deserved. The ' Souls ' did their best to stem the tide. We Eton reformers (of whom the world knows nothing) did our best. But the forces of nature were against us." And then O. B. suddenly turns to a conversation he has had with General Ricciotti Garibaldi, a democrat like himself, who had remarked that " Napoleon had only just failed in doing a greater work than Jesus Christ, with whom he might be compared." The only greater man was Julius Cæsar, " whom those donkeys murdered." Thus the statesman-mind took its wide sweeps through the fields of affairs, past and present, and was often able in the process to connect the general with the particular, the future of England or the genius of Napoleon with the life and works of O. B.

Not that truth was easy to weigh in the rough balance of the human reason, even in so simple a problem as the failure of the peers. " The most useful and important things " (he is writing to Lord Latymer) " are often inexplicable, and the principle of inheritance is one of them. It would be a terrible thing if the peers were lost to public life, the most valuable element in the country. But they must be chastened by misfortune and reformed."

The war came to direct such speculations into other channels. In August 1914, Oscar Browning was in the Apennines. Though he felt " rather ashamed at being out of England," and wrote offering to replace any elementary schoolmaster who had gone to the front, he realised that he was not likely to be wanted and decided to remain in Italy. Thus the exile to Rome, for which he had often wished at Cambridge, became an accomplished fact. Nor were his last years clouded by the horror of war. The holocaust of the youth and manhood of Europe hardly touched him imaginatively. He was shocked and grieved when he heard of the death of any of his former pupils. But wars were always cruel, and the historian from his training, the statesman from his nature, should never be a sentimentalist. So the cry of the " war to end war," which was " an insult to the intelligence of the English people," filled him with irritation, and when in 1917 he was asked to speak at a meeting in Rome in favour of the establishment of a League of Nations, he amazed a pacifist audience by saying that the annals of the world were paved with plans for universal peace, just as hell was paved with good intentions. It was right to make schemes, and they did good, but it was vain to suppose that they would succeed. Peace and War depended on causes outside of our ken and beyond our control, like the weather. " My dear Frank," he adds to his letter to Lord Latymer describing this event, " they are the will of God, and whatever He wills is both right and good."

To submit to the will of God, that was what Christian Science taught him and what he tried to do in so far as in him lay. All was for the best, even in the dark autumn of 1914. " In looking forward at the end of the old year," he writes in his diary on the last day of that December, when he was about to enter on his seventy-eighth year, " I find that in my mind this world and the next are inextricably joined together. I do not care whether I shall live to the end of this year, for it is indifferent to me whether I live in this world or the next. I only know that I shall live. This feeling has never been present to me before. Amen. Thank God for all His blessings."

III

These were not few. On all sides he saw indications that his reputation was growing. His lectures on the history of Mediæval Italy had increased it in Rome, his books had done the same in England and America. The Eighty Club elected him an honorary member on the ground of his long and distinguished service to the Liberal Party, and in 1921 the University of Cambridge had asked him to be their official representative at the Dante Commemoration held by the University of Bologna. As he told Lord Curzon, it was "a great and surprising honour." "I should have liked," he says, "above all things to go. They would probably have made me a Doctor and perhaps a Commendatore, and I should have met many Dante friends. But post-war railway travelling in Italy would have been too much for a man of eighty-four and the doctors peremptorily forbade it.

Six months later he had a still greater surprise. "My dear George," O. B. writes in February 1922 to Lord Curzon, "a wonderful thing has happened. Someone has given a portrait of me to Eton College and it has been accepted. Luxmoore told me this, and I thought that it must have been Lord Latymer. I wrote to ask him, and he told me that he had given it, but he would not let me know anything about it till he had heard where it had been hung. He said that they seemed very much pleased about it. I have written to Macnaghten, but he has not answered. Perhaps he has never received the letter. At any rate it is a marvellous occurrence and may be compared to the new Pope blessing the people in the Piazza. In one way I regard it as a tardy and inadequate reparation for a monstrous act of injustice. On the other hand it is the closing of a long feud and an acknowledgment that I am one of the most distinguished Eton masters. . . . I can hardly believe it."

So much for Eton and Cambridge. Everything was working out at last; and in the world he was gaining the kind of reputation he desired. He had written an article for the *Sunday Times* and been introduced in an editorial caption as the "famous historian and educationist." That is exactly, he observes with complacency, what he wishes to be known as, and it has taken him eighty years to achieve. The *Daily Mirror* too had published a poem of his in its poets' corner, in his opinion " the greatest honour which can befall any author." Thus he writes to Lord Latymer, who for fifty years had been his dearest and now was his " only friend," and adds that the selection of poems in that paper has been the best for years—" everyone a gem, including mine." On one of his many walks in Rome, " which often cover eight or ten miles," he takes up in a bookshop a copy of Pears' Shilling *Encyclopædia* and finds his name amongst the Prominent People; " that is," he explains, " the 3000 most distinguished people who have lived since the beginning of the world." He writes an epigram upon his being a " prominent person in Pears'," and circulates it amongst his friends. His biography in the latest edition of the *Encyclopædia Britannica* is also, of course, a tribute, but he confesses to Lord Curzon that he wishes it had not treated him rather as a personality than as a historian and " the greatest teacher " of his time.

When the doctor told him that he would live to be a hundred, he felt that he did not want to, because he was anxious to see what the next world was like. Yet " the third volume " was proving the most interesting of all. It enabled him to watch the whole careers of those whom he had known as boys, Lord Balfour at sixteen, Lord Curzon at fourteen. He writes thus to the Foreign Secretary, who is then engaged on " the dreary work of trying to reconcile national jealousies and rapacities," and asks him how he likes Austen for his colleague. " Of course he is an old and dear friend of mine," O. B. remarks, " honest and upright as the day, but not very clever. He owes his advancement to his character, and I am glad that I had a share in his education." Often to Lord Latymer, the only other correspondent to whom he habitually unburdened himself about politics, he laments the ignorance of Mr. Lloyd George, whom at other times he finds it convenient to extol as a product of the elementary schools. Count de Salis, our Minister at the Vatican, had spent an hour and a half with him, and told him that the Pope was indignant at the way we had left our ally Nicholas in the lurch and rejoiced in his being dethroned and imprisoned. " David," O. B. writes after recounting this conversation, " has been terrible, but then he knows nothing of history or foreign politics." Luckily the two Etonians in the Cabinet, Balfour and Curzon, had not committed themselves. He thought too that the King had been badly advised in writing to Kerensky: " George III would never have written to Robespierre." Politics were certainly of absorbing interest, though his views on English affairs might be just as great " rot " as those of Goldwin Smith when he lived at Toronto. And their interest for him culminated five months before his death. " My dear George," he writes on May 22, 1923, " this morning's *Piccolo* says that you are Prime Minister and I hope it is true. Please accept my warmest congratulations. I always told you that I should not be satisfied unless you were. I shall look forward with great interest to all the things you are going to do. I hope that one will be to make Poincaré suffer the fate of Castlereagh." When he found that history had taken another course, it was the last disappointment of his life. He told Lord Curzon that he considered the King had undertaken " a serious, and even a dangerous, responsibility, in helping to lay down the precedent that a member of the House of Lords cannot be Prime Minister. If the " Die-hards " had anything to do with it they aimed a more serious blow at the Upper House than anything in the

Parliament Act." However, O. B. was not a
Christian Scientist and an optimist for nothing, and
he adds : " I believe for myself, for reasons which
I will not enlarge upon, that Baldwin will not be
the success which people anticipate, that he will
have to resign and that you will be Prime Minister.
Of this I feel convinced, and then I shall sing
Nunc Dimittis."

Death was waiting for him. It was immaterial
whether he continued to live or not. Indeed the
phrase had no meaning. Death was nothing, a
mere transition from one sphere to another, a
" passing over." Or Death was a jolly old fellow,
with whom he had long been on excellent terms.
And in the meantime, since he could not yet
experience what the other world was like, he would
get what he could out of the one in which he
happened to be. It was a fine thing to live in
Rome and be appreciated, to have dinners given in
his honour on his birthdays, " a thing they never
did at Cambridge," to add a thousand words a day
to his History, to be received with deference in
the salons of Roman princesses, to be accompanied
everywhere by a valet, " who is noble and has a
coronet on his visiting cards." Every day it is
borne in on him more and more that he is the most
important Englishman in Rome, " and the responsibility is considerable." He is on committees,
patriotic, religious, social. Sometimes he takes the
chair, as at the annual meeting of the British and
Foreign Bible Society, when he delivers a speech
on the Society's activities in Italy. He is even made
Acting President of the British Academy of Arts,
and rules a Committee consisting of two Maltese
and an Anglo-Italian. They quarrel with him and
two resign. It is quite like old times. And when
the war is over, amongst the visitors who climb
the many flights to his flat in the Via Pietro Cavallini,

where in warm weather O. B. sits on the terrace overlooking the Tiber, and from his "curule chair," one of the many presents from Lord Curzon, talks of the things within his experience—amongst these visitors are undergraduates from Oxford and Cambridge. None give him more pleasure, even if they do come, as he remarks, to view an interesting ruin, in the same spirit as they visit the Coliseum.

Long before he had made the delightful discovery that youth still took pleasure in his society, even as he still liked young people about him. They clustered round him like bees, as he said. One gets a characteristic view of him one morning in the winter of 1915, when he was nearly seventy-nine years of age. In the middle of a letter to a friend he suddenly breaks off in a sentence. He explains why when he resumes : " At this moment I went to open the door for a boy of sixteen, a violin genius, whom I am helping to get a first-rate violin education. I took him to the Professor's for the first time and have just returned half an hour later." Then he proceeds with his letter. Again he has to break off. " At this moment," he continues subsequently, " the boy of sixteen (he is really seventeen) came back from the Professor. I had already given him five francs to buy some violin studies which the Professor had ordered for him, and now he wanted me to type a letter for him in Portuguese to his mother in Brazil. It took an hour and a half. This philanthropy costs both time and money."

An old pupil, who was in Rome after the war, remarks that his generosity and kindness of heart remained unbounded, and, as is customary with the truly generous character, the good deeds of the past were soon forgotten. "When I reminded him," he continues, " how he had defied convention by walking down King's Parade with a naked bottle of port under each arm—a gift for an invalid undergraduate—he refused to believe it. It was sad, however, that at the end of his life there were those around him who took advantage of his goodness. Cherished possessions would disappear in the most mysterious manner. One day it was a favourite fountain pen. After a long search I managed to buy its pair, but on my next visit that too had gone. But O. B. never regarded these continual disappearances as anything worse than losses, and I am glad that he could not."

So one day followed another, each filled with innumerable occupations. Only on Sundays was the routine broken. On that day he was in the habit of attending the Anglican service at eleven in the morning (at the " High " Church, not the " Low," as he explained), of reading Christian Science from two to three in the afternoon, and of going to the Waldensian Church in the evening. Occasionally he visited St. Peter's on great festivals. " The might and majesty of the Roman Church " never failed to impress his imagination, and there is some evidence that a year or two before he died he considered joining it. But it was from Christian Science that the inner light, which seemed to burn more brightly as senescence set its mark of bodily weaknesses upon him, drew its comforting radiance and warmth. " The root of my health and happiness," he tells Lord Curzon some two years before his death, " is Christian Science. Not the healing part, which I don't care for, but the moral principles and the rule of life. It is to me the essence of Christianity. I read my *Quarterly* every morning with bits of the Bible and of Mrs. Eddy. It certainly makes me happy and I believe keeps me well." O. B. was no dweller in the tents of orthodoxy.

IV

He had always been "overwhelmed with correspondence." Now from his Roman retreat he corresponded more indefatigably than ever. King's naturally remained his greatest interest, and his fellow-dons seem to have faithfully answered his many and none too legible letters. Sometimes he felt that the College "was not what it was." "The dons," he says in a letter to one of them, "are a low-minded lot and do not care for the College as much as they care for themselves." But such views might easily change. Letters from King's undergraduates, or better a visit from one or other of them, would make him more cheerful, and he would write to the same person in a very different strain. "I believe in the future of King's. It is a merry College, gay, go-ahead and ambitious, with a passion for originality something in the style of Rupert Brooke. I have hopes." He is pleased to hear that throughout the war meetings of the Political Society have been held at least once a term, so that the "apostolical succession" has been preserved. He is pleased also to think that after his death his ashes will rest in King's Chapel. The very idea of the "putrefying mass of corruption which coffins contain" has become hateful to him. Nor does Armageddon, an expression by the way that he detests, prevent him from exchanging bitter letters about the Training College, made still more bitter from the threat that the pension he draws from it may cease, owing to the war having dried up the sources of supply. A. C. Benson, with whom he communicates on this subject, "has always admired his handling of life," but he adds that "an unprovoked and violent attack without any knowledge of the facts of the case does not evoke either sympathy or admiration." And four months before his death O. B. feels constrained to write a severe letter to the editor of the *Cambridge Review*, which had published an article about him, saying that it was the only one out of at least a hundred which had given him pain, and that the writer was neither a scholar nor a gentleman. He pointed out that he kept up a close connection with Cambridge and often wrote for the Undergraduate papers, that he was one of the founders of the *Cambridge Review*, that he had always supported it, but that he should take care in the future that no copy ever came under his notice. "I hope this was not too severe," he adds, after telling another Fellow of King's what he has done.

His letters in this last period of his life are a sort of compendium of his whole career. Sir F. A. Bosanquet, his friend since boyhood at Eton, one of the few still alive who address him as Oscar, assures him that he is really as devoted to Eton as he is himself, though O. B. pretends to be as cosmopolitan as Gibbon or Lord Acton. "Yours," he adds, "has been the distinguished career. My lot has been to cultivate the *auream mediocritatem*." "What a marvellous memory you have got for little things as well as big," writes the last Vice-Provost of Eton. "Who could have imagined that W. D.'s doggerel of some sixty years ago could have revived your memories of my father's shaving soap?" Dean Inge thinks that he has every reason to feel contented in a "tottering world in which the happiest, next to the dead, are the aged and the childless." Bishop Welldon "never forgets their old friendship." Sir Walter Durnford, against whom the bitterness of ten years before is now passing away, hopes that he "can save the College" (the Training College) "which they both love." Viscount Bryce tells him that he is lucky in being able to see *Weltgeschichte* from a point of detachment. Frederic

Harrison, the only survivor amongst his contemporaries of the eighteen-seventies who was his senior, is able to congratulate him upon his zest, his erudition and his industry.

He corresponds with Sir Oliver Lodge on spiritualism and with Mr. Frank Harris on the personal idiosyncrasies of Swinburne. With Mr. H. G. Wells he takes up the cudgels for Napoleon. " I sent a copy of my Napoleon article to Wells, and he said that it was admirably written and *all true*. How he can say this after his account of N. in his World History must be left to his conscience to decide." Thus he comments to Lord Curzon, who shows no desire either to attack or defend O. B.'s hero. Letters that pass between him and Mr. Belloc about the battle of Blenheim excite calmer and more academic feelings. And then there were many nephews and nieces, greatnephews and great-nieces, to keep in touch with. " Dizzy was a blackguard," he says to a nephew whom he considered wanting in grace. " Mind you don't become one." " Caro papa ! " begins a letter from one of his spiritual children, who signs himself " vostro affezionatissimo e riconoscento figlio, Umberto Cialone." " Dear Old Chummy," commences one who had been a sailor and signs himself " Bert." And occasionally he had more august correspondents. Thus he is able to tell Lord Latymer what a " charming letter " he has had from Queen Mary " about her boy." " I don't wonder," he says, " at her being proud of him. I am sure that I am." A letter from the Pope is framed and hangs in his hall.

Certainly life was of absorbing interest, and not least those questions of morals which lay at the very basis of human relationship. *The Loom of Youth*, which O. B. considered a book of genius, enabled him to return to an old and favourite

subject, and to discuss once more with those who
had worked with him at Eton the vices of athleticism and the failings of the public schools.
Toleration had come with age. Schoolmasters had
a heavy responsibility. " Non est leve tot puerorum
observare manus oculosque in fine trementes," he
writes to one who had made a scientific study of
such questions. Nevertheless, the question was
one of immense difficulty. A year before he died,
O. B. records that he had just read a wonderful
book about the Northern Rhodesians, by his
friend the Reverend Edward Smith, " who tells
you everything and very seldom has recourse to
Latin." Depravity was not confined to men and
monkeys. A student of sexual pathology had
assured him that every male animal wished to
indulge in auto-erotism and only refrained from the
difficulty of doing so. To legislate against homo-
sexual practices was very often " to sanctify and
hallow them." There were things which laws
could not touch, and this was one of them. The
sanction for it must be left to each individual conscience. To the pure all things are pure. To the
good man there is no such thing as evil. He writes
a Latin poem which he sends to a friend :

Amor Improbus

Consors dierum, rex hominum potens,
Infestus auctor sollicitudinum,
    Tu fons voluptatis, sed idem
      Innumerabilium dolorum.

Seu pervicaci fronte superbias,
Seu pace cesses languidus improba,
    Prætendis ambages, perenni
      Nocte graves, Ereboque pressas.

Quis te resolvet ? quis propriam tibi
Dicabit ædem ? queis colet artibus ?
    Seu thure divino literis,
      Sive olidum patiaris hædum.

Sis forsan Orci vestibulum, igneas
Ostendis arces, radere nunc sinens
Extrema vestimenta, vultus
Olim alio reserabis ævo.

" The meaning," he explains, " is very subtle,
but I expect you will understand it. It is super-
ficially rather smutty, but intrinsically very religious
and spiritual. I think that it is very good, but
then I always think my own writings good." If
Lord Latymer did not agree with him, he could
always agree with Lord Latymer in thinking English
society " terrible " and in castigating the post-war
styles of dancing.

V

The portrait is finished and Oscar Browning can
be left to such a portion of immortality as destiny
has reserved for him in this world. But across
these high lights of his Roman period there
lay a dark shadow. That enormous vitality which
was a part of his genius, which indeed was
his genius, remained his to the end. Yet in spite
of all his courage and philosophy, the cancer was
at the heart of the rose. Christian Science (his
Coué, as he described it to Lord Curzon) might
teach him to be happy; nevertheless even whilst
he repeated that he was happier than he had ever
been, the old unrest and dissatisfaction, which his
mother had warned him against at Eton, were there.
The ambitions of his life, he felt, had been unrealised, one thing after another had eluded him, and
now in his old age he was poor, lonely, disappointed.
In some degree he might be paying the penalty of
bachelorhood. But there was no reason why he
was still plain Oscar Browning. In Rome, where
everyone had a title and " marchesi were three a
penny," he had none. " By what title shall I call

313

you ? " the Princess Colonna had asked him, and he had been obliged to reply, " Professor," though really he had " very slight claims to the appellation." The thing, however, might be remedied. If he were knighted " it would give great pleasure to many people all over the world," would lift him out of the ruck and make young men feel that his career was one which they might emulate. These views he expressed to Lord Latymer, adding that if he did not approve he would never think or speak of them again. And when Lord Latymer said that a knighthood would add nothing to his distinction he dropped the subject.

At length, three months before his death, he was, thanks to the Foreign Secretary's good offices with the Prime Minister, to be rewarded, in his own words, " with the first public honour which I have ever received from my own country." He was created an Officer of the Order of the British Empire, and the last letter which he ever wrote to Lord Curzon, within five weeks of his death, begins : " My dear George, I received the decoration yesterday from Kennard, who is Chargé d'Affaires. He presented it with great dignity and kindness. It is a splendid ornament in admirable taste." And only those who knew O. B. will realise that these lines were not written in irony.

Irony, that detestable literary artifice, had no place in O. B.'s armoury, and though in his lifetime he frequently excited the smiles which are its concomitant and indeed enjoyed the laughter himself, it should not be allowed to colour a presentation of him now that he stands as a historical figure, a man with great virtues and doubtless with great faults, a great man nevertheless, and with an unmistakable aura of genius about him. Genius is an inexplicable thing, and I have no confidence that these pages have reproduced the impression of it which O. B. indubitably conveyed, no matter how difficult, or egotistical, or vindictive he might appear to be on any particular matter. If one grants that genius is some vital force, generated by a peculiar sympathy between the poles of the intellect and the physical constitution of the cells of the body, some particular ratio between the grey matter of the brain and the red corpuscles of the blood, then O. B. possessed that electric fluid, encompassed that unknown ratio to which we owe everything that is greatest in man, everything that is indeed humanity's justification and hope.

O. B. has the lien on immortality of a great teacher, but it is a lien which can only be staked out for him by the disciple, and the greatest teachers of all are perhaps those whose disciples are unaware of their debt. The paradox was a favourite one of O. B.'s, and it is possibly another tribute to his greatness that, with a few individual exceptions, there has been no such recognition of the work he accomplished as has been given to men cast in a much smaller mould than he. And above all else, above his work and achievement, or rather making it the finest part of them, Oscar Browning approached life with a magnificent *élan* and courage which only a few can ever hope to command. Yet if the touch appeared sure, it was the result of will and self-discipline. At the beginning of this book I have related how gallantly he faced death in the summer of 1923. He had pondered over the enigma all his life, not a day had passed when he had not prepared himself for the end that comes to all. He professed to have no doubts that it was no terminus, only an additional dimension, and that the spirit would live all the more intensely after it had escaped from its prison of the flesh. Still, so long as he lived he had to deal with the life he knew, and until a fortnight before his death, when he was already suffering from a complication of ills which showed only too plainly that the mechanism of his body was worn out, he kept up entries in the diary which stretched back to a time before the Crimean War, and kept up too his reading—the last book to be mentioned being *Farington's Diary*. Yet he was a man, and it was only natural that he should show a human fear at the plashing of the dread Ferryman's oars, which now echoed in his ears. It might be a grand thing to die, but it was also a fearful thing.

At length he grew so ill that it was evident the end could not be far off. And on October 6th, when he had been in bed for nearly three weeks, he had reached the state of extreme exhaustion which at his great age made any chance of recovery hopeless. On that day, in the forenoon, all the members of his " adopted " family, " Mama " Antinori, her daughter Rosina, and her son Ettore, were in his bedroom, to be present, maybe with that Latin taste for ceremonial, at the last moments, when O. B. made signs to Ettore that he wished to speak to him. Ettore leant over the bed, and O. B., who found difficulty in speaking, asked him if he thought he was going to die. The young man reassured him as one might reassure a child, saying that he must not ask such questions but eat the chicken broth they had prepared for his lunch and get well again. O. B., apparently tranquil, said no more. But a moment afterwards he signed to the mother. She went to him, and then O. B. with sudden energy, shaking his hands with impatience and speaking in almost a normal voice, said to her : " Send that girl out of the room." " Mama " Antinori turned to obey his behest,

Rosina retired and the mother returned to his bedside.

But it was a Saturday morning and Saturn had had his last " go at him "—Oscar Browning was dead.

NOTE

I should like here to record my thanks to the many friends of Oscar Browning who have helped me in what has been an agreeable labour. Mr. Lowes Dickinson read through the foregoing pages in MS. and purged them of some of their grosser faults; for those that remain I am, of course, entirely responsible.

Professor C. R. Fay has contributed the last section of Chapter XV, and others to whom I am particularly indebted are Mr. Osbert Burdett, Mr. N. Wedd, Mr. J. R. Eling Green, the Rev. O. R. Vassall-Phillips, O.S.R., the Rev. B. Layer Hale-Wortham, and Mr. A. B. Hyde, Gymnastic Instructor at Dulwich College.

APPENDIX I

BIBLIOGRAPHY

HISTORY AND POLITICS :

The Netherlands of the Sixteenth Century : a Lecture delivered at Eton College. Pp. 40. London, 1869. 8vo.

Modern England, 1820–1874. Pp. 73. London, 1876. (Went into several editions and was finally brought down to 1885.)

Modern France, 1814–1879. Pp. 125. London, 1880.

Stories from English History : the Newbery Historical Readers Series, No. 1. London, 1882. 8vo.

The New Illustrated History of England. 4 vols. London, 1889–1890. 8vo.

The Life of Bartolomeo Colleoni of Anjou and Burgundy. Pp. vii + 93. London, 1891. 4to.

The Flight to Varennes and other Essays : Pp. vii + 348. London, 1892. 8vo.

Guelphs and Ghibellines : a Short History of Mediæval Italy from 1250 to 1409. Pp. ix + 213. London, 1893. 8vo.

The Citizen, his Rights and Responsibilities. Pp. 233. London, 1893. 8vo.

The Fall of Napoleon. Pp. viii + 327. London, 1907. 8vo.

Age of the Condottieri : a Short History of Mediæval Italy from 1409 to 1530. Pp. 275. London, 1895. 8vo.

Peter the Great. Pp. viii + 347. London, 1898. 8vo.

Charles XII of Sweden. Pp. xii + 368. London, 1899. 8vo.

A History of Europe in Outline, 1814–1848. Pp. 164. London, 1901. 8vo.

Wars of the Century and the Development of Military Science. Pp. xxxvii + 538. London, 1901.

The Foreign Policy of Pitt to the Outbreak of the War with France : Cambridge Modern History. 1904. 8vo.

Boyhood and Youth of Napoleon. Pp. 362. London, 1906. 8vo.

A History of the Modern World. 2 vols. London, 1910. 8vo.

A General History of the World. Pp. x + 799. London, 1913. 8vo.

A Short History of Italy, 375–1915. Pp. 79 + viii. 1917. 8vo.

PREFACES, Editions of Historical Documents, etc. :

Political Memoranda of Francis, Fifth Duke of Leeds. Edited with notes by Oscar Browning. London, 1884. 4to.

The Despatches of Earl Gower, English Ambassador at Paris from June 1790 to August 1792. Edited by Oscar Browning. London, 1885. 8vo.

England and Napoleon in 1803 : being the Despatches of Lord Whitworth and others. Edited by Oscar Browning. London, 1887. 8vo.

The Journal of Sir George Rooke. Edited by Oscar Browning. London, 1897. 8vo.

The State, by Woodrow Wilson. With an Introduction by Oscar Browning. London, 1899. 8vo.

Napoleon's Men and Methods, by Kielland. With a Preface by Oscar Browning. London, 1907. 8vo.

Despatches from Paris, 1784–1790. Selected and edited from the Foreign Office Correspondence by Oscar Browning. 1909. 4to. (Camden Third Series.)

Historical Handbooks. Edited by Oscar Browning. Rivington's, 1783–1876. 8vo.

EDUCATION :

An Introduction to the History of Educational Theories. Pp. x + 196. London. 1881. 8vo.

Prefaces, etc :

Milton's *Tractate on Education.* With an Introduction and Notes by Oscar Browning. The Pitt Press, 1883. 8vo.

J. F. Herbart : *The Science of Education and the Æsthetic Revelation of the World.* With a Preface by Oscar Browning. London, 1892. 8vo.

An Introduction to Herbart's Science of Education, by H. M. and E. Felkin. With a Preface by Oscar Browning. London, 1895. 8vo.

J. F. Herbart : *Letters and Lectures on Education.* With a Preface by Oscar Browning. London, 1901. 8vo.

With S. S. Fletcher : General Editor of Macmillan's *Manuals for Teachers.* London, 1899, etc. 8vo.

BIBLIOGRAPHY

BELLES LETTRES :

Life and Writings of George Eliot. Pp. xiv + 174. London, 1887. 8vo.

Goethe, his Life and Writings. Pp. viii + 144. London, 1891. 8vo.

Dante, his Life and Writings. Pp. vii + 104. London, 1893. 8vo.

R. *Browning's Poems* (Selections). With an Introduction by Oscar Browning. London, 1897. 8vo.

R. *Browning's Dramas.* With an Introduction by Oscar Browning. London, 1898. 8vo.

Impressions of Indian Travel. Pp. xvi + 236. London, 1903. 8vo.

Memories of Sixty Years. Pp. x + 364. London, 1910. 8vo.

Memories of Later Years. Pp. 223. London, 1923. 8vo.

Charles Vickery Hawkins, by W. E. Waddington and J. T Inskip. With a Chapter by Oscar Browning. 1896. 8vo.

CLASSICS :

Cornelius Nepos. With English Notes by Oscar Browning. Oxford, 1868. 8vo.

APPENDIX II

THE POLITICAL SOCIETY

FIRST MEETING HELD OCTOBER 23, 1876, IN MR. OSCAR
BROWNING'S ROOMS, KING'S COLLEGE, CAMBRIDGE

PRESIDENTS OF THE SOCIETY

OSCAR BROWNING, 1876–1908

(*Hon. President*, 1908–1923)

J. H. CLAPHAM, 1908–

MEMBERS, 1876–1908

(Names printed in italics are those of deceased members.)

O. *Browning* (*President*)
E. B. *Denison* (*Trinity*)
B. H. Holland (Trinity)
Hon. *A. Lyttelton* (*Trinity*)
H. Stephen (Trinity)
R. T. *Ritchie* (*Trinity*)
R. H. Brown (Trinity)
E. H. Dean (Peterhouse)
C. Lupton (Trinity)
Hon. J. W. Mansfield (Trinity)*
J. C. Tarver
Lord Colin Campbell (*Trinity*)
F. G. Bury (Trinity)
F. T. T. *Duka* (*Trinity Hall*)
J. P. Whitney
H. Hodgkin (Jesus)
J. K. Stephen*
J. E. C. Welldon
J. M. Paulton (Trinity Hall)

W. Crewdson
A. Strachey (*Trinity Hall*)
Hon. J. F. Wallop (Trinity)
R. Somervell*
A. Neville Rolfe (Trinity)
H. H. Harris
W. E. Willink
W. Gore Browne (Trinity)
F. Gelderd (Jesus)
F. L. Cox (Trinity)
A. H. Thompson (Trinity)
H. L. Stephen (Trinity)
E. R. *Christie* (*Christ's*)
L. J. Jones (Trinity)
G. Nugent Banks
S. J. C. Brinton (Trinity)
A. J. Oakley (*Pembroke*)
D. H. Battersby (Trinity)
T. M. Fowler
C. Strachey
H. Haines

* *Secretary.*

322

W. R. Sorley (Trinity)
*Walter A. Raleigh**
F. S. C. Crane
C. Ord
J. R. Tanner (St. John's)
J. W. Graham
G. H. Barclay (Trinity)
A. R. Ropes
J. Austen Chamberlain (Trinity)
H. R. Rathbone (Trinity)
J. H. Stone
A. Macnamara (Trinity)
G. E. Green (St. John's)
L. J. Maxse
C. R. Ashbee
G. L. Dickinson
A. S. Duffield (Trinity Hall)
*P. H. Sturge**
E. Jenks
Hon. L. R. Holland
J. F. Kendall
A. H. Studd
H. Vivian (Trinity)
*G. Townsend-Warner (Jesus)**
A. B. Cane (Trinity)
J. P. Malleson (Trinity)
T. M. Evans
A. F. Fox
C. Somervell
*W. J. Corbett**
J. H. Monk (Trinity)
E. R. J. Wyatt Davies (Trinity)
F. T. Galsworthy (Trinity)
D. F. Pennant (Trinity)
W. H. Moore*
G. H. F. Duncan (Trinity)
R. J. Wilkinson (Trinity)
W. D. Green
E. M. Kohnstamm (now Konstam)
G. H. Duckworth (Trinity)
W. H. Buckler (Trinity)
M. M. Macnaghten (Trinity)
S. H. Barber

C. G. Todhunter
L. Currie (Trinity)
H. N. Ferrers*
E. L. R. Thornton
C. P. Trevelyan (Trinity)
T. A. Bertram (Caius)
J. M. E. McTaggart (Trinity)
F. R. Keightley (Corpus)
F. Wisden
E. A. Newton
*C. V. Hawkins**
C. A. M. Barlow
A. G. Bather
J. W. Headlam
R. P. Mahaffy
H. J. Allen
J. H. Doncaster
H. C. Windley
P. H. Dyke
F. W. B. Smart
W. R. Gurley
V. N. Gilbert
J. R. de M. Abbott
W. F. Reddaway*
J. H. B. Masterman (Non-Coll.)
J. H. Clapham (*President*)*
J. T. Wardlaw
L. R. Holme (Jesus)
H. Clover
A. C. Chatterjee
E. C. E. Phipps
F. N. Mayers (St. John's)
F. E. B. Duff
G. M. Trevelyan (Trinity)
J. C. Wrigley
D. S. Macdiarmid
F. Pritchard
R. Geikie
R. Hosgood
E. A. S. Watt
S. McDougall
E. W. Newmarch
A. F. Wedgwood (Trinity)
H. C. Gutteridge*
J. R. Lee (Trinity)

* *Secretary.*

323

A. C. Pigou
A. M. Cohen
R. W. Seward
Anthony Wilkin
G. B. Mumford
R. H. Norton
K. Lipikorn
A. M. Gillespie
B. A. Spencer
W. Hedley
H. W. V. Temperley*
E. A. Parry
R. Narayanan
J. MacFarlane
H. O. Meredith
A. B. Gillett
G. H. M. Gray
A. R. Kennedy
P. Powell
G. B. Smith
T. F. V. Prickard
E. L. Merz
D. Davies
H. M. Peacey
M. L. Darling
J. E. C. Flitch
C. C. Michaelides (after-
    wards C. Graham)
N. Thornhill
T. Hamilton
C. R. Fay*
C. Seymour
G. G. Russell
C. S. Phillips
E. C. Wingfield-Stratford
R. F. Truscott
C. H. Goodall

E. Milner-White*
P. P. Dickinson
G. T. FitzGerald
K. M. Macmorran
H. Joseph
C. M. Lewis
C. E. Rickett
H. G. Marshall
C. K. Webster*
H. B. Spens
O. H. Burdett
F. V. Nancarrow
J. G. Bennett
C. A. Gordon
H. S. Wilson
K. Powell
R. W. B. Garrett
D. W. Corrie*
R. W. Coit
J. L. Deuchar
K. H. Flintoff
S. H. Smith
W. T. Lyon
J. C. Jolly*
H. S. Reitlinger
P. M. Shand
F. A. Holt
G. T. Corrie
A. G. Lias
N. Compton-Burnett
R. H. Willcocks
E. J. Nathan
G. E. Toulmin
J. B. Beresford
H. L. Farnell
C. T. Swift

During the war years, 1914–1918, the Society contained the whole College, and was the only College society of any kind.

* *Secretary.*

324

INDEX

INDEX